WIRED TO STEAL

Zionism and the Shaping of the Western Mind

By **Yoav Litvin**

with

Ilan Pappé

Foreword by **Robert M. Sapolsky**

OLIVE
BRANCH
PRESS

An imprint of Interlink Publishing Group, Inc.
Northampton, Massachusetts

First published in 2026 by

Olive Branch Press
An imprint of Interlink Publishing Group, Inc.
46 Crosby Street, Northampton, MA 01060
www.interlinkbooks.com

Library of Congress Cataloging-in-Publication data available
ISBN 978-1-62371-535-9

Printed and bound in the United States of America

Praise for

Wired to Steal
Zionism and the Shaping of the Western Mind

"This is the most comprehensive and timely book I know of that allows us finally to understand how the Zionist movement and the state of Israel dragged the Middle East and the world to this ghastly era of genocide, settler-colonial atrocities, Western complicities, and still expanding warfare. It required a neuroscientist and a historian—and much honesty—to unpack Zionism's combined criminality, cruelty, and colonial-imperial collusion with world powers over the past 100 years. This book's scientific evidence alongside the historical accounts allows us to understand how otherwise decent human beings have engaged in a non-stop rampage by Zionists, Israelis, and their global allies that peaked in the Gaza genocide with unprecedented cruelty against defenseless civilians, yet keeps expanding across the region and the world."
— Rami G. Khouri, American University of Beirut

"*Wired to Steal* goes deep to expose profound truths about Israel. Readers will learn how the vastly dehumanizing project of Zionism sold itself and why so many people bought it. This is a powerful book that undermines propaganda and elevates human possibilities."
— Norman Solomon, author of *War Made Invisible: How America Hides the Human Toll of Its Military Machine*

"Finally, a clear-eyed account of how Zionist ideology has weaponized Jewish trauma to justify settler-colonial violence. Whether you're new to the subject or have been engaged for decades, this highly original analysis reveals new layers of understanding. Crucially, it also charts a path forward. A vital read."
— Maha Nassar, author of *Brothers Apart: Palestinian Citizens of Israel and the Arab World*

"*Wired to Steal* approaches the study of colonial violence from a novel angle, bringing neuroscience to our understanding of power and domination. Yoav Litvin and Ilan Pappe trace the links between neural circuitry and historical acts of subjugation, showing how fear-driven defensive aggression and greed-driven offensive aggression are instrumentalized by leaders to secure popular support. By recasting territorial theft, occupation, and political repression as existential necessities, as with the case of Zionism, propaganda transforms these into moral acts of 'defense' and noble policies to ensure 'survival.' Through this innovative analysis of intergroup hierarchy, the authors reveal how biological impulses and national narratives intertwine to make conquest feel righteous and justified."
— Harriet Malinowitz, author of *Selling Israel: Zionism, Propaganda, and the Uses of Hasbara*

"When eight decades of slow and not-so-slow genocide in Palestine continue to be embraced by the very nations boasting of their enlightened righteousness, the urgent issue becomes 'how' this works, not 'what' or 'if'. With the combined expertise of preeminent historian Ilan Pappé and behavioral neuroscientist Yoav Litvin, *Wired to Steal* masterfully dissects the neurological mechanisms through which Israel's genocide has been normalized, but the book does not stop there: it challenges the very presumption that war is an inevitable scourge of humanity. Academically rigorous yet written in clear, concise language, the authors expose how we are manipulated—'psychologically hacked'—into the unthinkable, not as a theoretical exercise but as a hands-on tool to free us from these shackles. Nothing is taken on faith in this highly original and much-needed work.
— Thomas Suárez, author of *Palestine Hijacked: How Zionism Forged an Apartheid State from River to Sea* and *Palestine Mapped: From the River to the Sea in Early Geographic Thought*

"Litvin and Pappé write a uniquely courageous book, and explore a deeply worrying collective psychological state—worrying for its victims, of course, but also for perpetrators. They observe the origins and normalization of the genocidal rage currently pervading the Israeli body politic, follow the deliberate and systematic cultivation of a dehumanizing disposition, and make sense of a bleak and distressing reality. But there is hope: if a genocidal worldview and settler colonialism are a consequence of psychosocial conditioning, then they can be reversed."
— Lorenzo Veracini, Professor of History and Politics, Swinburne University of Technology

"What fuels Zionism? What perpetuates systemic injustice against Palestinians? These are the questions Yoav Litvin and Ilan Pappé interrogate in their riveting new book *Wired to Steal*, revealing how the colonizer's mind is trained to warp reality, dehumanize, and most importantly, how it can all be undone."
— Joshua Frank, co-editor of *CounterPunch*

Table of Contents

TABLES AND FIGURES

Foreword

A parable that I've heard from public health researchers:

> A public health scientist and an ER doctor bask on a riverbank. Suddenly, they see a person being swept downriver, flailing, their head bobbing beneath the surface. The doctor dives into the water, drags out the drowning person, and resuscitates them while the public health friend just sits there.
>
> Suddenly, another person is swept down river. The doctor dives in and laboriously saves them, the public health scientist again sitting passively. Then another, doc to the rescue again, public health friend immobile.
>
> Still gasping for breath from the effort, the doctor finally turns on the friend. "What's wrong with you? Why are you just sitting there? Why don't you help me and do something?"
>
> To which the public health researcher replies:
>
> "I am doing something. I'm figuring out why people keep falling in the river."

There are two broadly different ways of approaching how to understand, explain, or fix something: proximal versus distal orientations. How to fix the problem of people being swept downriver? Proximal intervention: pull them out of the water. Distal intervention: put up a sign upriver warning people about the slippery riverbank.

What caused an alcoholic to fall off the wagon? Proximal explanation: no self-control, lousy temporal discounting making it hard to foresee future consequences. Distal: chronic stress during early brain development producing an impoverished prefrontal cortex.

What caused a rampage that left hundreds of innocent civilians butchered, hundreds more taken hostage? Proximal explanation: depraved barbarity. Distal: growing up in the world's largest open-air prison as descendants of people whose homes were stolen by their captors.

Which brings us to the complementary question that anchors this book: What are the causes of settler colonialism? There are often unfruitful debates as to whether proximal or distal insights into human behavior are more useful. Fortunately, this vital book bypasses this choice with a remarkable collaboration.

In the hands of Ilan Pappe, an Israeli historian of the reality of Zionism, there is a proximal recounting of 150 years of expansionist plans stated only in private letters, underground terror groups expelling Palestinians, self-serving quasi-Talmudic hair-splitting as to what "should" means in a UN resolution, governmental bullshit reframing theft as completion of a Divine covenant. It is an ethos that, amid the erasure of Gaza and its people, can lead a senior Israeli government official to state, "There is no such thing as a civilian in Gaza" (an opinion endorsed by a substantial percentage of Israelis in multiple, credible polls). What are the proximal causes of settler colonialism? A people's heartlessness that conjures up the Hutu of Rwanda, the Serbs of the Balkans, the Janjaweed of Sudan. A heartlessness that turns the universality of "never again" into an ethnocentric anthem.

And in the hands of Yoav Litvin, an Israeli-American behavioral neuroscientist, we have a distal analysis: of the fine evolutionary and neurobiological lines between defensive and offensive aggression, of the ways that dehumanization of "Thems" helps to dispel cognitive dissonance, how the shame and humiliation of centuries of Jewish oppression and the stain of supposed Jewish ghetto sheepdom was vanquished with the invention of a credo of prickly pear pugnacity. Most of all, an analysis of a remarkably common trait among social mammals: victims of aggression are prone to displace aggression onto weaker bystanders (a response that even lessens the secretion of stress hormones into the bloodstream, something I've seen in my study subjects, savanna baboons living in the Serengeti). Among baboons, such displacement takes the straightforward form of a victim being de-stressed by spinning around and becoming a victimizer. But in a human, it's multilayered. There are the complex mechanisms of projection and transference that can make a Palestinian tending olive trees remind an Israeli of an SS trooper, thus where victimizing that farmer acts as a negative reinforcer for the shame of Jewish historical victimhood. Moreover, the human settler mindset is layered with a positive reinforcer as well, one consonant with more traditional colonialism: the straightforward greed of dispossessing your victims of land you covet. Theft. What are the distal causes of this historical version of settler colonialism? The biology and psychology of some of the ways in which multigenerational trauma metastasizes.

This collaborative intertwining of proximal and distal insights helps explain (but crucially, not forgive) the wellsprings of settler colonialism. This is a deep, richly insightful work of scholarship; I hope its influence will be widespread in dispelling myths of the flourishing of the Land of Milk and Honey.

~ Professor Robert M. Sapolsky (Stanford University, October 2025)

Part I - War as Culture: A Brief Survey

1. Introduction

> The only possibility of regaining one's balance is to face the whole problem, for all these discoveries, all these inquiries lead only in one direction: to make man admit that he is nothing, absolutely nothing—and that he must put an end to the narcissism on which he relies in order to imagine that he is different from the other "animals."
>
> ~Frantz Fanon, *Black Skin, White Masks* (p. 22, 1967)

For millennia, war has ravaged humanity and the planet, leaving behind devastation, trauma, and deep-seated inequality, perpetuating cycles of violence which echo across generations. Throughout history, thinkers and revolutionary leaders, among others, have sought to abolish war by understanding its causes, hoping to foster just, sustainable societies. Yet war endures.

A long tradition of critical inquiry examines war through historical analyses of anti-colonial, Indigenous, and Global South liberation movements. This work also draws on intellectual traditions including the Black Radical Tradition, Pan-Africanism, Marxism, feminism, intersectionality, and related critical lineages.

Wired to Steal builds on and complements these analyses with a scientifically grounded account of the neurobehavioral and psychological mechanisms that sustain and accelerate settler colonial domination and expansion. It approaches colonial war as a relatively modern cultural construct rather than as an expression of human nature, a collective behavioral practice shaped by identifiable psychological causes, mechanisms, and consequences, with particular attention to the forms, functions, and effects of Zionist aggression. At the center of this analysis is the Wired to Steal (W2S) model, which explains how constructs of domination harness greed and human emotional drives, particularly manufactured identity, fearmongering, and selective privilege, to produce, through conditioning, hierarchies that normalize violence and enable the ongoing theft of land and resources through a self-reinforcing, escalatory cycle. The book outlines what occurs within these violent formations, when and where they arise, how and why they develop, and under what conditions the cycle can be dismantled.

In his iconic *The Wretched of the Earth,* the Martinican psychiatrist and revolutionary theorist Frantz Fanon accurately described colonization as a process of dehumanization for both the colonized and the colonizer, though in profoundly different ways; the former reduced to objects or "animals" to be controlled, the latter morally compromised, anxious, alienated from their own humanity. Extending Fanon's insights, Aimé Césaire diagnosed this as moral and civilizational decay, Albert Memmi as ethical and psychological captivity, and Paulo Freire as an asymmetrical process in which the oppressed are denied humanity while the oppressor abdicates it.

It is worth asking what exactly is "humanity" and its negation, "dehumanization," in this context?

"Humanity" can be understood as relational and behavioral capacities which enable ethical social life and collective worldmaking, describing the set of behaviors that affirm mutual recognition, empathy, and dignity for individuals and collectives. "Dehumanization" signals the disruption or reversal of those social and behavioral processes, with oppression, dispossession, and genocide (i.e., destruction of a human collective in myriad forms) at its extreme.

Several thinkers have shed light on the potential motivations behind dehumanizing cruelty and subjugation, though their focus has fallen more on how ordinary people become capable of violence than on the structural dynamics of oppressive systems themselves. These include, among others, Arendt's (1906-1975) analysis of how ordinary people can perpetuate atrocity within a bureaucratic system; Fromm's (1900-1980) analysis of aggression and the psychological structures authoritarian societies produce; Milgram's (1933-1984) experiments, which showed how readily people inflict pain on others when instructed by an authority figure; Zimbardo's (1933-2024) account of how institutional power can convert ordinary people into punitive sadists, and Waller's (1961-) extension into behaviors during genocidal events, including dehumanization, in-group preference and moral indifference toward atrocity.

What remains inadequately addressed is the behavioral and neurological architecture through which colonial violence is produced, transmitted and sustained.

This volume develops these concepts through a five-part neurobehavioral framework utilizing Zionist settler colonialism as a contemporary case study, tracing how systems of domination emerge, unfold, culminate, and can ultimately be deconstructed. Part I frames behavioral analysis as a means to reveal underlying psychological and social mechanisms, subsequently outlining the nature of war as a collective human cultural construct. Part II proceeds to survey the shift from Jewish pacifism to Zionist settler expansionism through a neurobehavioral lens, examining how this trajectory moved from putative self-defense to the logic and practice of colonial genocide grounded in offensive aggression. Part III outlines the "Wired to Steal" model, a cyclical framework identifying the psychological and behavioral mechanisms through which Zionist domination operates, including identity formation, segregation, fear conditioning, and reward for aggression, culminating in the theft of land and resources from the Indigenous Palestinian people. Part IV links these processes to current events, analyzing the post-October 7, 2023, period as the culmination and normalization of long-standing colonial dynamics. Finally, Part V presents a prescriptive path toward reclaiming humanity through a cultural revolution, drawing on examples of resistance from the Global South and the imperial core and on the natural neurobehavioral rewards of human social interaction. It offers a concise survey of collective strategies for resisting oppression, with particular attention to Palestinian resistance to Zionist colonization.

Throughout, the book positions itself as an active participant in the ongoing process of storytelling, a fundamental mechanism for deconstruction and creation, highlighting its relevance for all those entangled in colonial dynamics and, by extension, for humanity as a whole.

This opening chapter presents a foundational framework for understanding war as a behavioral phenomenon which must be unpacked to allow for critical examination.

2. What is war?

a. Rhetoric and behavior

Language is central to how humans make sense of the world and communicate with one another. In modern times, political actors, supposed masters of language who wield words to promote their interests, often advance hidden and criminal agendas, shield crimes, perpetuate theft, and evade accountability. A critical examination of doctrine and ideology, undertaken later in this book (**Parts II, IV**), is essential to dismantling and resisting propaganda. This requires distinguishing between propaganda crafted for in-group versus out-group audiences, as well as between public political rhetoric and the discourse shared within ruling-class circles. However, it is important to recognize the limitations of rhetoric as a window into motivations and avoid assuming it provides a complete picture.

As the saying goes, actions speak louder than words, and indeed, behavior can be more revealing than narratives, which are often carefully crafted by professional spin doctors. Thus, in the first parts of this book we focus on the underlying behaviors associated with warfare, imperialism, and settler colonialism. As Fanon states in the first quote of this book, appropriate analysis must rest on a crucial scientific reality: stripped of the narcissistic exceptionalism manufactured by colonial structures, the human animal is subject to the same behavioral and neurological mechanisms as other social mammals. "Regaining one's balance" is contingent on dismantling this construct.

We recognize for some readers, linking an analysis of Zionist colonization and violence, as well as resistance to it, with scientific work grounded in the observation of animal behavior may be unfamiliar and not immediately intuitive. However, given the broad recognition of the value of neuroscientific approaches, it is important to note that their usefulness as both analytical and prescriptive tools is deeply rooted in the study of animal behavior.

The theory of evolution pioneered by Charles Darwin has fostered a comparative approach in which animals are often used to learn about humans. The disciplines of biology, physiology, medicine, psychology, and anthropology, among others, have thrived, leading to substantial advances in human knowledge, quality of life, health, and longevity.

Several interconnected academic fields engage in comparative work between animals and humans:

- Comparative psychology studies behavior and cognition across species to identify general principles and insights applicable to humans.
- Ethology observes animals in their natural environments to understand species-specific behaviors and evolutionary adaptations.
- Behavioral neuroscience examines the neural mechanisms underlying behavior using brain-focused methods like imaging and electrophysiology.
- Cognitive psychology investigates human mental processes such as perception, memory, attention, and problem-solving.

This book engages with these fields, particularly behavioral neuroscientific research in both animals and humans, which has deepened our understanding of the neural underpinnings of psychological and behavioral phenomena, including aggression and violence. In turn, this knowledge illuminates the recurring dynamics of war and peace, positioning evolutionary analysis as a potential tool for deciphering human historical development.

Broadly defined, behavior includes all observable and measurable actions, from basic reflexes to complex cognitive processes. Encompassing a range of actions and practices shaped by genetics, learning, memory, environment and social interactions, behavior can be categorized as follows:

- Explicit behavior refers to external, observable actions such as gestures, movements and vocalizations. Examples include walking, feeding, and grooming, all of which can be directly measured.
- Implicit behavior involves internal mental processes like thinking, memory, perception, and decision-making. While not directly observable, these processes are inferred through indicators and explored using tools such as neuroimaging.

- Social behavior encompasses interactions between individuals or groups, including communication, cooperation, aggression, empathy, and altruism. Studying these behaviors sheds light on social bonds and their influence on well-being, with significant implications in fields like sociology, anthropology, animal behavior, and, as argued in this book, political science.

Examining these categories in humans, a highly social species of primates, within a historical context allows political scientists and others to gain insights into the complexities of human behaviors, whether innate, learned, or both, helping to decode why individuals and groups act as they do. By focusing on actions rather than rhetoric, behavioral study cuts through the fog of propaganda, providing a clearer view of historical processes, recurring patterns, and unique developments, enabling a deeper understanding of unfolding conflicts with actionable solutions.

b. Comparative studies and dangers of anthropomorphism

> The difference in mind between man and the higher animals, great as it is, certainly is one of degree and not of kind.
>
> ~ Charles Darwin, *The Descent of Man, and Selection in Relation to Sex* (p.105, 1871)

When conducting comparative analysis between animals and humans, it is crucial to address the dangers of anthropomorphism: a propensity to attribute human traits, emotions, or intentions to nonhuman species. This was addressed by evolutionary biologists going back to Darwin's *The Descent of Man*, and including Konrad Lorenz, Niko Tinbergen, and others.

Evolutionary biologists and behavioral neuroscientists carefully engage in comparative work and do not assume equivalence as behaviors across species may arise from different mechanisms. Further, humans have developed elaborate social behavior which includes symbolic culture, language, and institutions. However, scientists do assume mammals share evolved and conserved anatomy, physiology, and behavior, including neuroendocrine and neurobehavioral circuits/mechanisms for stress, fear, anxiety, aggression, bonding, reward, learning, memory, and so forth, and that these provide invaluable insight into human behavior.

After all, human physicians and veterinarians often operate under the assumption of largely equivalent anatomy and physiology, particularly in related species to humans, such as primates and other mammals, affecting similar diagnoses and treatments. Indeed, studies of animals provide a powerful analytic tool, generating insights into both animal and human physiology and behavior, while often allowing scientists to examine systems that would be impossible or unethical to study directly in humans. While limited, comparative studies assist in drawing analogies at the mechanistic level.

Similarly, behavioral neuroscientists have built on this approach by studying social hierarchies, stress responses, aggression, and associated pathologies in a variety of species, while considering the evolutionary relatedness, or lack thereof, of model animals, whether in captivity or in the wild. With relevance to cognition, culture and context factored in, these models can illuminate biological mechanisms shared with humans. Properly grounded, comparative studies provide a robust framework for understanding collective human behavior and its pathological potential, while avoiding simplistic or misleading parallels.

This book carefully employs a comparative approach to construct behavioral models, applying findings from scientific research to shed light on mechanisms of war and aggression, with implications for settler colonialism in general and Zionism in particular.

c. War and human nature

> The expediency of aggressive or defensive tactics; and the fundamental laws of human nature: these are things that must most certainly be studied.
>
> -Sun Tzu, *The Art of War* (roughly 500–300 B.C.)

War is a form of violent, social aggression. Unlike interpersonal violence or homicide, war involves organized, cooperative, and often armed conflict, sanctioned by societies and waged by one group against another with the intent to kill. In its basic form, warfare is a strategy in which coalitions collaborate to aggressively seize and defend resources vital for reproduction.

Aggression, broadly defined, is any intentional behavior aimed at harming someone who wishes to avoid harm, while violence necessarily involves physical force intended to hurt, damage, or kill someone or something. While all violence is a form of aggression, not all aggression results in violence; aggression can also manifest in nonviolent forms, such as insults or threats.

Is collective violence an inherent part of human nature, or a relatively recent development? The answer to this question remains a topic of heated debate in scientific circles and carries significant political implications. If war is "natural," and existed as long as humanity has, and potentially before, achieving lasting peace would require an unlikely and potentially unstable transformation of societies, upending human nature. If it is predominantly cultural and modern, its abolition becomes possible and natural. If war is innate, overcoming it requires understanding and counteracting our biological instincts. If it is a cultural construct, dismantling it means analyzing and addressing its modern foundations.

"Deep rooters" contend that warfare has deep evolutionary roots, extending back millions of years to our primate ancestors, and has been a significant factor in shaping human psychology and behavior. In contrast, "shallow rooters" contend warfare is a relatively recent phenomenon in human evolutionary history, driven primarily by cultural shifts associated with the Neolithic Revolution, such as the rise of sedentism, (an inactive lifestyle), pastoralism, domestication of animals, agriculture, and food storage. These innovations created surpluses, leading to unequal resource distribution, the emergence of new types of social hierarchies, and a transition from collectivism to individualism. This shift disrupted mobile hunter-gatherer structures once held together by trust, empathy, and camaraderie, fueling emotions like aggression, fear, and envy, which in turn serve to sustain these stratified structures. Consequently, organized conflict has become significantly more common in the past 10,000 years.

Deep rooters point to chimpanzees, our closest relatives, who engage in lethal intergroup violence, often using tools as weapons, including raids and territorial expansion. These behaviors, they argue, enhance group success and indicate organized aggression predates humanity itself. There are even documented instances of "genocide" in chimpanzees, deep rooters claim, where mostly male chimpanzees raid rival communities, killing members, especially infants and weaker individuals.

A notable example occurred at Gombe Stream National Park in Tanzania, where, from the 1970s to the 2000s, the late primatologist and anthropologist Jane Goodall and others documented the Kasakela community systematically killing members of the neighboring Kahama community: the "Gombe Chimpanzee War." Over several years, coordinated attacks decimated the Kahama group, with the few survivors fleeing or being killed. Though these events have often been called "genocide," the term is controversial as applied here, as chimpanzees lack the political, cultural, or ideological motives that are part of the definition of human genocide.

Upon close, meticulous analysis, shallow rooters such as R. Brian Ferguson of Rutgers University refute these arguments, demonstrating chimpanzees and other primates do not engage in collective violence comparable to human warfare (more in **Part IV**). While male chimpanzees patrol boundaries and attack solitary males from neighboring groups, these behaviors stem from ecological pressures, resource competition, and human disruptions (e.g., food provisioning and its withdrawal) rather than innate warlike tendencies. Unlike humans, chimps do not form large-scale coalitions for conquest or political motives. Comparisons with bonobos, another close primate ancestor to humans known for their peaceful, female-dominated societies and intelligence, show they exhibit minimal intergroup violence. This underscores the role of social structure and environment in shaping aggression, challenging the idea that warfare is an evolutionary inevitability.

Ferguson further questions the validity of using chimpanzees or bonobos as models for human warfare, noting that both lineages have undergone significant evolutionary changes since diverging from their last common ancestor with humans. Unlike chimpanzees, humans have developed and evolved sophisticated strategies, technologies, and institutions for conducting war. Human warfare also involves moral and ethical considerations, long- and short-term political motivations, propaganda and the construction of "us vs. them" narratives.

As previously argued, animal studies can illustrate underlying biological mechanisms, such as fear, aggression, and other relevant behaviors, yet they cannot fully mimic and explain human war, which is layered with social, political, and symbolic dimensions. This difference stresses a critical nuance in which comparative biology can and should be used as a tool for insight, not as a direct template for human behavior.

Deep rooters argue that the paleo-archaeological record of hunter-gatherer societies, which documents small-scale raids and ambushes among various foraging groups, points to the long-standing presence of warfare in human social structures. They emphasize the Nataruk massacre, dating back to around 10,000 years ago, as proof of intergroup violence. This massacre, found near Lake Turkana in present-day Kenya, involved the killing of at least twenty-seven individuals, including men, women, and children, and serves as evidence of lethal conflict among prehistoric, nomadic hunter-gatherers. For deep rooters, this violence predates agriculture and sedentism, reinforcing their belief that war has deep evolutionary roots. Further, they point to Paleolithic cave paintings in France, around 25,000 years old, which depict figures seemingly pierced by spears, suggesting early warfare.

Skeptics argue the Nataruk site remains may reflect taphonomic processes (natural physical, chemical, and biological post-mortem changes), accidents, or predation rather than organized intergroup violence, making the "massacre" interpretation unsubstantiated. Further, shallow rooters challenge this view by pointing to the absence of unambiguous evidence of organized warfare before the Nataruk massacre in the late Stone Age. Moreover, they argue the intersecting bent or wavy lines in the Paleolithic cave paintings may represent shamanic forces, not weapons. Shallow rooters also highlight how many hunter-gatherer groups actively worked to prevent or minimize intergroup conflict. They contend warfare is more likely to occur in societies with hierarchical structures and monopolizable resources, rather than in egalitarian foraging societies. Thus, they see the Nataruk massacre as an anomaly, not a reflection of a widespread, ancestral tendency toward violence.

For most of human history, humans lived in hunter-gatherer societies which were generally egalitarian, as documented by anthropologists such as Douglas P. Fry at UNC Greensboro. Inequality emerged with the rise of agriculture and control and husbandry of livestock, which introduced the concept of resource accumulation. Growing surpluses fueled rising inequality, and the advent of inheritance within families solidified these imbalances, making inequality a persistent feature across cultures.

Why have hierarchical societies come to dominate more egalitarian ones? One of the reasons is hierarchy fosters militarism, which in turn enables conquest and expansion, strategies often used to survive resource shortages. In such systems, the ruling class shields itself from scarcity while the lower classes absorb most of the hardship.

In *War and Peace and War*, Peter Turchin explores the cyclical nature of empires, emphasizing how internal dynamics, particularly rising inequality, contribute to their decline. As empires expand and accumulate wealth, disparities in wealth and power emerge, leading to increased competition both between and within social classes. This erosion of social cohesion undermines collective action, making societies more susceptible to instability and collapse. Interestingly, Turchin claims the very factors contributing to an empire's rise, cohesion and shared purpose, can be eroded by gross inequalities and internal competitions which emerge during its expansion, ultimately leading to its decline.

An early example of warfare dates back to around 3200 BCE, when Pharaonic Egypt expanded into the Southern Levant, known as Canaan (modern-day Palestine/Israel, Lebanon, southern Syria, and Jordan). This expansion may mark one of the earliest instances of a tribal region being drawn into organized conflict, transforming centuries of peace into a battleground.

Such imperial wars are often mistakenly viewed as part of human nature. Reactionaries co-opt deep rooters' often cherry-picked claims to justify warfare and colonialism, extending the analysis to falsely depict Indigenous tribes as inherently violent "savages." However, in line with the shallow rooters' analysis, war is better understood as a relatively modern social cultural development which arose at specific moments in history motivated by particular systems of power, often tied to imperialism and colonial conquest, such as the case of Pharaonic Egypt's settlement expansion.

d. Human culture and propaganda

At its core, war can be understood as a strategic and practical social behavior, driven by the pursuit of resources, territory, power, and political objectives. Warfare shapes social relations, either reinforcing or challenging existing power structures.

In line with Richard B. Lee's seminal work showing many hunter-gatherer societies sustain low levels of violence through egalitarian norms, sharing, and nonviolent conflict resolution, Brian Ferguson argues that war is shaped by culture and historical conditions rather than by any fixed human nature. He argues what sets humans apart is not rigid social instincts, but flexible, intelligent minds with a remarkable ability to learn and adapt. This adaptability is what drives human behavior, including the inclination toward war. Ferguson points to societies which shape their own ways of fighting based on their beliefs and values. For example, while indigenous warfare may look similar in different regions, it is deeply influenced by each culture's unique traditions and moral codes, highlighting how global patterns of conflict take on local forms.

The controversy between deep and shallow rooters will not be settled here, though we clearly find the shallow rooters' evidence and approach far more compelling; war has undoubtedly evolved over time, predominantly shaped by culture and economic structures. If it existed in a rudimentary form before organized settlements, the shift to a sedentary lifestyle involving agriculture and resource accumulation certainly intensified and remodeled it. As a relatively modern form of large-scale social aggression, war exploits specific evolved emotional and behavioral mechanisms to serve particular interests.

Cultivated "culture," closely tied to the interests of society's leaders, plays a key role in shaping how people define "us" and "them," which in turn influences decisions about war and peace. Humans have a unique ability to think symbolically, and perceived shared values and norms often fuel war.

This leads to two central themes of this book. First, despite the complexities of political conflict and the relatively modern development of warfare, human brains still process and react to it using neural mechanisms shaped by millions of years of evolution, rooted in the challenges faced by hunter-gatherers on the savanna. Recognizing the behavioral expressions associated with war, namely defense and offense (**Part II**), is key to understanding the root causes and results of wars in their many forms, and potential pathways to resolution (**Part V**). Second, the unequal, hierarchical nature of power structures makes it crucial to distinguish between the psychology of the ruling class and that of the general population and the role of propaganda in promoting ruling-class interests (**Parts III, IV**).

Power structures in human societies shape how we understand and experience war and reflect the interests of those in control, creating narratives that serve these interests. Leaders frequently exploit powerful cultural ideas, such as honor, revenge, religion, ethnic identity, or status, to justify violence (what Fanon called "narcissism"). These distinctions are not universal; they shift depending on societal contexts and historical circumstances, illustrating how deeply rooted cultural narratives, including targeted propaganda, influence collective decision-making.

Cultural differences between stratified/individualistic versus egalitarian/collectivist societies also shape the motivations, behaviors, and propaganda of warring parties. In highly hierarchical societies in which power is concentrated in the ruling class, war requires little justification and can be waged purely for self-interest. In contrast, egalitarian, collectivist societies, in which broader consensus is necessary, readily accept defense yet are less likely to support wars that serve only a privileged few.

"Culture" and the power systems it upholds also play a crucial role in shaping peace. Societies that nurture values of creation, collaboration, interdependence, and environmental sustainability can foster conditions that reduce the likelihood of war. The human brain is not a blank slate; it readily forms "us" and "them" distinctions. Brain-imaging studies show that the anterior cingulate, a region associated with empathy, often exhibits greater activation when individuals witness the pain of someone of their own perceived group. People also tend to more quickly associate negative experiences with those they perceive as different. Yet, as Ibram X. Kendi argues in *How to Raise an Antiracist*, racial "bias" is not rooted in nature; it is rooted in racist ideas (p. 33).

Encouragingly, positive and close interactions with individuals from other racial groups can help override this fear response. Similarly, while culture can drive conflict, it also has the power to steer societies toward non-militaristic paths (more in **Part V**).

The impacts of war extend far beyond the battlefield, leaving deep psychological and emotional scars on individuals, communities, humanity as a whole, and planet Earth. War can stir intense feelings of fear, anger, trauma, grief, and a manufactured solidarity and empathy typical of faux kinships among strangers donning a similar uniform, all of which contribute to shaping both personal and collective identities. Understanding how war unfolds, examining the motivations behind its initiation, the propaganda that justifies it, and the broader implications it has on societies, can guide us toward a more peaceful future and offer insight into the complexities of human nature. To reclaim control and move toward lasting peace, we must expose how those in power manipulate systems for their own gain and look to societies less prone to war for insight and example.

e. Masculinity, femininity, and war

A useful example of a cultural construct is the relationship between gender and war. Human warfare has historically been dominated by men, yet this does not mean they are naturally predisposed to it. While men have often been the primary participants in war, cultural and historical variations challenge the idea that war is an inherently male pursuit.

Research on chimpanzees shows that although males sometimes engage in deadly violence, they are not inherently driven to kill. Instead, their aggression is shaped by factors like human disturbance, social organization, and personality. A comparison with bonobos, where females hold higher status and often form coalitions to restrain aggressive males, further highlights the role of social structures in shaping behavior.

Archaeological evidence challenges the idea that war was a dominant or natural part of early human societies and undermines the notion of an innate warrior masculinity. Ethnographic studies also show many non-state and hunter-gatherer societies resolved conflicts without war. Mobile forager bands, in particular, rarely engaged in warfare, often emphasizing cooperation over competition. In contrast, many sedentary societies actively socialize boys for aggression, promoting rough play, physical strength, and mock battles to instill competitiveness and bravery. This socialization, reinforced by adults, serves to produce warriors in societies where combat is framed as a masculine duty.

Here, as with war in general, we can see the primacy of nurture over nature in determining behavior. Indeed, femininity, like masculinity, is a cultural construct; its supposed inherent inclination toward peace is no more natural than the association of masculinity with war.

According to social role theory, women are expected to embody communal traits (warmth, kindness, nurturing), while men are expected to embody authoritative, independent traits. When women display dominance, they often face backlash for violating these norms, even if their goals serve the community. This backlash occurs in both mixed- and same-sex groups, underscoring how strongly culture enforces gender stereotypes.

Patriarchal systems can co-opt women who uphold their fearmongering and warmongering interests while marginalizing those who do not, a dynamic particularly evident in the entanglement of white feminism with colonialism. Jessie Daniels at the City University of New York reveals how both historical and contemporary feminist movements have often perpetuated violent, colonialist, male-dominant ideologies. Daniels highlights how early feminist advocacy for women's rights coexisted with support for colonial regimes, neglecting the role of race in shaping white femininity. Contemporary examples demonstrate appropriation and erasure of Indigenous activism while positioning white feminists as saviors of women of color without addressing systemic inequalities. Additionally, white feminism's reliance on neo-colonial practices, imposing Western ideals on non-Western contexts, and carceral solutions that disproportionately harm communities of color further entrench its complicity in colonial and neo-colonial, violent, and male-dominated structures.

Black feminist thinkers have long interrogated the cultural relationships between violence, oppression, and gendered power, offering critical and intersectional perspectives on war and aggression (**Part V**). Audre Lorde examined resistance in marginalized communities, highlighting women's relational and creative power. bell hooks argued patriarchal and white supremacist structures shape both interpersonal and systemic violence and explored how empathy and care can counteract these forces. Patricia Hill Collins's framework of the "matrix of domination" situates women's social roles as crucial for resisting structural oppression, while Chandra Talpade Mohanty examines how women navigate and reshape militarized contexts in postcolonial societies. Contemporary scholars like Joy James extend these insights to militarization and racialized state violence, linking femininity to strategies of survival, resistance, and ethics.

Women in the Black Panther Party further exemplify a unique blend of community empowerment and militancy. Leaders like Elaine Brown, Ericka Huggins, Assata Shakur, Kathleen Cleaver, and many others organized survival programs, education, and social services while participating in armed self-defense, demonstrating women's leadership could combine ethical collaboration and principled resistance. Together, these thinkers and activists debunk the white male capitalist stereotype of women as passive, demonstrating their instrumental roles in both community resilience and strategies for dismantling systemic violence (**Part V**).

Now that we have introduced the primacy of cultural constructs, as opposed to innate ones, particularly those of warfare, in shaping human collectives, we can move on to an example of such a collective. A similar logic of cultural identity formation shaped how European Jewish communities, grappling with centuries of exclusion, persecution, and powerlessness, laid the groundwork for the birth of political Zionism.

Further Reading

1. Memmi A. *The Colonizer and the Colonized.* Greenfeld H. Beacon Press; 1965.
2. Césaire A. *Discourse on Colonialism trans. Joan Pinkham.* Monthly Review Press; 1972 (Originally published in 1950).
3. Freire P, Ramos MB. *Pedagogy of the oppressed.* Sheed and Ward; 1972.
4. Fanon F. *The Wretched of the Earth* (C. Farrington, Trans.). Grove Press; 1963.
5. Ferguson RB. *Chimpanzees, War, and History.* Oxford University Press; 2023.
6. Glowacki L, Wilson ML, Wrangham RW. The evolutionary anthropology of war. *Journal of Economic Behavior & Organization.* 2020;178:963-982.
7. Baron RA, Richardson DR. *Human Aggression.* 2nd ed. Plenum Press; 1994.
8. Mirazón Lahr M, Rivera F, Power RK, et al. Inter-group violence among early Holocene hunter-gatherers of West Turkana, Kenya. *Nature.* Jan 21 2016;529(7586):394-8. doi:10.1038/nature16477
9. Borgerhoff Mulder M, Bowles S, Hertz T, et al. Intergenerational wealth transmission and the dynamics of inequality in small-scale societies. *Science.* Oct 30 2009;326(5953):682-8. doi:10.1126/science.1178336
10. Turchin P. *War and Peace and War: The Rise and Fall of Empires.* Plume; 2007.
11. Lee RB. Hunter-Gatherers and Human Evolution: New Light on Old Debates. *Annual Review of Anthropology.* 2018;47(Volume 47, 2018):513-531. doi:https://doi.org/10.1146/annurev-anthro-102116-041448

12. Ferguson RB. Why War? From the Pleistocene to the Present: an Anthropological Perspective. Editorial. *Public Anthropologist.* 2023;5(1): 1-6. doi:https://doi.org/10.1163/25891715-05010001
13. Hedges C. *War Is a Force that Gives Us Meaning* Anchor; 2003:224.
14. Darwin C. *The Descent of Man, and Selection in Relation to Sex.* John Murray; 1871.
15. Ferguson RB. Masculinity and War. *Current Anthropology.* 2021;62 (S23):112-124.
16. Chen Zeng T, Cheng JT, Henrich J. Dominance in humans. *Philos Trans R Soc Lond B* 2022;377doi: https://royalsocietypublishing.org/doi/10.1098/rstb.2020.0451
17. Kendi IX. *How to Raise an Antiracist.* One World; 2022.
18. Daniels J. The Trouble with White Feminism: Whiteness, Digital Feminism and the Intersectional Internet. doi: Available at SSRN: https://ssrn.com/abstract=2569369 or http://dx.doi.org/10.2139/ssrn.2569369
19. Lorde A. *Sister Outsider: Essays and Speeches.* The Crossing Press feminist series. Crossing Press; 1984:190 p.
20. hooks b. *From Margin to Center.* South End Press; 1984.
21. Collins PH. *Black Feminist Thought: Knowledge, Consciousness, and the Politics of Empowerment.* Routledge (originally Hyman); 1990.
22. James J, ed. *Warfare in the American Homeland: Policing and Prison in a Penal Democracy.* Duke University Press; 2007.

Part II - From Shtetl to Settlement: Jewish Pacifism to Zionist Settler Colonialism

1. Pacifism to empowerment: the cultural background for the birth of political Zionism

a. Before the Haskalah

By the mid-19th century, the locus of Zionism was in Central and Eastern Europe, where millions of Jews lived primarily in townships and villages, while their elites began to integrate into urban life. Zionism emerged within these communities as part of the broader cultural renaissance known as the Haskalah (the Jewish Enlightenment), which had begun at the end of the eighteenth century.

The vast majority of Jews were confined to rural areas within the Russian Empire's Pale of Settlement, where they faced severe legal, economic, social, and geographic restrictions. Their lives revolved around *halakha* (Jewish religious law), overseen by their rabbis and administered by the *kahal*, an internal council of lay leaders. This leadership provided spiritual guidance and local governance, managing everything from education and charity to legal disputes.

Isolated linguistically and culturally from their Christian neighbors, Jews in these parts of the continent spoke Yiddish and maintained a rich internal culture of storytelling, music, and religious devotion, including the rise of Hasidism as a popular spiritual movement. Economically restricted by imperial Russian law, they survived through peddling, trade, artisan work, and intermediary roles between peasants and nobles, positions which often made them scapegoats for broader social tensions. Despite growing hardships and periodic persecution, these communities sustained themselves through strong social bonds and a deeply rooted religious identity, forming a resilient social fabric.

Those among them who were religious and traditional, which were the majority in the nineteenth century, believed that suffering, whether personal or collective, was a form of divine punishment for moral or ritual failings. Traumatic events such as exile, persecution, forced segregation, or pogroms were often interpreted theologically, seen as God's response to communal transgressions. This worldview encouraged a posture of passivity and spiritual endurance, grounded in the conviction that redemption would come only through divine intervention, not human effort. In this context, rabbis typically emphasized repentance, Torah study, and spiritual resilience as the proper responses to adversity.

While only a minority of Jews lived in cities like Vienna, Prague, and Berlin, it was in these urban centers that the intellectual foundations of the Zionist movement took shape. These early Zionists sought to create a modern Jewish national identity, often departing from traditional religious life and connecting their vision to the contemporary European nationalist and colonialist movements of the era.

b. The Haskalah

The Haskalah (Jewish Enlightenment) began to challenge long-held beliefs. Emerging in late eighteenth-century Europe in Germany and Central Europe and later spreading eastward, the Haskalah was shaped by the ideals of the broader European Enlightenment. It promoted secular education, rationalism, and integration into modern society, while still affirming a redefined sense of Jewish identity. This intellectual movement encouraged Jews to view suffering and social stagnation not as inevitable divine punishment but as conditions that could and should be addressed through human initiative and reform.

Moses Mendelssohn, considered the father of the Haskalah, advocated for Jews to embrace modern languages, engage with non-Jewish culture, and modernize traditional Jewish education. The Haskalah encouraged Jews to desegregate away from insular religious study and to participate more fully in civic life, sparking debates about assimilation, tradition, and cultural survival that still resonate today.

The Haskalah fractured the traditional rabbinic hegemony which long dominated Jewish communal life. This rabbinic authority had reflected, in part, the historical limitations on Jews' access to secular education, the persistence of superstition, and the concentration of power among religious leaders, conditions reinforced by Jews' exclusion from mainstream European society and their reliance on internal solidarity for survival. The Haskalah encouraged a profound cultural shift within Jewish communities to rationalism, integration into European society, and engagement with modern ideas. As a result, the view that suffering was solely divine punishment weakened, and passive waiting for redemption gave way to active effort, including political, cultural, and even military initiatives (e.g., self-defense groups). The notion of human agency grew stronger, challenging earlier fatalism and reshaping Jewish responses to injustice.

However, even after the height of the Haskalah, many Jews who pursued secular education and sought greater integration into Western societies encountered deep-rooted prejudice and systemic exclusion, also within liberal democracies. These persistent barriers, in addition to the rise of romantic nationalist movements, the normalization of settler colonial expansionism as a solution for disenfranchised populations, and the rise of Marxism helped create fertile ground for the appeal of various movements for ethnic self-determination and empowerment.

c. The birth of Jewish political Zionism and other movements

The Haskalah marked a profound cultural shift in Jewish life. It broke down the boundaries of insular communities and exposed them to contemporary European political ideologies. Out of this transformation and as a response to its limitations emerged several modern movements, including Zionism, Bundism, and Reform and Conservative Judaism.

Zionism, a nationalist movement advocating for the establishment of a Jewish homeland in Palestine, represented a rebellion against both European antisemitism and the traditional Jewish pacifist view that suffering was divine punishment. It adopted a secular outlook which framed colonial expansion as a modern, legitimate response to exclusion and trauma.

Zionism's conceptual origins lie in two distinct religious environments. Among Evangelical Christians, especially in seventeenth-through-nineteenth-century Britain and the US, it took shape as a restorationist and millenarian idea. These Christians believed the return of Jews to Palestine would precipitate the Second Coming of Christ, the resurrection of the dead, and divine judgment. By the mid-nineteenth century, British Evangelical politicians saw this vision as aligning with imperial ambitions to wrest Palestine from the Ottoman Empire.

These Christian ideas inspired a similar impulse among Jewish intellectuals, driven by two intertwined motivations: the first was a response to rising antisemitism fueled by European romantic nationalism and colonialism, while the second was a desire to modernize Judaism and integrate Jews more fully into non-Jewish societies through universalist or revolutionary movements.

When assimilation, modernization, and political participation did not quell antisemitism, a core group concluded the only solution was to leave Europe and rebuild a version of Jewish Europe elsewhere, ideally in Palestine. By 1904, other destination options had largely been abandoned in the wake of the death of Theodore Herzl, who was the last leader to support these alternatives and particularly considered Uganda to be the best option.

Early Zionists drew from European romantic nationalism, colonial ideologies, messianic Evangelism and Judaism, and US-based concepts of white supremacy. They also adopted European orientalism, which led them to view Palestine as either an empty desert or one inhabited solely by nomadic peoples. In practice, both antisemites and Zionists saw a shared utility in concentrating Jews in Palestine; for the former, it meant scapegoating and expelling Jews; for the latter, it began as a colonial fantasy and evolved into a calculated strategy to confront what they framed as the "demographic threat" of the Indigenous Palestinian population.

Both groups also adopted racialized definitions of Jewish identity, reflecting the influence of nineteenth-century European pseudo-scientific racism (**Part III**). These ideas, which emerged among nationalist and race theorists in mid-nineteenth-century France and Germany, divided humanity into supposedly immutable "races." Physicians, anthropologists, and naturalists concocted flawed science to justify slavery, colonization, inequality, and white supremacist oppression, producing a framework that was adapted in settler-colonial societies such as the United States and Palestine, where they underpinned systems of segregation and dispossession.

Zionism was thus driven by two contradictory yet converging impulses: to protect Jews from antisemitism, and to reinvent Judaism within the romantic nationalist framework that had marginalized them. Over time, this redefinition came to frame the colonization of Palestine as the only viable solution to antisemitism.

Once Zionist leaders agreed, following heated internal debate, that Palestine was the sole legitimate destination and the center of the new nationalist vision of Judaism, confrontation with the Indigenous population became unavoidable. War as a continuous structure (versus episodic violence), as outlined by Rashid Khalidi in his book *The Hundred Years' War on Palestine: A History of Settler Colonialism and Resistance, 1917–2017,* thus became necessary and integral to the project and has remained so ever since, as in other settler colonial enterprises. By the end of World War I, Zionist aims were clearly articulated: to take over historic Palestine and build a Jewish state, regardless of Indigenous Palestinian resistance.

At its core, Zionism can therefore be understood as a white supremacist European project, borne of Europe's territorial ambitions in the Middle East and its failure to resolve antisemitism at home, opting instead to impose a racialized model of a so-called Jewish nation-state in the heart of the Arab world, at the expense of the Palestinian people. Notably, many Western European Jewish communities viewed Zionism as a project of Eastern European Jews and, among other reasons, supported or tolerated it as a means of preventing their migration to Western Europe.

Viewed through this lens, the evolution of Zionist aggression reveals its origins as a settler colonial project shaped by specific strategic objectives: territorial expansion and resource acquisition. Forging a new Zionist social collective required a profound cultural shift away from diasporic Jewish pacifism and toward militant, offensive nationalism, a shift that traces a direct ideological lineage from the Haskalah to modern Zionist thought.

How did this extreme transition take place? What were its steps along the way?

Addressing these questions requires unpacking warfare into its behavioral components: from individual aggression in defensive and offensive forms, to small-group territoriality and the maintenance of social hierarchies, and finally to large-scale social aggression. Cultural narratives, in turn, interact with these behavioral systems to shape action in ways that serve ruling-class interests.

To analyze this evolution, it is essential to begin with developments in Jewish communities in the mid-1800s, when Zionism emerged against the backdrop of the growing influence, and perceived failure, of the Haskalah. A key early component was the appropriation of self-defense traditions developed in response to nineteenth-century pogroms in Eastern Europe and forced ghettoization. Zionist leaders reinterpreted these practices not merely as survival strategies but as preparatory steps toward organized, exclusive, and forceful offensive takeover of Palestine, euphemistically termed ***kibush*** *ha'aretz* ("conquest/occupation of the land").

Zionism's behavioral trajectory thus began with defense, an active response to persecution that rebelled against traditional Jewish pacifism, in line with Haskalah ideals. The following section interrogates the behavioral expressions of defense in general, followed by how these manifested within European Jewish communities in particular.

2. Defense

Existence is a game of strategy, with aggression as one of its most potent tactics. From the roaring savannas of Africa to complex social webs of human civilization extending into virtual internet conglomerates, aggression can shape the balance of power, dictating who thrives and who falters.

Starting at the level of the individual, through groups, to societies, aggression encompasses much more than overt acts of force; it is a fundamental driver in the evolution, and at times devolution, of individuals and social systems, shaping patterns of survival and dominance. By fueling territorial behaviors between groups and structuring hierarchies within them, aggression lays the groundwork for how space, power, and social order are negotiated both across and within species.

Throughout the animal world, including in humans, aggression manifests in two primary forms: defensive and offensive. While both types may appear similar and can be masked duplicitously, they serve distinct purposes and are driven by different motivations; defensive aggression is rooted in survival, offensive aggression in control and domination.

Defensive aggression, an evolutionarily ancient and highly conserved behavior observed across all mammals, some other vertebrates, and even some invertebrates, is a reactive, instinctive, fear-driven response to an immediate threat. Its primary function is protection, whether of oneself, offspring, resources, or territory and it therefore ceases once the threat has passed. It is part of a broader defensive behavioral repertoire that includes both innate and learned components, primarily observed in vertebrates and a few invertebrates.

In contrast, most invertebrates, such as insects, rely on structural defenses, including protective armor, camouflage, and chemical deterrents like toxins or unpleasant tastes. While some do exhibit behavioral defenses, such as immobility or habitat selection, these responses are generally less developed and less varied than those seen in vertebrates, including mammals. Neurobehavioral research shows that human responses to threats share deep evolutionary roots with those of other mammals, reflecting common survival mechanisms.

Work spearheaded by Robert and Caroline Blanchard, at the University of Hawaiʻi at Mānoa, has demonstrated that in threatening situations, mammals stop non-defensive activities such as grooming, playing, foraging, feeding, and sexual behavior, and exhibit a range of defensive responses, including: (i) general avoidance of a threat and stimuli associated with it; (ii) flight from it; (iii) freezing as a means to reduce unwanted attention/detection; (iv) risk assessment as a transitory behavior to assess threat severity; (v) defensive threat as a display of force and a potential prelude to violence; (vi) defensive attack (the final two collectively termed "defensive aggression"). Social species (e.g., meerkats) may also display warning calls primarily directed at conspecifics (members of one's own species) living nearby.

For example, when confronted by a predator, a squirrel may freeze, retreat, puff up its tail, emit warning calls, chatter its teeth (defensive threat), or lunge at a predator (defensive attack), all signs of defensive behaviors aimed at staying alive rather than domination. The goal is immediate survival, avoiding conflict when possible while ensuring safety when necessary.

Studies on mammals including humans reveal that defensive behaviors vary based on threat type and context, reflecting adaptations to natural dangers such as predators, conspecifics, and environmental hazards. Among these three types of threats, predators likely drive the greatest variation in defense strategies across prey species. Studies across different cultures (e.g., United States, Brazil, United Kingdom) show consistent human responses to threat scenarios, paralleling animal behaviors. The translation of animal defensive patterns to humans highlights evolutionary adaptations in threat response mechanisms, with implications for understanding normal and pathological behaviors.

The manifestation of these behaviors depends on several factors: (i) context – an animal will typically flee a threat within an environment in which escape is possible, yet when trapped it will freeze/fight; (ii) stimulus intensity – whereas ambiguous stimuli (such as predator odor in rodents) elicit risk assessment behaviors and are often associated with a state of anxiety, discrete threats (presence of predator) elicit flight, avoidance, defensive threat, and attack and are associated with a state of fear; (iii) defensive distance – the distance between predator and prey shifts defensive coping strategies from avoidance to escape, with short distances and contact culminating in defensive aggression (see **Figure II.1**).

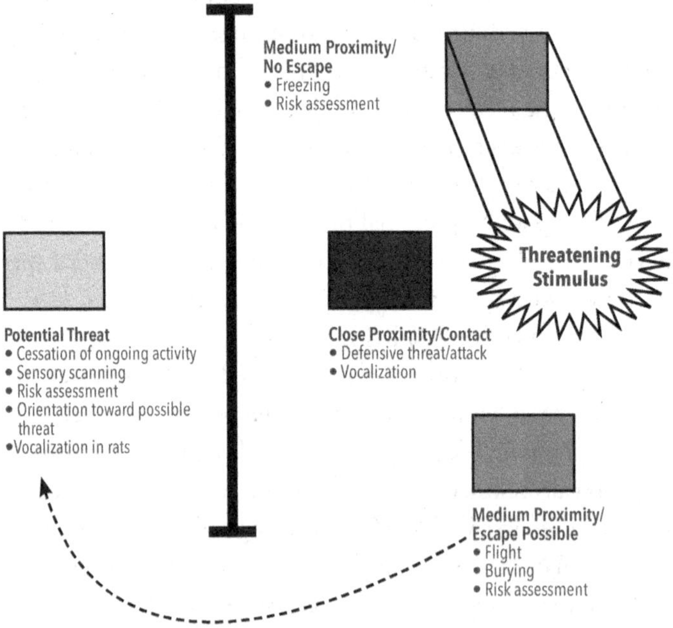

Figure II.1. Defensive behaviors are affected by context and intensity

Innate defensive behaviors may become conditioned to specific environments or cues. For instance, associating danger with particular neighborhoods, or reacting to auditory or visual stimuli such as approaching footsteps or dim lighting. These responses may intensify when context and cue combine, as in hearing footsteps in dangerous parts of town.

Such "fear conditioning" is a behavioral paradigm in which an organism learns to associate an otherwise neutral stimulus (e.g., a particular place, a sound or a light) with an aversive one (e.g., pain). After repeated pairings, the neutral stimulus alone elicits a behavioral and physiological fear response, such as freezing or increased heart rate, respectively. Fear conditioning is widely used in research to study the mechanisms of learned fear and anxiety, with defensive behaviors modeled in various kinds of paradigms (more in **Part III**).

While defensive behaviors are adaptive in particular situations, their chronic and potentially pathological expression has significant and far-reaching effects on both individuals and society, with lasting consequences across mental, physical, and social dimensions. On the individual, chronic fear and stress can contribute to anxiety disorders such as post-traumatic stress disorder (PTSD) and can lead to major depression, while also impairing brain function, including cognition, emotional regulation, and self-control. Further, it can increase heart rate and blood pressure, raising the risk of cardiovascular diseases such as strokes and heart attacks and is linked to metabolic issues, including obesity and diabetes.

Behaviorally, chronic fear may turn to unhealthy coping mechanisms like overeating, smoking, abnormal defensive aggression (more in **Part III**), or excessive alcohol drinking, while neglecting exercise and social interactions. Chronic activation of fear and stress disrupts sleep, reducing both sleep quality and duration, further exacerbating health problems.

Together, these effects have profound implications for both individuals and society. Chronic fear is weaponized to justify lethal defensive aggression, as the following sections illustrate, while also making populations more susceptible to propaganda that promotes offensive aggression.

3. Defending the Pale and early Zionist "defense"

Pogroms in Eastern Europe and Imperial Russia, especially following the 1881 assassination of Czar Alexander II by the revolutionary group *Narodnaya*

Volya ("People's Will"), and during the waves of violence in 1903–05 and 1917–20, made clear to many Jews that such attacks often occurred with the tacit approval of the authorities, and at times were even actively incited by them. Jews were scapegoated for the political instability, with various groups exploiting the unrest to incite violence, especially in the southwestern regions. As such, some Jews came to see self-defense, including the protection of property, as physically and spiritually necessary.

During this period, many Jewish inhabitants had become secular yet were not emancipated, i.e., they still experienced legal and social restrictions and lacked equal rights, citizenship, and freedom to live and work among non-Jews. As a result, their experience of antisemitism and the violence and trauma it entailed was filtered through a modern lens. Unlike the traditional views of highly segregated communities that framed suffering as divine punishment for sin, these Jews, who enjoyed some freedoms and were affected by the rise of European romantic nationalist movements, felt a deep sense of shame at their continued humiliation and powerlessness, especially as their hopes for integration were violently shattered.

In response to this onslaught of violence, Jewish people chose several strategies to defend themselves. First, those who had the means and ability chose to escape (identical to other mammals' chosen defensive behavior), leaving for Western Europe, the Americas, Australia, Palestine, and other destinations. Second, many self-segregated further in communities: shtetls (fortressing, a form of freezing when escape is not possible). Third, a minority organized self-defense units to repel antisemitic attacks, an example of defensive aggression (threat and attack) behavior in mammals. This form of rebellion was a means of active protection as well as to restore pride amid profound trauma and loss. Finally, some joined the armies of new nations, such as the Polish army.

Both Zionist and non-Zionist Jews had been contemplating self-defense since the late 1860s, particularly in the Ukrainian regions of Czarist Russia. These efforts were often sporadic and rarely organized on a large scale. The most effective action likely took place in Odessa in 1871, led by students with some popular support. Early on, Zionist groups took charge of these initiatives, framing them as a defense of Jews in Europe and also as preparation for defending the future Zionist colony in Palestine.

However, there was a clear distinction between Zionist and non-Zionist approaches to defense. Non-Zionists viewed defense primarily as a survival mechanism en route toward integration into European society, whereas Zionists embraced antisemitic arguments justifying Jewish segregation and combined these with romantic nationalism, European colonialism, and messianic Christianity and Judaism, framing defense as a crucial preparatory stage for the eventual return to the "Land of Israel."

Rabbi Zvi Hirsch Kalischer (1795–1874), an Orthodox German rabbi and early advocate for Jewish resettlement in Ottoman Palestine, promoted the idea of Jewish self-defense before the emergence of the formal Zionist movement. In his 1862 work *Derishat Tzion*, he emphasized the necessity of deploying armed guards, especially at night, to deter threats to property, crops, and livestock from neighboring Arab communities. He urged the formation of guard units and argued that, if these settlements were attacked or destroyed, a dedicated force should be ready to respond decisively. His stance reflected a broader belief in proactive defense measures as essential for the survival and stability of Jewish communities in the region:

> We need armed guards to fend off the Arabs and if they destroy what will be planted ... we need police to destroy them. [*Sefer Ha-Haganah*, volume 1, part 1. p. 23]

Rabbi Judah Alkalai (1798–1878) was a pioneering figure in early Zionist thought who bridged traditional Jewish messianism with practical Zionist nationalism and colonialism. In his letter: Ivri Anochi ("I am a Hebrew"; *Kitvei Harav Yehuda Alkalai*, Part 2, year 9, volume 6, November 22, 1872), Alkalai rejected passive waiting for divine redemption, advocating for active Jewish settlement in Palestine and emphasizing land purchase, agriculture, and organized self-defense as essential steps to hasten the restoration of Zion. His ideas laid important groundwork for later political Zionism by promoting the notion that human initiative was necessary to fulfill the biblical promise of return and sovereignty.

The First Aliyah ("ascension" in Hebrew) refers to the immigration of approximately 30,000 Jews to Ottoman Palestine between 1882 and 1903, primarily from Eastern Europe. Driven by economic hardship, antisemitic policies, and violent pogroms, these immigrants were also inspired by early Zionist thought. A key influence was Leo Pinsker's 1882 pamphlet "Auto-Emancipation," which argued that Jews must achieve their own political and national independence rather than wait for acceptance or liberation from the non-Jewish world.

In 1882, an exceptional group of about 200 Yemeni Jews arrived in Palestine, challenging the Eurocentric character of Zionist settler colonialism. Inspired by reports of new Jewish immigration, they viewed it as a sign heralding the return of the Messiah and came as religious pilgrims. Unlike the European Jewish settlers, they were quite able farmers and were viewed by the European settlers as suitable substitutes for the Arab workers, whose employment was seen as undermining the wish to Judaize Palestine. Most of them went to one of the first colonies, Kineret, yet were not allowed to live within it, only nearby it; i.e., they were denied access to the public space of the colony. After seventeen years of discrimination, they had enough of the white supremacist racism and moved to another colony, Rehovot, where they built a neighborhood called Marmoreque, which exists to this very day.

Back in Europe, the pogrom in Kishinev in April 1903, in which upper-class Russians also took part in the slaughtering of Jews, moved the Jewish communities to upgrade self-defense training and organization in a more structured way. Two weeks after the pogroms, the *Aguddat Soferim Ivrim* ("Hebrew Writers League"), released a statement written by Aḥad Ha-Am, advocating for an institutionalization of defense in Jewish communities.

Aḥad Ha-Am, a key figure in "cultural Zionism," had already called for Jewish self-reliance, defense and dignity in the face of persecution in his 1891 essay "An Open Letter to My Brethren in the Spirit." By the early twentieth century, this call resonated more widely, as a spirit of defiance began to stir within Jewish communities, especially after the pogrom in Kishinev, driven by the rising momentum of Zionist thought. Its most forceful poetic expression came from Haim Nahman Bialik, another member of the *Aguddat Soferim Ivrim*, who later became the national Zionist poet. Bialik's *The City of Slaughter* is a scathing critique of Jewish passivity, in which victims are bitterly portrayed as "calves to the slaughter."

Both Zionists (*Poalei Zion*) and non-Zionists (*the Bund*) supported this attempt to organize self-defense. These efforts evolved organically from grassroots necessity and reflected a collective transformation in mindset, organization, and identity. In Odessa, amid rising violence, Jewish communities began organizing collective self-defense.

Among the most prominent and energetic leaders was a young Vladimir Jabotinsky, whose experience of the 1903 Kishinev pogrom had profoundly radicalized him. He would later become the chief architect of a more militant, nationalistic, capitalist, and increasingly fascistic vision of Zionism. In his brutally honest 1923 essay "The Iron Wall (We and the Arabs)," Jabotinsky argued that Zionist colonization of Palestine could only succeed through segregation and overwhelming offensive military force, since no native population would willingly accept its own dispossession. He openly embraced settler colonial logic, viewing Palestinian people as subjects to be broken, not engaged. This framing laid the ideological groundwork for Israeli militarism, leading up to and including the escalated genocide since October 7, 2023 (**Part IV**), embedding the belief that security and deterrence must always precede any diplomatic effort, and that only overwhelming power, not mutual recognition, can bring about stability.

As Mihaly Kalman details in his work *Hero Shtetls: Jewish Armed Self-Defense,* across agricultural colonies, shtetls, and urban centers, Jewish communities formed self-defense units composed of local youth, laborers, artisans, and occasionally demobilized soldiers. These units, often created in the aftermath of violent pogroms, patrolled neighborhoods, guarded synagogues and schools, and manned garrison points in preparation for anticipated attacks. Many were organized with specific functions; combat detachments, intelligence operatives, medical teams, and house guards, ensuring operational flexibility and localized control.

These efforts relied heavily on community mobilization. Funding came through voluntary donations, communal taxation of the wealthy, and conscription of local Jews into defense duties. In times of crisis, schools and synagogues transformed from educational and spiritual centers to strategic hubs including functioning as storehouses for weapons, meeting places for planning, and shelters during outbreaks of violence.

Self-defense units underwent regular training in tactics, topography, defensive installations, and weapons handling. Many towns and villages were divided into defense zones, and shofar blasts were used as warning signals and to rally troops, enabling better coordination in times of emergency (akin to conspecific alarm cries in many mammals). Communications centers were established to facilitate real-time updates during attacks, and efforts were made to consolidate these units into larger, regionally coordinated frameworks, fostering leadership and strategic cohesion.

To anticipate threats, intelligence units monitored antisemitic propaganda, political agitation, and suspicious movements in nearby towns. Night patrols and alarm systems created protective nets across entire regions, minimizing the possibility of surprise attacks.

Though often under-equipped, Jewish self-defense groups acquired arms through local purchase, smuggling, and at times through cooperation with sympathetic Cossacks or *druzhinniki* (volunteer militias). Some were even able to procure rifles and machine guns, and tactics such as warning shots and preemptive patrols were deployed to deter would-be attackers. Plans were developed in advance to structure engagement and defense when violence erupted.

In some areas, Jewish defense units managed to collaborate with local militias, garrisoned troops, and, in the early twentieth century, also Bolshevik forces, particularly to guard factories, escort trade shipments, and root out bandit gangs. Efforts were made to legalize self-defense by incorporating them into broader military structures, offering a degree of formal recognition and protection.

At first, many defense groups declared political neutrality within local politics, aiming to focus solely on community protection. However, amid revolution and civil war, neutrality proved increasingly unsustainable. As violence intensified, cultural and political advocacy emerged as an essential part of the struggle; Jewish journalists, artists, and intellectuals documented atrocities and highlighted acts of heroism, pushing for greater rights and political legitimacy through the lens of Jewish suffering and resilience.

As these units gained confidence, some began to assume quasi-state functions. They levied taxes, administered local justice and organized labor cooperatives to sustain their operations. In places where state authority had collapsed, they filled the vacuum, acting as both protectors and administrators of their communities.

That said, not all resistance was segregated. In some regions, Jewish and Christian residents worked together to repel bandit attacks and maintain order. These alliances, often encouraged by local military commanders, demonstrated that solidarity in the face of lawlessness could transcend religious lines, at least temporarily.

Beneath the rifles and watch posts lay a deeper transformation. Generations of persecution had instilled passivity and dependence on outside powers, yet the birth of Jewish self-defense marked a revolution of the mind. Inspired by Europe's romantic nationalism, Jewish communities reclaimed ancient warriors like Bar Kochba and Judah Maccabee as symbols of resistance, forging a new identity rooted in dignity, strength, and self-determination.

In the Pale of Settlement, Jewish responses to violence reflected a broader shift from victimhood to agency. Through armed resistance, community cohesion, strategic alliances, and cultural transformation, Jews in the Pale turned vulnerability into defiance, planting seeds of collective agency in one of the most hostile environments in modern Jewish history.

These seeds were cultivated by the Zionist settler colonial movement.

a. The defense of Golovanevsk: an example of the full defensive behavioral repertoire

An example of self-defense forces being utilized effectively occurred in Golovanevsk in the Pale of Settlement in December 1917. Amid a power vacuum and rising tensions, local Jews organized a self-defense unit under the guise of a Committee for Public Security. The unit, composed of local youth, shopkeepers, and clerks, acquired weapons from nearby towns and deserters. Training included map reading, military tactics, and proper use of weapons. At the same time, efforts were made to coordinate these units under a unified structure and to set up communication hubs for better coordination during emergencies.

On December 18, during a market day, thousands of peasants began looting Jewish stalls and shops. The Ukrainian unit stationed in the town and the militia remained passive, reluctant to defend the Jews.

The Jewish self-defense unit intervened by disarming some militiamen and firing warning shots into the air. When the crowd continued looting, one self-defense member shot (or threw a grenade at) a woman carrying looted jewelry, causing the *pogromshchiki* (a person who participates in or instigates a pogrom) to flee. This decisive action saved the Jewish community from further violence and looting. Although the incident resulted in seven or eight attackers being killed, the self-defense unit's efforts were crucial in repelling the pogrom and restoring order.

This example illustrates several key aspects of a defensive behavioral repertoire. The unit was initially formed in direct response to rising tensions, as avoidance and flight were dismissed, viewed not only as defeat but as unsustainable long-term strategies. When the threat became more immediate, the defenders responded with a preemptive threat, firing warning shots (defensive threat) to signal both their readiness to defend and their preference to avoid full-scale violence. When the danger escalated into an actual pogrom, i.e., stimulus intensity increased and defensive distance decreased, the unit responded with lethal defensive attack, aiming to ensure survival and repel the attackers. The violence ceased only when the *pogromshchiki* fled, underscoring the aggression was rooted in defense/fear, not offense/control.

b. The construction of "self-defense" in Zionist discourse

It is both intriguing and important to examine the concept of "self-defense" during the period known in Israeli historiography as the First Aliyah (1882–1905), as well as how it was later portrayed. This account helped lay the groundwork for the evolution of individual self-defense into a more explicit and active form of defense of segregation and collective offensive aggression.

Formulation of the "self-defense" narrative was concocted and manifested best in the *Haganah* ("defense" in Hebrew) book, the official history of the main paramilitary group established by the Zionist settlers in 1920 and active until 1948. The book was published by the Israel Defense Force (IDF) in 1954. Significantly, it was written in hindsight by leading Israeli historians who were quite aware of the importance of the chronicle for domestic consumption. (Its Hebrew edition was never translated to other languages.)

The principal message was that defense was an act of survival against an existential threat and thus valid legally, morally, and politically (ibid, pp. 9–10). Loyal to romantic nationalist ideologies, it located the actions of the settler from 1882 to 1954 within a long historical continuum of Jewish resistance to foreign occupation from biblical times. Although the book describes a conventional story of self-defense, it frequently manufactures a fantasy that this was a unique Jewish way of defense, one that did not exist anywhere else, accompanied by sentences such as the "nation of Israel is the bravest among the nations" (ibid, p.13).

According to this narrative, bravery was lost, with other laudable national qualities, once the "nation" was exiled. Jews became defenseless and always found themselves at a disadvantage of being the few against the many. While they believed in the pre-exile mythology where the divine authority defended them and would help them return to Palestine and redeem the land and defend it, this vision never materialized substantially until the arrival of Zionism.

The plot takes quite a surprising twist. Anecdotal events in the life of the very small Jewish community in Palestine become a glorious chapter in the continuum of a history of self-defense. However, it claims self-defense is particularly effective if the nation lives on its postulated homeland. Self-defense in exile is lauded yet not deemed effective and therefore does not ensure the nation's survival. This disparaging view on exile has been analyzed recently by scholars such as Amnon Raz-Krakotzkin and Gabi Piterberg as the negation of the exile, which became a very important component in antisemitic Zionist propaganda.

The *Haganah* book focuses on the period 1850 to 1882, a time when the Jews of Europe tried to assimilate in European society, including a willingness to serve in European national armies as a misguided concept of self-defense. However, service in these armies heralded a new era of Jewish self-defense which would mature only in Palestine. Again, the message was that Jews were involved in self-defense, though it was not effective because it did not include the wish for *Herut* (freedom), namely Jewish national independence linked to land.

According to the book, this is why Jewish communities were largely unable to withstand the new wave of pogroms which began in Russia in the early 1870s, a wave triggering a collective Jewish "mental crisis" or communal trauma. Aligning with antisemitic doctrine wherein Jews were cast as perpetual outsiders in Europe, destined for self-segregation in their own homeland, the proposed solution was Zionism, or more concretely, the establishment of "self-defense" through a belligerent colonial project in Palestine. This, concludes Ben Zion Dinur, chief editor of the first volume of *Sefer Toldot HaHaganah*, was the only way to reawaken the uniquely effective and extraordinary spirit of the Jewish people, one unparalleled by any other nation, rooted in their mythological pre-exilic past. His account mimics settler colonial trajectories rooted in manifest destiny ideology, and beautifully encapsulates the dynamic relationship between defense and offense:

> The many who will ensure with their sword the freedom and independence of the people—existed, but the path to it was one of difficult ascent in three stages: from self-defense to organized defense, from organized defense to struggle, from struggle to war.
> *Sefer HaHagana*, part 1, volume1, page e (ה)

c. The myth of defense: from individual survival to collective co-optation

The *Haganah* book distinguishes between two stages in the issue of defense in the period 1882–1905. The first stage was the *Ma'avak* (in Hebrew, "struggle") and the second *Shmira* (in Hebrew, "guarding"). Language is important here. *Ma'avak* is active, yet depends on context, while *Shmira* is passive. Here the struggle was necessary because the Palestinians, according to the book, considered the settlers to be aliens who constitute an existential danger. Thus, the initial struggle was to secure a foothold.

Once established, the new enclave required protection (*Shmira*: the act of guarding). This process mirrors the broader stages of settler colonialism, specifically its Russian form carried out by Cossacks, and colonialism in general: first, an invasion by force, then defense of stolen positions.

According to the book, it supposedly took two years to push back and force the existing native population to reconcile with the presence of the settlers, though, of course, this acceptance has never truly occurred. (Later, the Israeli propaganda would blame British officers, Islamic Imams, and Arab culture generally as inciting the locals to resist the Zionist project.) In the initial stage, the colony demonstrated its ability to retaliate with double the force against local resistance (ibid, p. 71). The book praises the strong sense of solidarity and the willingness to support other colonies, recognizing this as an existential necessity.

However, it concludes that the defense strategies based on employing local Palestinians or other initiatives from the older colonies would not have been sufficient to ensure the survival of the Zionist project in Palestine. To achieve this, segregation, including exclusivist Zionist defense, had to be tied to the "national vision" (ibid. p. 114), a colonial strategy calling for distinctly offensive tactics.

The shift from individual self-defense to the defense of seized land, and ultimately to offensive conquests, was driven by the emergence of a new "psychic entity": a manufactured collective identity with a will to resist and defend, framed and marketed as a revolt against exile. This collectivization, now tied to territorial and resource ambitions, marked a decisive turn from personal protection to organized offensive aggression. It fueled further expansionist pursuits and self-organized by defining and solidifying internal hierarchies while casting Indigenous Palestinians to the very lowest rung as the perpetual "other" and an enemy to be permanently subdued.

Over time, the notion of "defense" transformed from its original role in Czarist Russia, protecting Jewish communities, into a deliberate strategy and culture of offense—conquest, territorial control and domination, driving out and murdering existing Indigenous Palestinian inhabitants, heavily influenced by Russian and other forms of colonial expansionism coupled with defense of segregation. What began as a response to existential threats against Jewish communities gradually evolved into the defense of exclusive settler colonies in Palestine, often in disregard (and mockery) of local customs and populations. Over time, this defensive posture shifted further, becoming a justification for preemptive and offensive actions. The creation of organizations such as HaShomer ("the guard" in Hebrew) and later the Haganah institutionalized this transformation, embedding militarized expansionism into the foundation of Zionist ideology.

d. Segregation to domination in Palestine (1882-1903)

The progression from small, vigilante-style guard units to organized paramilitary organizations was rapid and deliberate, driving a social process of collective identity formation and the consolidation of internal hierarchies structured around the pursuit of land, with conflicts usually instigated by competing claims to it. Through mass mobilization, political advocacy, training, public demonstrations, and strategic planning, Zionist settlers built a layered system. Over time, these groups coalesced around offensive tactics, transforming from scattered community watch efforts into a coordinated military apparatus capable of enforcing segregation and pursuing strategic expansion.

The first wave of Zionist colonization, known as the First Aliyah, led to the establishment of twenty colonies on land bought from big landowners. These transactions transferred control of rural spaces to Zionist hands, even though tenant farmers had lived and cultivated the land there for centuries and now faced eviction and colonization. The settler invaders employed local guards in order to triumph in inevitable clashes over water, grazing spaces, and other resources. Both they and their main benefactor, Baron Rothschild, chose Palestinians for guarding missions because it was cheaper to employ them than to convert settlers into guards. There was also the belief that this employment would help maintain friendly relations with the Arab neighbors.

The land for these colonies was acquired from either absentee or local landlords. For centuries, villages in the region had maintained a complex, inclusive system of relationships with landowners, where tenants and landowners shared mutual benefits, a structure distinct from the exclusivist feudal system in Europe.

From the mid-nineteenth century, it was possible to purchase land in Ottoman Palestine. However, until the arrival of Zionism, changes in traditional land ownership arrangements had not resulted in eviction of villagers. The arrival of Zionist settlers, however, disrupted these established dynamics. Water sources, orchards, and gardens near roads and pathways had long been treated as communal spaces where people would pick fruit, drink from wells, and share resources. The European invaders, however, viewed the locals with typical white/European supremacist racism and their customary practices as theft, redefining long-standing traditions as criminal acts ("Theft and leakage were part of the Bedouin tradition, and the weakness of the Turkish police allowed them to spread."; *Sefer Toldot HaHaganah* [The *Haganah* book], volume 1, part 1, p. 72). This framework rejected the norms of the Indigenous population, treating local practices such as land-sharing, communal agriculture, and traditional animal grazing as backward or illegitimate. Lands acquired from absentee landlords were enclosed and defended as private, fenced-off territory, with little tolerance for Indigenous presence or movement across them.

Though inspired by Jewish self-defense in the Pale of Settlement, Zionist "defense" was rooted in a vision of exclusive existence within segregated, European-style colonial enclaves, a transitional phase of settlement expansion with elements of defense and offense.

Indeed, in the early days of Zionist settlement in Palestine, colonists encountered persistent tension with the local Palestinian population associated with the transition from local traditions of inclusivity to Zionist European segregation practices. The primary sources of conflict included land disputes, control over pastureland, spring water, wells, and instances of theft and raids. These challenges pushed the settlers to develop increasingly organized and strategic "defensive" systems, evolving from basic self-protection to militarized structures capable of offensive operations. Once the Balfour Declaration of November 2, 1917, became known to the local Palestinian society, the conflict moved to more political issues: mainly a constant resistance to the notion that Palestine would one day, in one form or another, be a Jewish state.

One striking example illustrates this tension: The sheikh of the village of al-Tulayel, one of the 530 villages destroyed during the 1948 Nakba, visited one of the earliest Zionist settlements established on his land, Yesod Ham'alah. Out of curiosity, he went to see what had been done with the land. Tragically, a Zionist settler attacked and injured him, and he later died from his wounds. He had come only to observe, not to take anything.

Initially, Zionist settlers relied on informal methods to protect their communities. In agricultural colonies like Petah Tikva and Rishon LeZion, local guard systems were created to monitor threats from neighboring Arab villages. These guards, often young men from the settlements, worked in rotating shifts, as seen in Zichron Ya'akov, ensuring round-the-clock surveillance. Cooperation was common across settlements; when one was attacked, others would send reinforcements, illustrating an early form of collaborative defense, potentially inspired by self-defense units in the Pale of Settlement.

To bolster these efforts, settlers constructed structures such as walls and towers, particularly in frontier communities like Gedera and Metula. When attacks came, settlers responded with armed resistance, guarding their lands with rifles and pistols, as recorded in confrontations in Petah Tikva and Rosh Pina, the latter facing conflict with the Zangaria tribe. The necessity of readiness led to training in combat and the strategic placement of guards, especially during high-tension periods.

While conflict was frequent, interactions between Zionist settlers and Palestinian communities were not purely hostile. There were moments of mutual respect and cooperation: some Palestinian neighbors protected Zionist settlers during attacks, and peace treaties were sometimes negotiated after clashes. Some settlers aimed to protect their honor and property without needlessly humiliating or harming Palestinians. Influential figures like Rabbi Abraham Isaac Kook called for peace and unity, advocating moral conduct even in the face of provocation.

However, the underlying tensions over land ownership, identity, and political control remained unresolved. Zionist actions, particularly land seizures and the establishment of segregated settlements with guard units, were viewed by Palestinians as provocations, leading to cycles of resistance and reprisal. Slowly, Zionist strategy moved from exclusivist defense to a system of asserting dominance, justified through the language of survival yet implemented through expanding offensive militarization.

What defines and drives offense as opposed to defense? How do defense and offense contribute to dynamics within and between social groups? Can these behaviors coexist or are they mutually exclusive?

Before tracing the next phase in the evolution of Zionist military strategy, it is instructive to look beyond human conflict back to the animal kingdom, where the distinction between defensive and offensive aggression offers valuable insight into this complex social dynamic.

4. Offense

Offensive aggression is proactive, calculated, goal-driven, and aimed at dominating others, controlling resources, or eliminating a perceived threat. Offensive aggression is bold and direct, and in contrast to defensive aggression it is not instigated by fear but reduced by it. The offender advances, growls, stares down opponents, or takes physical action to intimidate or subdue, persisting until they yield.

A vivid example can be seen in two male elephant seals crashing their massive bodies together on a crowded beach, each vying for dominance and the right to mate. Winning these power struggles ensures access to mates and resources, guaranteeing continuation of the individual's genetic line.

The bodily targets of defensive and offensive aggression also differ, reflecting their distinctive functions: defensive attacks often aim for vulnerable areas to inflict maximum harm and ensure escape and subsequent survival, while offensive attacks are typically directed at less lethal zones, those protected by defensive features like a lion's mane or a rat's back. Attack of these areas allows individuals to signal strength and resolve challenges to status without causing serious injury to either attacker or victim, preserving the group's cohesion, strength, and overall fitness.

The neural circuitry underlying defensive and offensive aggression is highly complex and evolutionarily conserved across vertebrate species. It is modulated by an interplay of neurochemical systems, including serotonin, dopamine, vasopressin, oxytocin, and adrenal and gonadal steroids, among others. These systems interact within a core network of brain regions that highly overlap with a network responsible for sociality.

Behavioral differences between offense and defense reflect distinct underlying neurobiological and physiological systems. Of particular interest, both defensive and offensive forms of aggression activate the body's autonomic fight-or-flight response system, yet the hormones involved differ. Defensive aggression is associated with glucocorticoids, the body's main stress hormones, which are involved in the response to adversity and self-preservation. Successful defensive aggression can serve to lower glucocorticoid levels by reducing the intensity of a threat or increasing distance from it. This response is negatively reinforced, i.e., when a defensive behavior leads to stress reduction, it becomes more likely to occur in similar situations.

In contrast, offensive aggression is linked to testosterone, which is released into the bloodstream in response to both mental and physical challenges and drives proactive, dominance-seeking behavior. This behavior also activates the mesolimbic dopamine system, the brain's reward pathway, triggered, for example, by eating, sex, and addictive drug use. Studies in both animals and humans have found that the anticipation and execution of aggressive behavior can trigger dopamine release in a brain region called the nucleus accumbens, positively reinforcing the behavior and increasing the likelihood of its repetition, particularly when it leads to outcomes like social dominance, competitive success, or material gain. The so-called winner effect further amplifies this process: repeated victories elevate both dopamine and testosterone levels, leading to increased aggression over time.

This association helps explain why some individuals may be drawn to aggression not simply out of necessity, self-defense, or its consequent reduction in stress, but because it produces a positive, neurochemical payoff, particularly in social environments where power and dominance are valorized or materially rewarded (see **Figure II.2**).

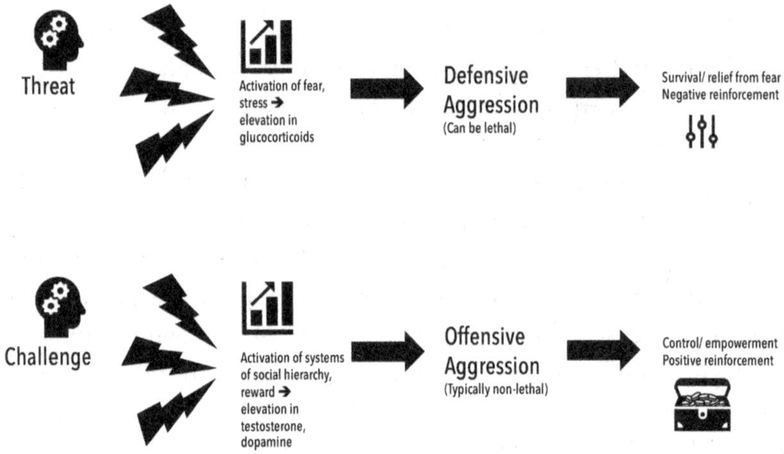

Figure II.2. Defensive and offensive forms of aggression–drivers and results.

A withdrawal-like pathological state may develop due to the addictive nature of offensive aggression, similar to that following drug abstinence, and is characterized by stress (elevation in glucocorticoids), fear/anxiety, increased impulsivity, and a tendency to relapse. Therefore, aggression can form an escalatory, pathological addiction cycle with deadly results in certain unbalanced or manipulated social situations, thereby linking offensive aggression to defensive aggression. Understanding the interplay between systems of fear, reward, and aggression is crucial for unpacking both personal and structural forms of violence, from bullying to militarism (more in **Part III**).

Crucially, biological systems are rarely clear-cut, and offense and defense can overlap and exist on a continuum, even in situations with a power imbalance. In both animals and humans, defensive strategies can escalate and even transform into offensive behaviors when an opportunity arises to assert control and seize territory with no or little negative consequences. Likewise, offensive behaviors may become defensive responses as power dynamics change and unexpected threats emerge. Territorial disputes can escalate from defense of in-group territory to conquest of out-group areas. Similarly, in hierarchical social structures, lower-ranking individuals may initially submit to avoid conflict yet can seize the moment to challenge a dominant rival when conditions change.

Humans exhibit similar patterns. In self-defense scenarios, individuals may first attempt to avoid or de-escalate and then attack to gain advantages. Conflicts in workplaces, politics, or legal disputes often begin with defensive strategies like negotiation or damage control, yet can escalate to lawsuits, public confrontations, or power struggles if resolution efforts fail.

In warfare, defensive strategies are used markedly to protect territory or resources. However, if the defending force gains a strategic advantage or if the opportunity arises, it may launch counterattacks or offensive operations to push back the original offender and secure a more favorable position to prevent future assaults.

That said, settler colonial projects are anchored in a culture of land and resource theft by colonizers, driven by an oppressive power dynamic that sustains the colonized in a perpetual defensive stance. Without a profound cultural shift (**Part V**), resistance to settler colonialism, in all its forms, is thus defensive.

a. Aggression within collectives: the roles of dominance and hierarchy in social group cohesion

Group stability and cohesion are essential for the survival of many social mammals, especially during territorial conflicts, in which larger groups tend to dominate smaller ones, as their collective strength deters smaller groups from initiating aggression due to fear of defeat. This dynamic means being part of a small group is especially dangerous, as it is less likely to successfully defend itself against invaders. Therefore, there is an evolutionary advantage to resolving intragroup dominance struggles in a non-lethal manner, as eliminating a potential ally weakens the collective, making the group more vulnerable to external threats.

Within social groups in defined territories, offensive aggression in the form of dominance struggles establishes hierarchies, where both dominant and subordinate subjects contribute to overall group stability and survival. These conflicts help regulate access to resources without constant fighting, with higher-ranking individuals enjoying priority access while lower-ranking ones must wait or find alternatives.

Accordingly, dominance struggles are often tempered by behavioral signals; postures, vocalizations, and threat displays communicating strength and intent, helping to defuse tension before violence erupts as a final resort. The large canines and muscular builds of male baboons, for example, facilitate ritualized displays of dominance, such as baring teeth, lunging, or mock fighting, allowing individuals to ascertain their position without resorting to serious injury when power imbalances are clear. Dominant animals typically possess high social intelligence and strong impulse control. They can resist provocation, build strategic alliances, and discern which conflicts are worth engaging in and which are better avoided. Notably, while some studies on baboons were conducted on captive animals, many findings have been independently confirmed through field observations in the wild, including work documented by Jeanne and Stuart Altman, Dorothy Cheney, Robert Seyfarth, Barbara Smuts, Hans Kummer, Robert Sapolsky, and others.

The stress hormones glucocorticoids play a key role in reinforcing social hierarchies. After a conflict, the losing animal experiences a rise in glucocorticoid levels, which plays a part in encoding the memory of social defeat and drives submissive behavior associated with fear, reducing the chance of future confrontations with the same opponent. In contrast, the dominant animal receives a rewarding surge of testosterone and dopamine and a reduction in glucocorticoid levels, reinforcing aggressive behavior and status maintenance.

Subordinates may subsequently redirect aggression toward individuals ranked even lower, which helps reduce their own glucocorticoid levels. This downward displacement of aggression stabilizes the hierarchy yet comes at a social cost: the lowest-ranking individuals, with no targets below them, remain chronically stressed. Persistently elevated glucocorticoids in these individuals are linked to negative health outcomes, a pattern consistent with findings in humans, in which chronic social stress (e.g., bullying) is a major contributor to depression and other stress-related illnesses.

Parallels to human social behavior are clear: a balance between fear and control, i.e., defense and offense, respectively, establishes and maintains intragroup social hierarchies, with each level solidifying its status through stress reduction by assertion of dominance over those below.

The mechanisms through which these narratives are reinforced in human societies, often via propaganda, encourage offensive aggression toward those lower in the hierarchy, while deflecting attention away from the ruling class as the true source of systemic aggression.

In line with this biological phenomenon, Frantz Fanon, in *The Wretched of the Earth*, lucidly described how the colonized, unable to direct suppressed aggression toward their oppressors due to the dramatic power imbalance, often turn it inward, manifesting violence within their own community.

> The colonized man will first manifest this aggressiveness which has been deposited in his bones against his own people. (pp. 52)

Fanon's notions correspond with what W.E.B. Du Bois (1868–1963), the American sociologist, historian and activist who pioneered the study of race as a structural rather than biological phenomenon, called a "public and psychological wage": the social status, deference and institutional privileges conferred by racial belonging that bind the most economically marginal in-group members to the hierarchy rather than to those below them (*Black Reconstruction in America*, 1935).

This is precisely how white supremacy works, including its Zionist version, in which Black and Brown Zionist Jews are often the most vehemently oppressive and racist toward the quintessential outgroup: Palestinians, due to lack of access to their immediate oppressors, the white European Zionists.

That said, displacement of aggression is not the only route to reducing stress or fostering social cohesion, in both animals and humans. Affiliative behaviors, such as grooming and coalition-building, also lower glucocorticoid levels and help curb intra- and intergroup aggression. Research on baboons shows that strong, lasting social bonds reduce stress hormones and promote cooperation, underscoring the diverse roles aggression and social bonding can play in shaping and sustaining social structures.

However, we should be careful not to simplistically portray hierarchies as benefiting only those at the very top. Present in many human contexts, hierarchies serve essential functions in social organization, coordination, and collective action. They reflect and perpetuate cultural norms and values, as the behaviors and traits rewarded within these structures become embedded in personal and collective identities.

Hierarchies promote efficiency by streamlining decision-making, clarifying roles and responsibilities and ensuring effective resource allocation. They also maintain social order by establishing expectations and providing mechanisms for conflict resolution. Additionally, they offer opportunities for mobility, incentivizing productivity, and achievement.

Hierarchies play a significant role in shaping social identity and fostering a sense of belonging, influencing how individuals perceive themselves and their place within a group (more in **Part III** on how the ruling class sustains hierarchies). This structured environment strengthens social cohesion and offers a framework for social recognition, where those who achieve higher status may receive validation, respect, and resources, enhancing their self-esteem and reinforcing their social identity. However, as evidenced in both animals and humans, hierarchies can impact feelings of exclusion. While higher-status individuals may feel valued, those in lower positions can experience marginalization, affecting both individual well-being and group dynamics.

Lastly, hierarchies are not necessarily vertical; they can be horizontal, with minimal levels of authority and members holding roughly equal standing, though influence may still be distributed unevenly.

b. Aggression between collectives: Territoriality and segregation

Now that the differences between defensive and offensive forms of aggression have been outlined, including some examples of forms within collectives, it is useful to expand to aggression between collectives, common in animals and human societies, particularly those associated with territory and/or resources.

Territoriality in animals involves actively defending a specific area to secure exclusive access to resources such as food, mates, and shelter. By marking boundaries and engaging in defensive behaviors when intruders encroach, animals can reduce direct conflict between groups, ensuring their survival and reproductive success within those borders.

Territoriality in humans can be seen in the protection of personal space, where individuals maintain physical distance from others and feel discomfort when that space is invaded. This behavior is also reflected in property ownership, where homes, land, and personal belongings are fiercely defended, often through legal systems or physical confrontations when disputes arise. At work, people often establish territorial boundaries around their designated spaces, such as offices, cubicles, or desks, and also extend this behavior to projects and responsibilities they manage. Territoriality also manifests in personal relationships, where disloyalty can result in severe, even lethal punishment.

On a broader scale, territoriality extends to national borders, where countries and other entities defend them through military presence, laws, and diplomacy, sometimes resulting in conflicts or wars. As stated in **Part I**, individual and small-group territorial behaviors are strongly influenced by cultural context. In modern Western individualist societies, these behaviors are often reinforced by "us vs. them" narratives. Fragmenting society through segregation draws physical, structural, or emotional boundaries that divide people into "us" and "them," shaping how groups relate and reinforcing often hostile social dynamics. "Us vs. them" narratives exclude groups from the social hierarchy, introducing higher potential for lethal or otherwise sadistic territorial or resource-related confrontations via defensive aggression; recall defensive aggression can be lethal as it is rooted in survival whereas offensive aggression is typically nonlethal as it maintains hierarchies rooted in control.

Segregation cultivates a parochial mindset, where the priority becomes surpassing or dominating the "other" at the expense of improving conditions within the group. It reinforces in-group loyalty while undermining ideals of equality, eroding empathy toward those lower in the social rung, and especially those in the out group. This is the danger of segregation: it creates a volatile gray zone between offense and defense, where the line dividing survival and theft becomes blurred. In this space, "defense" becomes a convenient justification for severe violence, made all the easier by the erosion of empathy toward out-group members.

Such "us vs. them" narratives serve ruling-class divide-and-conquer strategies by undermining trust and fragmenting solidarity. As a result, the working class, which is global in nature and lacks significant territory, faces greater difficulty in organizing against capitalist or other forms of exploitation. On the other hand, in collectivist cultures, spaces are shared, fences are largely absent, trust is enhanced, and territorial aggression is significantly curtailed (see **Figure II.3**).

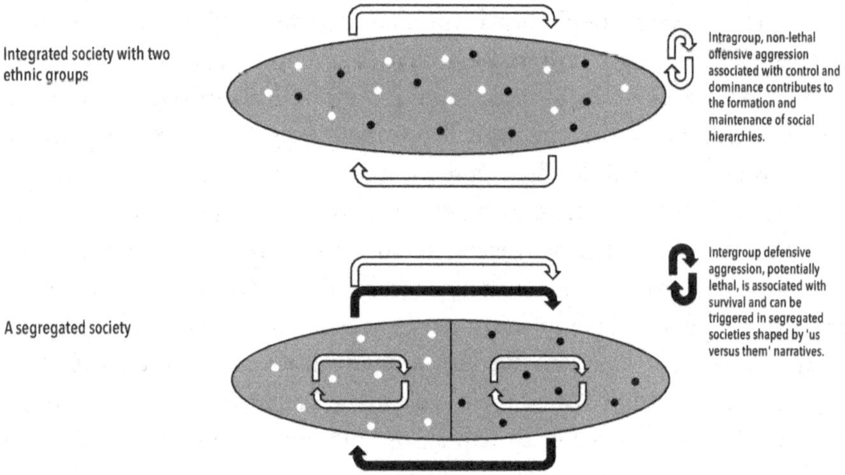

Figure II.3. Aggression in Integrated and Segregated societies

In the extreme segregation and oppression of a prison environment, a particularly violent "us vs. them" dynamic is often manufactured as a method of control, producing both offensive and defensive behaviors within a hyper-top-down structure. A ruthless hierarchy emerges in which individuals must submit; those who comply may be co-opted by dominant forces, while those who resist or fail to conform are eliminated, either as a demonstration of power and status or because they are simply deemed useless. This social formation fosters aggression and survivalism characterized by chronic fear, anxiety, hypervigilance, and the constant possibility of lethality, conditions intensified by confinement.

It is thus unsurprising that the United States, the world's only superpower is also the largest incarcerator, housing around 2 million prisoners across state and federal prisons, jails, immigration detention, juvenile facilities and territorial prisons. Scholars such as Michelle Alexander in *The New Jim Crow* argue that this extraordinary scale of incarceration functions as a system of racialized social control, systematically marginalizing Black, Indigenous, People of Color (BIPOC) under the guise of criminal justice and reinforcing broader patterns of inequality.

5. From Empathy to Violence

In his book *The Altruistic Brain: How We Are Naturally Good,* Donald W. Pfaff of The Rockefeller University argues that altruism and kindness are natural and innate. Pfaff's elegant framework—Altruistic Brain Theory (ABT)—delineates the human brain as biologically organized toward prosocial behavior. He proposes a neurobiological sequence in which: (i) humans perceive another person's situation; (ii) neural processes blur the distinction between self and other; (iii) the other person's welfare becomes neurologically salient to us; (iv) motivation to help is generated, and; (v) altruistic action follows. Enhancement factors, according to Pfaff, include nurturing upbringings, exposure to cooperative social norms, strong role models, and environments that reward trust and reciprocity. On the other hand, suppressive factors include violent environments, chronic stress, dehumanizing propaganda, and cultural norms that emphasize competition, hierarchy, or out-group hostility. In such contexts, the neural wiring for empathy may still be present though it is overridden and/or inhibited.

Indeed, intergroup violence is facilitated by several psychological and neural mechanisms that, through conditioning and rewards for aggression, help individuals overcome their natural aversion to harming others.

Moral disengagement occurs when individuals shift responsibility and suppress personal moral standards while acting as part of a group. Findings show this is associated with reduced activity in the prefrontal cortex (PFC), a brain region involved in executive function, self-referential thinking, and moral reasoning, making it easier to justify harming others. We will revisit this important brain region several more times throughout this volume.

The Canadian-American psychologist Albert Bandura (1925–2021) identified and systematically described moral disengagement as the cognitive mechanisms through which individuals disengage their internal moral standards to perpetrate harm. These include moral justification, euphemistic labeling, displacement of responsibility, and dehumanization of victims.

Importantly, Bandura's framework operates primarily at the cognitive level. The neural findings above provide the biological substrate for these mechanisms, showing moral disengagement involves measurable suppression of the brain regions responsible for self-regulation and moral reasoning.

Dehumanization leads individuals to perceive outgroup members as less than human, often evoking emotions such as disgust and fear. This is linked to increased activity in threat-related areas such as the amygdala (fear) and insula (implicated in disgust as well as empathy), alongside reduced PFC activity, which impairs the ability to empathize with others.

Neural responses vary depending on the perceived justification for violence: Justified violence (e.g., against enemy combatants) evokes less moral sensitivity than unjustified violence (e.g., against civilians), with the lateral orbitofrontal cortex (LOFC) showing increased activity in response to unjustified harm, indicating feelings of guilt. Here we begin to see how segregation can reshape perceptions of others as threats, making offensive aggression appear as legitimate "self-defense."

Importantly, attacks by outgroup members on ingroup individuals elicit strong moral and neural reactions, reflecting an evolutionary bias toward defending one's ingroup members. This includes heightened lOFC activity, signifying greater moral concern.

In human societies, power struggles may be fought with weapons, words, influence, or some combination thereof rather than just claws and teeth, yet the stakes, control over resources and social standing, remain similar.

Human resources extend beyond basic survival needs to include reputation, wealth, and other socially valued assets that can function as social plumage, signaling status, desirability, and potential reproductive advantage. Displays of status, such as clothing, cars, titles, or social media presence, can serve as signals of one's place within a hierarchy, similar to the dominance displays observed in animals. Yet what makes these signals credible?

According to Amotz Zahavi's "handicap principle," costly traits can serve as honest signals of fitness precisely because only individuals with sufficient resources can afford to maintain them. The price ensures only individuals with high fitness can afford to produce and/or maintain the trait, making it a reliable signal to others for purposes like attracting mates or deterring rivals (e.g., a peacock's extravagant tail, or strutting behavior in deer).

These behaviors have adaptive significance, allocating resources like wealth, power, and social connections while affecting social cohesion. However, cultural variations shape how territoriality and dominance are perceived and handled. Some economic systems emphasize collective ownership and collaboration, while others prioritize individual rights, class, and competition. Moreover, cultures influence how conflicts are resolved, with some preferring confrontation and others opting for indirect or collaborative approaches.

The near-universal development of laws governing ownership and the establishment of centralized authorities to enforce them reflects the significance and complexity of resource control in human societies. In parts of the West, these legal structures have been associated with substantial reductions in interpersonal lethal violence over the past several centuries. By contrast, collective aggression, measured by war-related deaths per 100,000 people, exhibits large fluctuations that complicate claims of a consistent long-term decline. While there has been a decline since World War II, similar reductions have occurred throughout history, making it unclear whether this represents a lasting trend.

Notably, the widespread use of modern weapons in lethal human conflicts, particularly those that enable mass murder with a joystick (e.g., drones), diminishes the effectiveness of evolved defensive responses and obscures the cues that typically distinguish offensive from defensive intent. This issue is particularly relevant in legal contexts, such as self-defense claims in homicide or assault cases. It is also relevant in political situations in which two or more sides contend their aggression was in self-defense.

To manage territorial and dominance-related conflicts, humans can rely on conflict-resolution methods like negotiation, mediation, and legal action, aiming to reduce direct aggression and find mutually agreeable solutions. Research highlights several intervention strategies such as promoting shared identities, encouraging people to see members of different groups as part of a common in-group, enhancing mentalization, or the ability to understand others' thoughts and feelings, and reducing negative attitudes toward outgroups (more in **Part V**).

These strategies target both the psychological drivers and neural correlates of intergroup violence, offering pathways to reduce conflict and promote empathy across group lines.

Equally important is the conscious avoidance of dehumanizing language by media and public figures, as repeated exposure to such rhetoric fosters internalized dehumanization and erodes empathy. Encouraging mentalization, i.e., viewing outgroup members as individuals with unique circumstances, can counteract this effect and foster understanding, especially when facilitated through direct or indirect intergroup contact. Reducing negative attitudes toward outgroups also involves training cognitive control to manage implicit biases and harmful emotional responses like schadenfreude (the pleasure or satisfaction derived from another person's misfortune).

Cooperative efforts framed around shared challenges such as public health crises can further unite disparate groups and redirect hostility toward collaboration. Preventing moral disengagement requires avoiding rhetoric which blames outgroups for societal issues and instead reinforces individual accountability, which can preserve moral sensitivity even in group contexts. Media narratives play a crucial role as well; rather than fueling fear or division, they should spotlight stories of cross-group cooperation and shared humanity. Finally, active rehumanization, through cultural transformation, including empathy-building efforts and perspective-taking, can reverse the psychological distancing that leads to violence.

Understanding how empathy and social cohesion can be cultivated provides a crucial contrast to settler-colonial strategies that rely on construction of identity, segregation, conditioning, and rewards for aggression to secure resources and maintain hierarchical control, often under the language of "self-defense."

6. Strategies of settler colonial theft

The contradictions of poverty, racism, and inequality inherent in capitalism within European settler societies have continually driven waves of landless migrants toward colonial frontiers, fueling dispossession and settlement of Indigenous lands. As Patrick Wolfe notes,

> Territoriality is settler colonialism's specific, irreducible element … Settler colonialism was foundational to modernity.
> ~ Patrick Wolfe, "Settler Colonialism and the Elimination of the Native." *Journal of Genocide Research*, 8(4), 387.

a. Methods of conquest

The ultimate aim of warfare under imperialism and colonialism has been the seizure of land and resources and their subsequent privatization, with agriculture symbolizing the settler's ideal of permanence and control, while the collective, nomadic way of life and identity representing a threat to be eliminated.

Segregation and offensive aggression have served both as tools for displacing nomadic peoples and for transforming previously rooted communities into nomads through destruction of their permanence. This dynamic has shaped settler societies across the Americas, Africa, Australia, and Asia, including Palestine. When settler colonial frontiers are exhausted, assimilation becomes (reluctantly) the mechanism for erasing Indigenous identity, a trajectory Palestinians inside the 1948 borders have endured and one those in the Occupied Palestinian Territories (OPT) may face if Israel's expansionist drive is ever checked in what Patrick Wolfe calls "structural genocide," which accounts for mass homicide as well as subtler methods like forced assimilation and cultural disappearance.

The interplay between defense and offense has been manipulated by the ruling class to justify violence and dispossession of entire populations. In exclusivist human societies that manufacture "us vs. them" narratives, segregation erodes empathy and severs the behavioral, emotional, and moral ties that typically manage conflict. These include dehumanization — through religion, racism, economic rationalization (the claim that Indigenous peoples were not making productive use of the land), civilizational and developmental reasoning (the claim that Indigenous peoples were at a lower stage of human development and required European tutelage), or the portrayal of native resistance as savage aggression — which lowers the threshold for invader violence; threat inversion, which recasts the dispossessed as aggressors; divine mandate, which removes moral agency and lowers the bar for 'permissible' violence; historical erasure, which denies the out-group's existence and culture; and fear conditioning, which activates defensive neural circuitry bypassing reasoning and making violence seem necessary.

Dehumanization changes who you see, threat inversion changes what you think happened, divine mandate removes your choice for violence, historical erasure removes the victim entirely and fear conditioning changes how your nervous system responds. They work together because they target different systems simultaneously, making the whole more resistant to disruption than any single mechanism would be.

The concept of territorial ownership itself reflects a deep power imbalance. Those who take land through offense, typically colonizers, rely on systemic and institutionalized force, while those defending it, usually the native population, are limited to reactive and defensive forms of resistance. Scholars such as Patrick Wolfe point to a separation between "dominion," reserved exclusively for European sovereigns, and the more limited native right of "occupancy," often defined in terms of practical use like hunting or gathering, associated with Palestinian Bedouins, and agriculture, as practiced by Palestinian Fellaheen farmers. The conceptual divide between ownership and use underscores how settler colonialism depends fundamentally on the displacement and erasure of Indigenous societies.

European "discovery" in Turtle Island created a legal framework granting colonizers exclusive rights to land transactions, pressuring Indigenous communities to sell under duress. Similarly, Palestinians with Israeli citizenship have faced structural barriers to land ownership: over 90 percent of land is state-controlled, and policies favoring Jewish citizens, such as those enforced by the Jewish National Fund (JNF), effectively limit access to housing and development. As a result, Palestinian communities suffer from housing shortages, overcrowding, and underdevelopment. The property rights of Palestinians in the OPT who live under military rule are far more restrictive.

b. Racism and the colonial relationship

The construction of race by racists is a strategic social tool to dispossess, divide and conquer Indigenous populations, defining a loyal "us" and a dehumanized "them" from whom land and resources can be seized, often under the guise of divine right. Race fragments resistance by reframing social hierarchies around a manufactured construct, obscuring material exploitation behind a false narrative of human differences that do not exist and are not the true source of oppression, inequality, or poverty.

To sustain these hierarchies, colonists in the eighteenth and nineteenth centuries relied on the pseudoscientific theories of craniology, phrenology, and the blood quantum regime to claim racial superiority and justify Indigenous dispossession and erasure.

In his 1950 work *Discourse on Colonialism,* Aimé Césaire observes how colonial aggression reduces the colonized to "things" to be exploited, while also brutalizing the colonizer. Similarly, Fanon in *The Wretched of the Earth* shows how colonial structures fracture the humanity of both groups: the colonizer defined by brutality, the colonized as a dehumanized "other."

The dynamic between colonizer and colonized shows how perceptions of threat drive offensive and defensive aggression, ultimately leading to theft. Offensive aggression, advantageous for the colonizer, serves as a proactive strategy to dominate perceived threats. In contrast, defensive aggression is the colonized people's only available response and the colonizer's tool for further genocide and dispossession. The behavioral patterns, motivations, inhibitions, target selection, and relative lethality associated with each form of aggression align closely with these historical roles.

This dynamic is regularly manipulated by targeted propaganda shifting blame away from the ruling class to affect public support in forms of state-sponsored or vigilante offensive and defensive aggression.

It is likely this logic and structural dynamic was promoted by imperialist forces to drive domination and war in the Levant as early as 3200 BCE (see **Part I**). In modern times it underpins white supremacist imperial, colonial, and settler colonial systems of power deeply rooted in Western so-called modernity, which impose a hierarchy of civilization that categorizes communities outside its norms as "primitive," "barbaric," "non-Christian," "non-Judeo Christian," or "uncivilized." These labels position members of outgroups, i.e., the "other," as an inferior, dehumanized threat and obstacle to progress. Framing certain groups as "others" enables a shift from inclusion within hierarchical structures, where resource sharing is expected, to exclusionary, and at times eliminatory, forms of territoriality. This shift creates opportunities for the ruling class to monopolize resources and territory without an obligation to share its accumulated wealth.

From this framework, genocide often arises, as the propagandistic drive for "progress" demands the destruction of those deemed incompatible with modern so-called enlightened ideals, frequently through colonial domination. When carried out under conditions of extreme power imbalance and impunity, such narratives can obscure and legitimize acts of genocide, ultimately driven by the unlawful seizure of land and resources. This is why the genocide of Indigenous peoples has often been disguised as defense and/or an effort to "civilize" them. These narratives function as conditioning tools which suppress moral resistance while employing the lethality associated with defensive action. Far from being an aberration, genocide is woven into the fabric of modernity, leaving devastation in its path, particularly for those living on the margins.

International law reflects and incorporates these principles; collective offensive aggression as expressed by the acquisition and annexation of territory through conquest, is prohibited by the UN charter and establishment and expansion of settlements on such land is a violation of international humanitarian and human rights law. In contrast, Article 51 of the UN Charter explicitly recognizes self-defense, including armed defensive aggression, as a right.

These principles are fundamental to settler colonialism, and Zionism has followed them from its inception until today. In contrast to liberal Zionist sleight of hand (more in **Part IV**) and in line with the genocidal forthrightness of today's Zionist leaders, the founders of the movement were exceptionally honest about its motivations and intentions (and racism). In the words of David Ben-Gurion (1938), founding figure of the State of Israel and its first prime minister:

> "Let us not ignore the truth among ourselves ... politically we are the aggressors and they defend themselves... The country is theirs, because they inhabit it, whereas we want to come here and settle down, and in their view we want to take away from them their country. ... Behind the terrorism [by the Arabs] is a movement, which though primitive is not devoid of idealism and self sacrifice."

The pursuit of control and power led Zionist leaders to instrumentalize the Jewish defensive response to antisemitic persecution in Europe into an offensive strategy for territorial acquisition. This shift culminated in a settler-colonial project in Palestine, carried out at the expense of its Indigenous Palestinian population.

Segregationist practices once imposed on Jews in Europe were rebranded by Zionists as "Jewish ideals," reinforcing exclusionary "us vs. them" dynamics, which served the Zionist ruling class who knew they could never control the native Palestinians. Coupled with the material and psychological rewards of aggression, this created a cycle of greed that propelled the move from defense to offense (more in **Part III**). Meanwhile, Zionist propaganda dehumanized Palestinians, making it easier to justify increasingly lethal forms of "defensive" violence with the ultimate goal of either complete subjugation, or death.

How did this transformation unfold? Next, and for the remainder of Part II, we examine the evolution of Zionist settler behavior.

7. From Jewish survival to Zionist theft - a new identity

The massive pogroms in Czarist Russia in the late nineteenth century, along with the efforts of Jewish self-defense groups to protect their communities, played a significant role in bolstering the Zionist movement. In addition to the physical and material devastation it wrought, antisemitic violence created a profound identity crisis among Jews, who were othered, dehumanized, exploited, disenfranchised, abused, and eliminated.

Unlike leftist groups, e.g., the Bund, which persistently advocated for integration as well as Jewish cultural and political autonomy within Europe, Zionists promoted the antisemitic premise that Jews were outsiders in European society and, at least to a certain extent, responsible for their own suffering. A solution was manufactured and packaged as a familiar manifest destiny ideology underpinning settler colonialism, which asserted that Jewish people were a distinct people whose exile from Palestine thousands of years ago demanded a return to, and offensive conquest of, an ancestral homeland as a means of securing safety and self-determination.

As a result, Zionists were widely unpopular among most European Jews, who saw the ideals of the Enlightenment, emancipation, equality and integration, as their ultimate goal. For many of these Jews, the notion of a "return" to a land they knew only through ancient religious texts was not only unfamiliar, delusional, and irrelevant but also immoral, religiously forbidden, and indeed antithetical to Jewish notions of return.

The Zionist movement sought to forge a "new Jew" with a modern understanding of antisemitism, one which embraced force and a connection to the land, symbolized by the gun and the plough, respectively, as the solutions to oppression. This marked a stark departure from traditional Jewish beliefs, which saw hardship as divine punishment for sin and thus discouraged integration within global oppressive networks. This shift paved the way for the formation of "us" (Zionist) and "them" (Indigenous Palestinian) groups, and a transition from defense to offense, from a need for safety to a craving for control through territorial acquisition.

In his 1882 pamphlet "Auto-Emancipation," Leon Pinsker, a Zionist ideologue from Belarus, argued for a Jewish homeland as essential for the defense and dignity of the Jewish people:

> The proper, the only solution, is in the creation of a Jewish nationality, of a people living upon its own soil, the auto-emancipation of the Jews; their return to the ranks of the nations by the acquisition of a Jewish homeland.

Pinsker further stated:

> The Jews are not a living nation; they are everywhere aliens; therefore they are despised.
> ~ Pinsker, "Autoemanipation" (p. 11, 1906); Translated by Blondheim, D. S. The Macabaean Publishing Company.

Pinsker illustrates how the Jewish identity crisis contributed to the emergence of a Zionist society intent on constructing a hierarchical structure around the supposed return to and defense of a fabricated, mythologized collective identity. This identity aimed to unify a diverse and often fragmented set of communities under a single national framework based on constructed race and territory, akin to fascistic ideological structure of Blood and Earth (*Blut und Boden*).

In the eyes of the mostly secular Zionists, this so-called sanctified pursuit justified collaboration with antisemitic forces in service of Western colonial interests, paradoxically employing the language of "defense" to legitimize offensive tactics rooted in the very ideology that had fueled the persecution of Jews in Europe, namely white supremacy.

In *The Jewish State* (1896), Theodor Herzl emphasized the idea of a Jewish state as a necessary defense for Jewish people and castigated those who objected:

> The Jews who wish it will have their state. We shall live at last as free people on our own soil, and die peacefully in our own homes. The anti-Semites will be our best friends; they will persuade the Utopians that we are right.

And:

> The Jews are a people, and they wish to remain a people. The Jews will have a state, and their defense will consist of their unity and the strength of their own land.
> – Theodor Herzl, *The Jewish State* (p. 157, Courier Corporation, Apr 27, 2012)

Thus, the concept of "defense" became one of the earliest, and continues to be one of the most effective, Zionist propaganda tools, skillfully merging Jewish longing for safety with a syncretization of white supremacist and messianic ideologies to justify oppression and land theft.

Contrary to the reality of an historically continuous Palestinian society with an educated and politically engaged urban elite and a flourishing web of rural communities, this portrayal allowed Zionists to evict Indigenous Palestinian people without moral qualms or restraints, framing the establishment of "Jewish only" settlements as a civilized, divine right.

In this context, any physical or ideological threat to the manufactured Zionist collective became existential, used to justify an often-brutal, so-called defensive response. Yet in reality, this was an offensive project of deliberate genocide of, and theft from, the Indigenous Palestinian "other."

These dynamics were present from Zionism's early days and continue to drive its expansionism to this day.

a. The Defense of Petah Tikva (1878): the failure and lessons learned

An early episode of conflict, while not unique, represents one of the first instances of Zionist defense of segregation in the Yishuv and underscores the inseparability of agricultural settlement/ colonization from security considerations in late Ottoman Palestine. The defense (and initial and temporary collapse) of Petah Tikva served as a catalyst for the development of later Jewish organizations, including Bar Giora (1907), Hashomer (1909), and eventually the Haganah (1920).

Petah Tikva, established in 1878, holds the distinction of being the first modern Jewish agricultural settlement in Ottoman Palestine. Founded by religious Jews from Jerusalem, the settlement embodied the nascent ideals of Zionism before the emergence of organized Zionist movements in Europe. However, the early years of the colony were marked by extreme hardship, particularly due to geographic, political, and security challenges, culminating in an early episode of abandonment following a violent confrontation.

The land chosen for Petah Tikva lay northeast of Jaffa, near the Yarkon River. While it was agriculturally promising, the area was also notorious for its marshy conditions, making it a breeding ground for malaria. Although it should be said that nearby existed a village, Melbes, a small mud village, whose inhabitants were dispersed after the lands were bought by the settlers. Several villages like this disappeared from Palestine very early, during the first phase of colonization (1882–1926).

The health hazards associated with the marshy conditions soon took a toll on the settlers. Compounding these difficulties was the legal and administrative ambiguity surrounding land ownership in the Ottoman Empire, where overlapping or contested claims were common.

According to the *Haganah* book, almost immediately, the settlers faced hostilities from surrounding Arab villages, notably Yehudia. The tensions were rooted in both land disputes and the broader geopolitical dynamics of the region. While the Jewish settlers had acquired the land through formal channels, local Arab populations often regarded the transfer of land to outsiders as illegitimate, particularly if it affected customary grazing or cultivation rights.

Security incidents escalated over time, including the theft of livestock, destruction of property, and armed confrontations. These attacks were not centrally coordinated yet reflected a pattern of local resistance to Zionist land acquisition and settlement, seen as a threat to the existing order. Most of the attacks were carried out by peasants who were driven away from their fields and habitats as a result of the colonization.

In the absence of Ottoman state protection, the settlers turned to self-defense, though they had little military training or equipment. They organized patrols, often composed of unarmed or lightly armed men from the colony.

In some cases, they hired local Arab guards, a common practice at the time, though such arrangements were fragile and could quickly deteriorate under stress or changing alliances.

In late 1878, tensions peaked in a violent confrontation with residents of nearby Arab villages, reportedly including a group from Yehudia. The attackers damaged property and fields, and the settlers, weakened by illness and unprepared for sustained conflict, were unable to repel them effectively.

Faced with both security threats and a public health crisis due to malaria, the residents made the strategic decision to abandon the settlement and return to Jerusalem. This marked the temporary suspension of the Petah Tikva project, though not its end.

The settlement was revived in 1883 with the assistance of new immigrants, particularly from Eastern Europe, and with the financial support of Baron Edmond de Rothschild. The revived settlement incorporated lessons learned from the earlier failure, chief among them the necessity of organized and well-resourced defense, i.e., further entrenchment of an exclusivist, aggressive settler mentality, rather than an attempt to rectify differences through inclusivity.

More practical and popular were the ideas of leading members of a new wave of colonization, the Second Aliya, who were impressed by the offensive way the Russian empire expanded its territories, by occupying faraway posts and then demanding, in the name of defense, the entire territory spanning the official Russian territories to the new outposts.

b. Proud Guardians of the Homeland (1905-1918)

The mission of expanding the offensive nature of the Yishuv was entrusted to the Second Aliya (1905–1914). About 30,000 Jews arrived in that period yet only about 7,000–10,000 remained in Palestine. (The Jewish population as a whole was roughly 80,000 out of 800,000 inhabitants.) Immigration was influenced by socialist, Zionist and European colonial ideologies, which shaped the vision and goals of the immigrants.

Many of the 30,000 immigrants, mostly from the Russian Empire, were instrumental in building early Zionist institutions, founding kibbutzim, and shaping the exclusivist Jewish labor movement in Palestine. Their arrival also infused the Jewish settlement with a heightened sense of militancy, spearheaded by some of Zionism's most well-known leaders such as Joseph Trumpeldor, a former Russian army officer who became a key figure in early Jewish military efforts and cofounder of HaShomer ("the Guard," the first Jewish defense organization in Palestine); Yitzhak Ben-Zvi, a future president of Israel and an early leader in Jewish self-defense efforts, involved in organizing HaShomer; Israel Shochat, a founding member of HaShomer; and David Ben-Gurion. Though primarily a political leader, Ben-Gurion, who later became Israel's first prime minister, was deeply involved in shaping the Zionist labor movement and supporting self-defense efforts.

Russian influences forged a unique political culture in Israel that fused revolutionary zeal, secular nationalism, cultural hybridity, and a deep-rooted commitment to militarism. The leadership of this group arrived with a background in clandestine revolutionary movements, which instilled a political ethos rooted in radical transformation and activism. One of the key contributions was the emergence of the secular Jewish identity which originated in Russia and prioritized nationalism over religious tradition and played a central role in forging the "new Jew/ Hebrew" identity that Zionism championed. This identity shift was accompanied by a pride in force, influenced by experiences with pogroms and revolutionary struggle, which became central to Israeli notions of self-defense and sovereignty. Cultural continuity with Russia was also evident in the reverence for Russian literature, music, and artistic sensibilities, many of which were translated into Hebrew and embedded in Israeli cultural life. Furthermore, elements of Russian nationalism, such as the romanticization of homeland and emphasis on territorial identity, shaped practices like the Hebraization of names and places.

The most aggressive stance, evident in the belligerent sections of the *Haganah* book, is encapsulated in a subheading titled "Alien Work (Avoda Zara)—A Cancer in the Body of the Yishuv" (ibid, p. 135). Usishkin, a leading ideologue of the *Yishuv*, the term Israeli historiography uses for the broader settler community, described Arab labor as a "malignant leprosy." As the book states, the Second Aliyah ideologues sought to "prevent violating the sanctity of Israel by the Ishmaelites," an encapsulation of the "othering" of the Indigenous inhabitants which became a central pillar of Zionist ideology, motivation, and expansionism.

By 1905, as the colonies became more autonomous under Zionist organizational oversight, "defense" evolved into a hybrid system employing both locals and settlers. Financial considerations increasingly gave way to ideological segregationist imperatives, particularly the drive to "Hebraize" or "Judaize" every aspect of life, including security and military organization.

Three years earlier, when still in Europe, those who would lay the foundations to the new kind of militarized Zionist presence were thinking in terms of national armies with territorial objectives. "The People's Legion" was the first such idea and was focused on an attempt by Theodore Herzl to persuade the British authorities in Egypt (Egypt was under British occupation since 1882) to allow the establishment of a Zionist colony in El-Arish, on the border between the British Sinai and Ottoman Palestine. With the total rejection of the idea by Earl Cromer, the High Commissioner of Egypt, nothing came out of this initiative.

c. Early Aggression in Palestine

The development of "defense" in the Yishuv was driven by the logic of settler expansion followed by defense of gains, as Zionist efforts to establish exclusive Jewish settlements with restrictive land use increasingly met with resistance from local Arab communities and were further complicated by fluctuating Ottoman and then British policies. Over time, the defense system transformed from informal self-defense groups into a structured and organized military force.

During the Second Aliyah (1904–1914), highly idealistic settlers modified the tradition of organized Jewish defense, drawing on European Jewish self-defense units, Cossack settlement models, Zionist youth movements, socialism, and Russian revolutionary tactics. In 1905, the Jaffa Group, led by figures like Israel Shochat and Yitzhak Ben-Zvi, laid the groundwork for Bar-Giora (1907) and later HaShomer (1909), which sought to centralize and professionalize the defense of Jewish settlements. HaShomer embodied ideals of bravery, independence, and communal defense, transforming the colonies into fortified outposts where farming and security were inseparable.

These groups operated on principles of community mobilization, military training, and armed preparedness, marking a significant shift from scattered resistance to systematic protection. The goal was not only defense but also to cultivate a "new Jew" identity: self-reliant, strong, and rooted in the land. Later, the Nili Group (1915) and eventually the Haganah emerged as major players in Zionist defense infrastructure, incorporating intelligence, coordination, and growing military capability.

i. Bar Giora: institutionalizing defense of segregation

The main political party of the settlers, Poalei Zion, established a group called Bar Giora. Bar Giora was founded on Simchat Torah night in 1907 by a group of eight members, including Israel Shochat, at Yitzhak Ben-Zvi's apartment in Jaffa. The organization was named after Simon Bar Giora, a Jewish leader during the Great Revolt against Rome, demonstrating yet again the inherent necessity of linking Zionist expansionism with Jewish mythology. It was a small, secretive group with strict discipline and limited membership, stating its purpose as "the occupation of the labor market": namely an offensive against the Arab workers wherever they were. Decisions required unanimous agreement, and members were bound by a strong sense of loyalty and secrecy.

The group adopted the slogan "In blood and fire Judah fell, in blood and fire Judah will rise," referencing the ancient Kingdom of Judah, which was destroyed through violence and conquest. This statement asserts that just as Judah fell by violent means, its restoration and rebirth would also come through struggle, conflict and sacrifice, framing colonial violence as part of a divinely sanctioned mission. This demonstrates a stark dissonance between the names of organizations tasked with "defense" and their mission statements, which openly advocated offensive actions such as the takeover of the labor market.

Bar Giora concentrated its efforts in the Lower Galilee, where Jewish settlements perceived themselves vulnerable to attacks from Bedouin tribes and local Arab villagers. Members of Bar Giora took over the guarding of Jewish settlements such as Sejara (Sajara), Mascha (Kfar Tavor), and Yavne'el, replacing Arab guards with Zionist ones.

The group emphasized physical training, horseback riding, and the use of weapons, preparing its members for self-defense and settlement protection. Bar Giora represented the shift from reliance on foreign guards to Zionist self-reliance and independence in security matters. It fostered a new settler identity to replace the Jewish one perceived as antiquated and weak, one of courage and heroism among settlers, contributing to the broader Zionist movement's goals of establishing a Jewish homeland.

Bar Giora's establishment and activities marked a turning point in the history of Zionist settler self-defense, setting the stage for the organized military efforts that followed in the decades leading to the establishment of the State of Israel.

ii. HaShomer: the fortification of "us" and "them"

The leaders of the small settler community were impressed and in 1909 expanded the organization and founded a new one: HaShomer ("The Guard" in Hebrew). Again, while the name conveys defensive duties, the formative documents and slogans were offensive. *Kibush* ("conquest" or "occupation" in Hebrew) was the key word in their documents, occupying the land and the labor market. The first step was to take by force the security business from locals, still trusted by the older generation of settlers who also spoke Arabic and were more assimilated than the second wave which came after 1905.

HaShomer expanded its activities to protect settlements across Palestine, including areas in the Galilee, the coast (Sharon), and the inner plains (Judea). It introduced organized defense strategies and played a significant role in the broader Zionist movement. HaShomer continued until 1920, when it was replaced by the Haganah, ("defense" in Hebrew), a larger and more comprehensive so-called defense organization. Hashomer's legacy influenced the development of the Haganah and later the IDF.

Beyond Cossack colonial influence, HaShomer also adopted Bedouin clothing, weaponry, and tactics, blending foreign European militaristic traditions with native adaptations, which may be interpreted as duplicitous, orientalist attempts to co-opt the appearance of local hierarchies. This fusion produced a distinct syncretized identity, casting Zionists as frontier warriors defending their people while simultaneously embodying the merger of so-called defense with European offensive aggression and territorial expansion.

The Cossack model remained influential beyond HaShomer, shaping the Third Aliyah's (1919–1923) vision of segregated colonies. Figures like Meir Ya'ari championed settlements modeled after Cossack strongholds, further solidifying the link between Zionist segregation and "defense" in Palestine and Cossack history. Ultimately, this synthesis of Cossack militarism and Bedouin resilience forged an enduring ethos of self-reliance and expansion, defining the Yishuv's approach to "defense."

HaShomer did more than just occupy the labor market. It established segregation and militarized systems for the colonies, which used offensive aggression as revenge and retaliation, as well as means for evicting Palestinian tenants from land purchased by the Zionist movement. The outward discourse focused on defense, though the actions, as well as the internal discussions among the leadership, were unmistakably segregationist and offensive.

HaShomer's strength lay in its non-local structure, which allowed it to coordinate with neighboring settlements during times of conflict. This was evident when settlers from various colonies united to intervene in local altercations with their Palestinian neighbors.

Using a physical defense structure was a central part of the new organizational effort. The symbol of defense in Israeli mythology is a wall and guard tower, which became widely recognized in the 1930s. Yet in fact, it had already been evident in the early colonies such as Gdera ("fence" in Hebrew), where a wall was built in 1884 as part of the attempt to defend the colony.

As mentioned, walls and towers, a Cossack/Russian colonial tactic that heavily influenced members of the Second Aliyah, are designed to segregate communities, hindering the natural formation of social bonds and hierarchies that are inherent in human societies. They erode trust, amplify fear, and ultimately facilitate territorial expansion and dispossession through genocide under the pretext of "defense."

Significantly, some of the tactics used by Zionists on Indigenous Palestinian people were employed against Jewish people in Europe during the same period. It is also noteworthy that none of the Palestinian villages had walls, which made their subjugation and occupation by Zionist colonizers extremely easy. Also, the notion of guards was quite alien to most Palestinian villages, though it quickly became an organic feature of all Zionist colonies.

Some leaders of the older settlements viewed this approach as overly offensive and provocative. Indeed, before the establishment of HaShomer, the First Aliyah had managed to establish a modus vivendi with the local population. Yet the new settlers argued that the wall was the best safeguard against lawlessness, despite the police proving quite effective. Segregation and apartheid were early, instrumental tools for constructing "us vs. them" groupings, reinforcing and deepening the colonial mindset. As previously noted, the real issue was that after the land was purchased, former tenants were denied access to it and soon realized the new ownership could lead to their dispossession. Given this, it is unsurprising they did not welcome the settlers.

The offensive aggression was carried out by specialized units known as *Havurot ha-Kibush* ("Occupation/conquest Gangs" in Hebrew). Their violence was directed at Palestinians and Jewish settlers who continued to employ Palestinian laborers, demonstrating Zionist objectives were not focused on Jewish safety, but on exclusivist territorial and resource acquisition. Those who refused to comply faced severe threats, including death.

In one instance, an ultimatum was issued, demanding Jewish employers cease hiring Palestinians within twenty-five days (Israel Giladi, HaShomer). In another case, a group called "The Grandchildren of Pinchas" directly threatened Jewish employers in Rehovot in 1913 for continuing to hire Arab workers.

A group that acted alongside HaShomer was the Gidonim, founded in Zichron Ya'acov. They were only active for four months, and interestingly they wished to defend the old colonies from the members of the Second Aliyah (see work by Rachel Elboim-Dror). As part of the second generation of the First Aliya, they were owners of sizeable lands and had relatively good relationships with the Palestinians around them. Further, they insisted on employing Arab labor and expressed sympathy with the goals of the Arab national movement, even supporting some of its efforts to assist the British in occupying Palestine.

Reminiscent of contemporary branding of dissenters to Zionism, Gidonim members were labeled as "antisemites" by members of the Second Aliyah because they criticized these newcomers for undermining relations with local Palestinians. Ultimately, the Gidonim became a footnote in the history of Zionist colonization, while it was HaShomer that laid the foundation for the settlers' future military organization and expansion.

d. Moving to "Offensive Defense": Expanding the Foothold

The main objective of the Zionist movement in the years leading to the First World War was to expand its territorial foothold in Palestine through the purchase of land from local and absentee landlords. As mentioned, prior to Zionist colonization, change of ownership did not dislocate villages that were on these lands; the Zionists were the first-ever purchasers who demanded the eviction of the villagers. This was a very structured effort and was combined by the twin action of replacing Arab guards with settlers and driving by force the tenants out of the land purchased.

The effort moved in sequence from one area to the next: first in the northeastern valleys, then with the establishment of the colony of Rehovot, followed by expansion to the coast where Zionists took over guarding and enlarging the colony of Hadera, and finally into the southern plains. The missions were all defined as *Kibush*, i.e., occupation/conquest of the guarding missions and the land and by demanding renumeration from the veteran settlers. (It was much more expensive to hire HaShomer members than the local Arabs.)

Yet before the First World War, these attempts were still vehemently opposed by the older generation of settlers, which led to the eviction of HaShomer from the three veteran colonies by 1913.

The First World War brought with it compulsory conscription of those settlers who had obtained Ottoman citizenship and contributed further to Zionist accumulation of military experience that would serve the settler community during the years of British rule (1918–1948). This was achieved among other methods by establishing a "Hebrew Battalion," an idea conceived by Vladimer Ze'ev Jabotinsky, which joined the invasion of Palestine by the Allied forces.

i. The Jewish Legion: a Zionist-imperial collaboration

The Jewish Legion was a military unit formed during World War I by Zionist volunteers eager to support the British war effort while advancing Zionist aspirations. Conceived by Jabotinsky in December 1914 as the first official military cooperation between Zionists and Western imperial forces, the idea of a Hebrew military force gained traction with support from Yosef Trumpeldor, a decorated veteran of the Russo-Japanese War. Although British authorities initially resisted creating a combat unit and instead sanctioned the Zion Mule Corps, a labor battalion of 650 men led by Colonel John Patterson that served in Gallipoli, continued lobbying eventually led to the formation of three Jewish battalions within the Royal Fusiliers, an infantry regiment that guarded artillery units and engaged in frontline combat, colonial campaigns, and ceremonial duties. These units, drawing volunteers from Britain, the United States, Canada, and Palestine, trained rigorously and participated in the British campaign against the Ottoman Empire, notably contributing to the victory at the Battle of Megiddo in 1918.

While the Legion fostered camaraderie and a shared Zionist purpose among its members, it also contended with logistical hardships and skepticism from British officers. Nonetheless, its symbolic and practical impact was significant. The Legion energized the Zionist movement; many of its veterans became central figures in the Yishuv and the Haganah. Figures like Jabotinsky and Trumpeldor emerged as enduring icons of Zionism, and the Legion itself became a foundational chapter in the narrative of Jewish state-building.

ii. The Establishment of the Haganah

The First World War ended with the occupation of the entirety of Palestine by Britain, which had already declared in its Balfour Declaration (November 2, 1917) its commitment to building a Jewish homeland in Palestine. This pledge was incorporated into the Mandate charter granted by the League of Nations, contradicting the general principle of all mandates that Indigenous peoples or newly established nations in the Arab world should have the right to self-determination.

By 1920, the British were already busy dealing with the challenges this contradiction produced, as the local Palestinian leadership began to coalesce into a national anti-colonialist leadership, organizing until 1920 mainly nonviolent resistance to the pro-Zionist intentions of the British government in Palestine. Yet it was already clear that the first High Commissioner, the pro-Zionist Anglo-Jew Herbert Samuel, had begun translating the Balfour Declaration into concrete support for the Zionist movement, helping to lay the foundations for a future Jewish state.

The Palestinian resistance became more widespread and at times increasingly violent. In April 1920, a provocative march organized by Jabotinsky in the old city of Jerusalem ignited the first significant clash between the local Palestinian population and the settler community. This was not a random clash, it was widespread, intense, and lasted a while, claiming the lives of a relatively high number of Arabs and Jews. It also coincided with attacks on Jewish settlements in the Upper Galilee by local forces which regarded the area as part of the greater Syria colonized by France. The few Jewish colonies there decided not to join this anti-colonial struggle against France, and this led to a punitive action by the rebels against the isolated settlements, before the British could impose proper rule on that part of Palestine.

A second wave of protests erupted in May 1921. By that time, the Palestinian leadership was fully aware that the formation of nation states in Lebanon, Syria, and Iraq would not be replicated in Palestine due to the Balfour Declaration.

Protests deteriorated to violent clashes, and both waves of early Palestinian resistance to the Zionist colonization of the country had led to the decision among the political leaders of the settlers' community to replace HaShomer with a more institutionalized military organization, which they called *Ha-Haganah* ("the Defense" in Hebrew).

The Haganah, founded officially in December 1920, was part of a broader infrastructure that the British authorities allowed the settlers to construct, essentially a state within a state, complete with its own trade unions, educational system, health care, and defense institutions.

The Zionist Trade Union, the *Histadrut*, became the most powerful institution in the settler community and it was responsible for regulating the defense of the settlers under the new organization, the Haganah.

The first issue the group dealt with, and which it thought HaShomer and other outfits had failed in doing, was the national spread of the defense units to the level of the smallest settlements. This effort demanded taxing the settlers, increasing the request for donations from the outside, and a clearer structure of training.

What is interesting in the narrative of the *Haganah* book is that one of the reasons given for the need for a more regulated system of defense was to avoid the brutal, vengeful acts that had been perpetrated by individuals against

Palestinians (including women and children) during the clashes of 1920 and 1921. This is eerily reminiscent of contemporary uses of "human rights" as pretexts for aggression. Yet from its inception, the Haganah operated under the directive that "revenge is possible if it is done in the right way" (namely, not harming women and children; Volume 2/part 1, p. 150).

The British authorities insisted they could provide the defense needed for the settlers' community. For that purpose, they provided training and weapons. And while they never recognized the Haganah as a legal structure, the weapons and training helped to strengthen this main paramilitary outfit of the settlers' community.

The *Haganah* book discusses the years 1920 to 1929 as dreary, in which defense was routine and not particularly exciting. It treats known episodes of cruelty, such as the assassination of anti-Zionist dissident Jacob Israël de Haan (an Orthodox Jew) and the planting of bombs in Arab neighborhoods, as the exceptions to the rule (Volume 2/part 1, pp. 252–253).

These years were devoted to accumulating weapons and intensifying training of the settlers as future soldiers. This period helped the Haganah become more effective when the third Palestinian attempt at stopping the colonization of Palestine and the implementation of the pro-Zionist policy by the British government erupted in 1929.

iii. *al-Buraq* Revolution (1929)

The Palestinians refer to 1929 as the *al-Buraq* Revolution because it was triggered by the Jewish insistence on changing the status quo around Haram al-Sharif, indicating in the eyes of the religious Muslim leadership a wish to replace the mosques on the mount with a third temple.

The outburst was triggered by the dispute over the old city in Jerusalem, yet it had deeper roots that go back to the very beginning of the Zionist colonization of Palestine. The most important of which was the pauperization of the Palestinian countryside in areas where lands bought by Zionists were then built up into settlements, forcing thousands to emigrate to the towns that could not provide proper housing or employment, due to the Zionist strategy of using only "Hebrew labor." Thus, this was not only a religious/national rebellion but also a socioeconomic one.

In the shanty towns that emerged near them later, the Syrian preacher

Izz al-Din al-Qassam would be able to recruit young men to form the first guerrilla movement in the struggle against Britain and its pro-Zionist policy.

The protests and the violence spread from Jerusalem to many other places and in Hebron led to the massacre of sixty-seven Jews, which became engraved in the collective history of the Israeli Zionists as ultimate proof of the so-called barbarity and cruelty of the Palestinian "others," justifying their brutalization since.

During the events of 1929, the Haganah already appeared as an organization with all the insignia of an army and was quite successful in both defending settlements and launching offensive attacks on Arab communities. Again, the *Haganah* book lists some of the atrocities committed by Haganah members, excusing these as exceptions that do not prove the rule (Volume 2, part 1, p. 368).

One of the key takeaways for the Zionist leadership after the events of 1929 was the need to redefine "defense," not merely as protecting communities but as securing the foundations of a future Jewish state (*hamedina she-baderech)* (ibid, p. 515).

So-called defense in the period leading to the revolt of 1936 to 1939 was focused on smuggling weapons and manpower, immigrants, to Palestine. (There was a quota on Jewish immigration since 1930.)

iv. On the Way to Arab Revolt, 1930–1936

In the early 1930s, the main military body of the Zionist settler community, the Haganah, was challenged by a new organization: the Irgun ("the organization" in Hebrew), claiming that its raison d'etere was the lack of offensive initiatives by the Haganah against both the British and the Palestinians. The rivalry pushed the Haganah into a more offensive mindset, and its dynamic of overtly fascistic politics, pulling the supposedly "reasonable" camp rightward, has remained central to Israeli "democracy."

In 1932, one of the leaders of the Zionist community, Haim Arlozorov, wrote to Chaim Weizmann that the time has come to use the military power to take over the country and build a minority rule (namely non-democratic) as the British would not help to deliver the Jewish state (Volume 2, part 1, page 609):

> There is no way of realizing Zionism without a transitional phase during which a minority nationalist revolutionary Jewish regime will rule the country…[this government] will take over the state apparatus, the administration and the military force.

This statement is particularly striking when examined in the context presented in the *Book of the Haganah*. Again, it is brought as an exception that does not prove the rule. In fact, the book points to "anti-militarism" as one the important features that distinguished the Haganah from the Irgun. By anti-militarism, the aim was to emphasize the organization's informal character, eschewing the uniforms, rituals, and hierarchical mannerisms often associated with European fascist movements. However, the book editors hastened to explain this was not pacifism. In fact, pacifism was identified in the early 1930s as a sickness that the Haganah had to cure. (They called it "extreme pacificism.")

It is worth repeating that Jewish people were largely pacifist before the Haskalah, a condition Zionists antisemitically viewed as pathological. Pacifism, they claimed, was prevalent among the settlers because it was a global phenomenon. Pacifists were dismissed as delusional, incapable of grasping the necessity or the appealing aesthetic of brute force in advancing the Zionist project. The antidote was a growing wave of young "New Hebrew" settlers determined to erase the so-called national disgrace of the defenseless exile. Joining the Haganah became their way of reclaiming strength and agency (Volume 1, part 2, p. 624).

The shift from "Jew" to "Hebrew" among Zionist settlers marked a deliberate break from the religious and diasporic past in favor of a new national identity. By adopting the term *ivri* (meaning 'Hebrew') over *yehudi* (meaning "Jewish"), Zionists cast off the perceived weakness of exile, embracing an image of the bold, self-reliant settler rooted in the land. This transformation involved rejecting rabbinic Judaism, Yiddish, and diaspora culture as obstacles to nation-building.

Influenced by Russian distinctions between *yevrey* ("national") and *yiudey* ("religious"), Zionists emphasized secular nationalism. Acts of Hebraization such as renaming individuals and places symbolized the severing of Jewish and European ties. The "secular Jew" emerged, retaining ethnic continuity while shedding religious identity. At its core, the Zionist project sought to revive a mythic Hebraic past centered on strength, labor, and land as the foundation for a modern national self.

v. The Arab Revolt: from "restraint" (*Havlaga*) to "response" (*Teguva*)

The revolt (1936–1939) erupted after failed attempts by the Palestinian leadership to persuade Britain to retain Palestine as an Arab state and keep its obligation under the mandate of allowing the majority and native people of the land to gain independence in their own homeland.

Skirmishes in Tel Aviv and Jaffa moved the Palestinian leadership to declare a general strike and a campaign of protests and petitions against the pro-Zionist policy of the British Mandate.

The strike, i.e., civil disobedience, can be seen as a form of defensive behavior, specifically, avoidance used to assert the group's significance within an established social hierarchy. At this stage, Palestinians were "otherized" in relation to the expanding Zionist settler population, yet they remained a vital part of the British Mandate's social and political fabric.

Almost half a year later, it seemed the civil disobedience did not change a thing, and under pressure of several groups, Palestinians moved into resistance via armed struggle (more in **Part V**). The group *Qassmiyun* applied particular pressure. These were disciples of Izz al-Din al-Qassam, the Syrian preacher turned guerrilla warrior mentioned earlier. A second group consisted of young members of the emerging urban middle class, who began organizing in Palestine's major cities. A third group comprised local rural leaders, who leveraged their clan-based ties to mobilize and, in many ways, lead the revolt. In the Arab world, enthusiastic young people volunteered to local outfits that entered Palestine to help the rebels.

Serious operations only commenced after it was evident that the Arab world stood behind the cause. They formed a "committee for the defense of Palestine," which was active from Damascus in trying to recruit fighters and weapons. When Britain began persecuting Palestinian leaders in 1937, they found refuge in Damascus and other Arab capitals.

The new phase included guerrilla attacks on British personnel involved in the installation and transportation of the Iraq Petroleum Company (IPC) oil pipe. As the *Haganah* book admits, this stage of the Palestinian revolt was not directed against the Zionist settlers but mostly against the British (2/2 p. 762). This was a hard revolt to quell, and it took the British army and air force nearly three years to defeat it, through an emergency military regime that was based on collective punishments, arrests without trial, torture, destruction of villages, executions, and deportation. A huge number of soldiers had to be recruited to carry it out from all over the empire.

Zionist forces adopted many of these tactics from the British and continue to deploy them against Palestinians and others to this day, while also monetizing and professionalizing them for export to regimes around the world.

The *Haganah* book explains that the revolt brought an end to a doctrine framed as *Havlaga* ("restraint") or at times referred to as "passive defense." It describes moments when it was decided to deviate from the defensive restraint in the face of a particularly brutal Palestinian attack or operation, instances which led to great joy among the settler community: "The joy and excitement of the people when learning about the end of the Havlaga is beyond comprehension," wrote one of the leaders at the time (2/2 p. 671).

One of the main triggers was the fortification of the Revisionist movement's military wing, led by Jabotinsky: the Irgun. As previously noted, Jabotinsky had criticized the Haganah for what he saw as its passivity toward the Palestinians. Reflecting this ideological split, the Irgun operated independently and refused to coordinate with the Haganah. Although the Haganah attempted to bring the Irgun under its command, these efforts ultimately failed.

This posed a significant challenge as Zionist leaders, notably David Ben-Gurion, concluded after the first year of the revolt that the Yishuv needed to become "a formidable military presence" in the country (2/2, p. 737). By 1937 the Haganah had already grown to 25,000 members, while at the revolt's peak in 1939, Arab fighters numbered only about 15,000, supported by roughly 300 volunteers.

This enthusiasm and the criticism from the Irgun led to the increase in attacks on Palestinians, while at the same time, at least according to the *Haganah* book, the leaders of the settlers were engaged in a "moral" discussion about "collateral damage" (namely the growing number of non-armed

Palestinians in the Haganah operations). One Haganah leader wrote, "Our orders were not to hurt women and children," yet admitted there were situations where avoiding civilian casualties was "impossible." An early 1937 issue of the Haganah newspaper (no. 673) stated that killing innocent people during operations was acceptable, an unavoidable consequence of retaliation. At the same time, the paper and other publications insisted revenge must never be the motive, exposing a contradiction between stated ethics and operational realities.

Another reaction of the Jewish leadership was *Homa and Migdal* ("Wall and Tower"): the strategy of building new settlements on land seized, purchased, or unaccounted for, by constructing in one day a tower and a stockade as an established fact. *Kviat uvdot ba-shetach* ("establishing fait accompli on the ground") became a structural method of expanding geographically the Zionist presence in pre-1948 Palestine and later in the occupied West Bank. The British authorities often tolerated these settlements once they were built, because removing them would provoke confrontations. The importance of this was not just having new colonies but also the demand of the right to own space between them. Fifty-two colonies were established in such a manner. The *Haganah* book described this imitative behavior as the occupation of the country.

vi. The Haganah as a counterinsurgency force

The *Haganah* book in a typical contradictory manner has very little respect for the military performance of the Palestinian rebels yet fails to explain why the British needed massive forces and a long period of time to quell the uprising. By August 1938, much of Palestine's urban space and roads were under the control of the rebels.

The Zionist perception at the time, and also that of the *Haganah* book, was that this was pure "terrorism." This led to the realization in the words of the *Haganah* book, that the settler community cannot rely on the British soldiers "to dirty their hands" in facing that "terrorism."

The *Haganah* book strongly asserts that retaliatory violence against Arab assaults, without discrimination, was largely perpetrated by the Irgun. Notably, in Jerusalem, this resulted in a higher number of Arab casualties compared to Jewish ones. In contrast, the Haganah's preferred strategy involved close collaboration with the British military and police, which the Haganah argue ultimately brought an end to the "terror."

Language became important once more. At the time, and in retrospect, the Haganah claimed it moved from what it called *Havlaga* ("restraint/containment") to *Teguva* ("reaction"), or in its own words, it left behind passive defense (*Haganah Passivit*). This was an accurate description of its actions, though it also reflects a sense of self-righteousness that later manifested in words attributed to Golda Meir: "We can forgive the Arabs for killing our children. We cannot forgive them for forcing us to kill their children."

One of the main reasons, in the Haganah's own perception, of an inability to move to what it called active defensive strategy was the lack of necessary tools to implement it. The year 1937 was devoted to developing this capacity. In 1938, at least nominally, the Haganah distinguished itself from the Irgun. The Irgun's approach involved indiscriminate and widespread killings of Palestinians as a response to both Palestinian resistance and British actions against Zionist terrorists.

The *Teguva* reaction became "retaliation" (*Tagmul*). and the headquarters published a few master documents stressing the need to not kill women and children and not target populated civilian spaces. The doctrine of *Tagmul*, arising during this period, later influenced Israeli responses to Palestinian actions, specifically in labeling them as terrorism. Already in the 1930s, and increasingly by 1948, local commanders and troops began to view villages and neighbors as enemy bases, a distinction that gradually lost legitimacy. The groundwork for *Tagmul* was thus established in this era.

According to the *Haganah* book (847), the transition from passive to active defense happened gradually. For a while this was energized by the night squads, a concept introduced and masterminded by an ardent pro-Zionist senior British officer, Reginald Orde Wingate, who for a while persuaded the British army in Palestine to attach Zionist fighters to British commando units in their nightly attacks on Palestinian villages, using ruthless methods with the alleged aim of deterring villages from hosting "gangs" that were involved in the revolt. Wingate taught them the art of collective punishment against Palestinian villages. In June 1938, for the first time, the Haganah troops experienced the taste of occupying a Palestinian village: a Haganah unit and a British company jointly attacked the village of Ghribyya, on the border between Palestine and Lebanon, and held it for few hours.

Amatzia Cohen who took part in the operation remembered that a British sergeant taught them how to use bayonets in attacking the defenseless villagers.

> "'I think you are totally ignorant in your Ramat Yochanan [the training base for the Haganah] and you do not know the elementary use of bayonets when attacking dirty Arabs, when your left foot is in the front,' he shouted at Cohen and his friends after the occupation was completed."
> – A Memorial Book for Amazia Choen produced by Kibbutz Ramat Yohanan, 1939 (p. 59)

Wingate envisioned a Jewish state as crucial for the British Empire's strength in the Middle East. However, British policy shifts in 1939 halted this initiative. Nevertheless, its impact was significant; it directly inspired the creation of the Plugot Sadeh ("field squads," known as POSH) by Jewish settlers a year later. As noted in the *Haganah* book, POSH units exemplified the transition from passive defense to active defense strategies (Volume 2, part 2, p. 967). British military instructors observed that the settler squads they trained were insufficiently hardened. In an effort to rectify this, they attempted to instill techniques employed against Irish populations in Northern Ireland by the "Black and Tan" units.

vii. Britain as an Enemy, 1939-1945

Palestinian leaders felt a temporary sense of relief when Britain backed away from the Peel Commission's initial recommendations at the start of the revolt, which had proposed partitioning Palestine, annexing the Arab areas to Transjordan, and transferring populations to create a more homogeneous Jewish enclave in historic Palestine. Yet the revolt ultimately failed to prevent British support for Zionist settlement, though it influenced subsequent policy adjustments.

The 1938 Woodhead Commission reviewed partition options and concluded a viable Jewish state could not be created under the Peel framework. Subsequent deliberations led Britain to abandon partition proposals and, in

1939, issue the White Paper, which significantly restricted Jewish immigration and land purchases.

The White Paper and subsequent regulations promulgated by the British government in Palestine imposed severe limitations on further Jewish immigration and purchase of land, even on building settlements on land already purchased.

In response to the 1939 White Paper, which signaled a dramatic shift in British policy toward endorsing an Arab-majority Palestine with a Jewish minority, the Haganah made facilitating illegal immigration one of its chief priorities.

Defense, the leaders of the Zionist community now declared, was a willingness to fight by force both the British policy and an Arab rule, should Britain impose it in the future. In reaction, British policy changed; from 1939 onward, the Haganah was outlawed, its leaders arrested and deported, and its weapons confiscated. Yet as we enter the years of the Second World War, these British operations were quite limited and ineffective.

Each newly established unit, most notably the *Palmach* (an acronym for Plugot Mahatz, "strike companies", founded in 1940 and inspired by POSH), was described both at the time and in retrospect as marking the shift from passive to active defense. At the same time, it was closely associated with *kibush ha'aretz* ("the conquest of the land").

Approaching the Mandate's conclusion, the Haganah increasingly prioritized retaliation against Arab and British entities. These actions were designed as punitive measures, deterrents, and to terrorize perceived enemies. Meanwhile, the Irgun and the emerging Stern Gang, acting as more extreme counterparts, pressured the Haganah with bolder, more offensive and violent retaliatory operations.

viii. The Impact of the Second World War

There were three major impacts of the Second World War and the Holocaust on the strategy of the Haganah. The first was translating the decision of the Zionist leadership to push for an end of the British Mandate into military actions, through armed struggle as well as diplomacy. Second, to utilize seasoned Jewish soldiers, some originating from the Palestine settlements and battle-hardened, to establish a modernized and structured military force. And finally, to appropriate events such as the Warsaw uprising and the battles of the Jewish partisans, as part of the settlers' overall struggle for independence. The war also led to development of a local military industry along with more systematic purchase of arms and weapons aboard.

The doctrine was still officially defined as active defense and retaliation, though with the formation of the Palmach, this approach took on a new character. As the elite commando units of the Haganah, the Palmach operated with considerable autonomy, free to improvise and disregard constraints in their actions against both the British army and the Palestinians.

While initially engaged in supporting Britain's efforts to counter Nazi expansion into the eastern Mediterranean, the organization underwent a post-war transformation. It first concentrated on the British army, then evolved into an exceptionally harsh and violent entity, responsible for massacres and severe atrocities against the Palestinian population. An additional assignment during the war was to collect data on all the Palestinian villages, with the help of either local collaborators or members of the Palmach who were disguised as locals or pretended to pay visits to nearby villages, taking advantage of the traditional hospitality.

A project known as "the village files" documented information intended to furnish knowledge for the eventual acquisition of villages. Ever since the early 1940s, the intelligence service of the Haganah collected detailed information about every village in Palestine. It was collected by spies sent to the villages and included an assessment of the lands' quality, the quantity of harvest and fruit trees, interrelations inside the village, and the villages' history. The reports included lists of those who had been suspected of being involved in actions against the settlers. These lists later were used to identify these people, after the occupation of their villages. Some of them were executed on the spot, others were sent to labor camps. What the files proved was that the expedited ethnic cleansing during the Nakba had already been extensively prepared in the early 1940s.

Yet during the war, the Palmach was busy training, accumulating weapons and preparing for the moment the British mandate would come to an end, as did other factions like the Irgun and the Haganah as a whole. The revolt's suppression severely weakened the Palestinians, leaving them with a critical shortage of capable military personnel and leaders. Furthermore, the absence of a political elite within Palestine meant there was no strategic planning for the immediate future, compounding the detrimental effects of the repression.

ix. Resistance to Illegal Immigration and the struggle against Britain

The Arab Revolt led to a drastic shift in British policy, as London imposed strict limits on Zionist land purchases and immigration. This new approach was formalized in the 1939 White Paper.

The Haganah reacted by establishing, at the end of April 1939, an organization known as *Mossad le-Aliya Bet* ("the Institute for Immigration"). Its main modus operandi was to hire ships and try to smuggle them into Palestine, which occasionally led to confrontation with the Royal Navy. All in all, dozens of such maritime operations ended successfully and helped to increase the number of settlers in Palestine. The clandestine nature of these operations added another dimension to the Zionist project that would later be translated into institutional agencies such as the Mossad and the Shin Bet.

Until 1945, the Haganah was careful not to enter direct confrontation with the British; although around 1942, the Zionist leadership under Ben-Gurion reached the conclusion that the Zionist project did not require British help anymore and it should aspire to bring the Palestine mandate to an end. This decision echoed similar patterns in other settler colonial projects such as those in the United States and South Africa, where settlers, having secured a foothold with the help of the British Empire, ultimately turned to direct confrontation with the very power that had enabled their colonization.

The offshoot organizations from the Haganah, the Irgun, and the Stern Gang did not accept this policy and began a campaign of guerrilla warfare and terror against British personal and installations. For a short while the Haganah strongly opposed these attacks and even assisted the British in trying to prevent them, a period knows as *Hasezon* ("the Season"), namely the hunting season of the Zionist militants aided by the Haganah.

Ben-Gurion's position during World War II was summed up in his famous 1939 maxim, which outlined his strategy of supporting the British in their fight against the Nazis while simultaneously opposing British policies in Palestine: "We will fight the White Paper as if there is no war against the Nazis, and we fight the Nazis as if there is no White Paper."

For that reason, Ben-Gurion went along with the idea of helping the British through the establishment of the Jewish Brigade.

x. The Jewish Brigade

The primary motive behind establishing the Jewish Brigade Group, as it was officially called, was to train a larger number of settlers in the skills and discipline of a regular army. The brigade was initiated by the Zionist leadership and approved by the British army only in July 1944. Composed entirely of volunteers from the settler community, it bore distinct Jewish and Zionist insignia.

With a force of 5,000 troops, it saw three weeks of combat before transitioning to serve as an auxiliary force supporting British military rule in various parts of Europe. The Brigade exploited this assignment for inducing Holocaust survivors to choose Palestine as their destination, rather than staying in Europe or moving to the Global North.

Apart from the Brigade troops, Zionist emissaries were very active in the Displaced Persons Camps (DPS), where survivors of the Holocaust were held. Non-Zionist organizations such as the Joint and the Bund were trying to help these Jews to immigrate to the US; this was fiercely opposed by the Zionist emissaries, who in a sly manner recruited the refugees to the Haganah so as to threaten them with the allegation of deserting military services as part of the pressure of pushing them toward Palestine. (This episode is fully described by Yossi Grodzinsky in *In the Shadow of the Holocaust: the Struggle between Jews and Zionists in the Aftermath of the World War II*, Monroe, Maine: Common Courage Press, 2004.)

All in all, the attempt to bring a large number of European Jews over to Palestine after the Holocaust was entirely successful, which led to the decision a bit later to attempt to bring the Jewish communities in the Arab world to Palestine.

Encouraging more Jews to come as settlers was against British policy, so the Jewish Brigade was actually working against the British, as much as aiding them in the war effort. Yet the most important impact was that this Brigade became the backbone of the regular army of the new state built in 1948: Israel.

After the war, this strategy shifted as the Haganah joined forces with the Irgun and the Stern Gang to form *Tenuat Ha-Meri Ha-Ivri* ("the Hebrew Rebellion Movement"), active until July 1946. The movement carried out eleven major operations, including freeing detained immigrants, and sabotaging railway lines, police stations, radar installations, bridges, and dozens of British aircraft, as well as attacking railway workshops. The most notorious action of the *Tenua* was the bombing of the King David Hotel in Jerusalem in 1946. Ninety-one people were killed, including seventeen Jews; the rest were Palestinians and British personnel.

The negative reaction to the blowing up of the hotel encompassed also members of the political leadership of the Zionist movement, and it was decided to dismantle the *Tenua.* The two other organizations continued to perform terrorist attacks against the British.

xi. Transition to the IDF and the Nakba.

When the British decided to withdraw from Palestine in February 1947, the future of the country was handed over to the United Nations, then dominated by Western powers, leading Palestinians to feel they had little chance of fairly representing their case. Hence, the UN offered a solution without consulting the Palestinians of dividing the country into two: a Jewish and an Arab state. While the US briefly accepted that a solution could be imposed on the Palestinians, President Truman, under the pressure of the Zionist lobby, retreated from such a position.

The Haganah in the last days of the British mandate focused on the military methods of taking over the country on the one hand and preparing for the possibility of a military confrontation with neighboring Arab countries, on the other. These preparations coalesced in a master plan, known as Plan Dalet, or Plan D, completed on March 10, 1948.

Plan D was based on two key assumptions: first, that any military action by neighboring Arab countries to prevent the establishment of a Jewish state would not begin before the official end of the British mandate, on May 15, 1948, and that such efforts would be limited, as the Arab armies were primarily focused on securing the new regimes recently freed from colonial rule.

Part of the reason for the optimism about the weakness of the military challenge on the borders was the tacit agreement between the Jewish Agency and the Emir Abdullah of Transjordan. It was not a written agreement, yet it was quite clear the Arab Legion, which was the best army in the Arab world at the time, would limit its operation in return for getting part of Palestine (the area that became the West Bank) without firing a single shot.

The second assumption was that the rejection of the idea of partition opened the way for a military takeover of Palestine as a whole and that part of it could be achieved before the end of the mandate, even if, legally, Britain was still responsible for law and order.

After Plan D was adopted, it was first implemented in Palestine's urban centers. In the weeks leading up to May 15, 1948, Zionist forces carried out urbicide in cities such as Haifa, Jaffa, Bisan, Acre, Safad, and Tiberias: towns that were partly mixed Arab-Jewish or entirely Arab. These areas, along with surrounding villages, were systematically de-Arabized. Similar fates befell the neighborhoods of West Jerusalem and its nearby villages.

By May 15, 1948, approximately 250,000 Palestinians had been expelled, with much of the displacement accompanied by massacres. The most infamous was the Deir Yassin massacre, where hundreds of men, women, and children were killed in a village that had a non-aggression agreement with the Haganah yet was strategically located in an area designated by Plan Dalet to be exclusively Jewish.

The ethnic cleansing operation before and after the 15th of May 1948 was accompanied by more than thirty massacres, partly intentional, to accelerate the uprooting of the population, partly because of unintentional encirclement of villages, where initially the tactics were meant to leave one flank open for the villagers to flee. In some cases, it was revenge due to a previous clash with that village.

Up to May 15, 1948, the Palestinian military response to Plan Dalet consisted of two forces. Local paramilitary groups: A few thousand ill-trained and ill-equipped, mainly rural youngsters focused on defending their villages and neighborhood but were no match for the better trained and numerically superior Zionist forces. The second force consisted of several thousand volunteer soldiers in an army known as the Army of Salvation, made of young people from Syria and Iraq who had infiltrated Palestine and tried to help the local Palestinians.

On May 15, 1948, all the Zionist military organizations fused into a new state army, the Israeli Defense Forces, (IDF), which now faced two fronts. One was the ethnic cleansing front, where IDF troops continued to systematically expel the Palestinians; the second front confronted regular Arab forces coming from Egypt, Jordan, Syria, and Lebanon. (There was also an Iraqi contingent that assisted the Jordanians.) As mentioned previously, a pre-1948 tacit agreement with Jordan limited the operations of the Arab Legion and the Jordanian army, which focused on taking over what became known as the West Bank and fighting over Jerusalem, as the negotiations failed to produce an agreement on the city's future.

The military effort on both fronts lasted more or less until the beginning of December 1948. There were additional operations that stretched Israel's control over the Negev and Um Rashrash, a village on the Red Sea that became the port of Eilat. In the process, Israel ethnically cleansed tens of thousands of Bedouins living in the Negev desert, an operation which continued until 1950.

By the end of the operations, half of Palestine's Arab population (750,000) became refugees and half of its villages (531) were wiped out, as were most of its urban spaces. On the ruins of the villages, the Jewish National Fund planted recreational forests or built Zionist settlements.

Every part of historical Palestine that had been occupied and had a Palestinian population was put under military rule that continued until 1966. The military rule was based on British mandatory regulations that granted absolute power to the military in running the life of the population, including the ability to punish individually or collectively any criticism or resistance to the rule.

Table II.1. The evolution of aggression in the Zionist *Yishuv* in Palestine.

PERIOD / EVENT	YEAR(S)	DESCRIPTION	PRACTICES
First Aliyah	1882-1903	The first wave of Zionist colonization inspired by antisemitism and early Zionist thinkers	Segregation, land acquisition, defense using local Arab guards inspired by early self-defense in the Pale of Settlement. Colonies organized patrols, often unarmed, and sometimes hired local Arab guards, though these arrangements were unreliable and vulnerable to instability.
Second Aliyah and Early Defense Groups	1904-1914	Influx of idealistic settlers revived Jewish self-defense ideals. Inspired by European models and socialist-revolutionary movements.	Engaged in organizing Jewish self-defense groups like HaShomer to protect settlements, and offensive actions, including forcibly replacing Arab workers with Jewish laborers and employing "Occupation Gangs" to evict Palestinian tenants from purchased land.
Jaffa Group	1905	Formed by pioneers including Shochat and Ben-Zvi.	Marked the transition toward centralized Zionist defense.
Bar Giora	1907	Secretive defense group named after Simon Bar Giora.	Focused on self-defense in Lower Galilee. Promoted Jewish-only guarding and military training.
HaShomer	1909-1920	Successor to Bar Giora.	Formalized defense operations across Palestine. Replaced Arab guards with Jewish ones.
The Jewish Legion	1915-1918	World War I military unit under British command. Fought at Gallipoli and in Palestine.	Demonstrated Jewish military potential and reinforced Zionist goals.
Haganah Formation and Early Activity	1920-1936	Established after Arab riots. Main defense body of the Yishuv. Passive strategy during 1929 riots, later semi-merged with Irgun.	Redefine "defense," not merely as protecting communities, but as securing the foundations of a future Jewish state.
Arab Revolt and Active Defense	1936-1939	Used "wall and tower" tactics for rapid settlement. Special Night Squads and Field Companies marked shift to offensive defense.	"Restraint" (*Havlaga*) morphs to active defense (*Teguva*). Groundwork created for retaliatory methods (*Tagmul*).

(continued on next page)

Legal Units and British Cooperation	1936-1939	Thousands of Jews served as *notrim* ("guard police") under British supervision.	Haganah training and armament. Thousands of Jewish guards, *notrim* ("guard police"), were recruited as part of the British police force, enabling training with government-issued weapons. Zionist guards protected vital infrastructure like railways and built a barbed wire fence along the northern border to curb Arab infiltration.
World War II and the Palmach	1941-1945	Palmach created as Haganah's elite strike force. Trained fighters for special operations and future conflict.	Acted as the Haganah's elite strike force, training fighters for future conflict and solidifying retaliation (*teguva*) as their policy.
Jewish Brigade in British Army	1944	Fought in WW II. Gained valuable experience and built ties with British and Allied command.	Gaining valuable combat experience and strengthening ties with international allies.
Resistance to British and Illegal Immigration	1945-1948	Hebrew Resistance Movement launched attacks on British targets. Haganah organized Aliyah Bet, smuggling in Jewish refugees.	Hebrew Resistance Movement (1945) included the Haganah, Irgun, and Lehi, which coordinated attacks on British installations to protest restrictive immigration policies and the White Paper of 1939.
Transition to IDF and Nakba	1947-1948	Haganah led operations during war. Conducted both defensive and offensive missions.	Occupying the urban space of Palestine in April and May 1948 and expelling before the establishment of the IDF, 250,000 Palestinians and taking over the parts allocated to the Jewish state in the partition resolution.
Establishment of the Israel Defense Forces (IDF)	1948	Haganah transformed into the IDF, the official military of the new state of Israel.	Continuing the ethnic cleansing of Palestine, while repelling an attempt by neighboring Arab states to salvage the Palestinians. By December 1948, 750,000 Palestinians were uprooted, 531 villages destroyed, 11 towns de-Arabized and on their ruins, settlements were built and forests were planted.

Further Reading

1. Khalidi R. *The Hundred Years' War on Palestine: A History of Settler Colonialism and Resistance, 1917–2017.* Metropolitan Books; 2020.
2. Pappé I. *Lobbying for Zionism on Both Sides of the Atlantic.* Blackstone Publishing, Inc.; 2024.
3. Blanchard DC, Litvin Y, Pentkowski NS, Blanchard RJ. Defense and aggression. In: Berntson GG, Cacioppo JT, eds. *Handbook of Neuroscience for the Behavioral Sciences.* John Wiley and Sons, Inc.; 2009:958-974.
4. Blanchard DC. Of Lion Manes and Human Beards: Some Unusual Effects of the Interaction between Aggression and Sociality. *Front Behav Neurosci.* 2010;3:45. doi:10.3389/neuro.08.045.2009
5. Blanchard DC. Translating dynamic defense patterns from rodents to people. *Neurosci Biobehav Rev.* May 2017;76(Pt A):22-28. doi:10.1016/j.neubiorev.2016.11.001
6. Blanchard DC, Hynd AL, Minke KA, Minemoto T, Blanchard RJ. Human defensive behaviors to threat scenarios show parallels to fear- and anxiety-related defense patterns of non-human mammals. *Neurosci Biobehav Rev.* Dec 2001;25(7-8):761-70. doi:10.1016/s0149-7634(01)00056-2
7. Blanchard RJ, Blanchard DC. Bringing natural behaviors into the laboratory: a tribute to Paul MacLean. *Physiol Behav.* Aug 2003;79(3):515-24. doi:10.1016/s0031-9384(03)00157-4
8. Sapolsky RM. *Why Zebras Don't Get Ulcers: The Acclaimed Guide to Stress, Stress-Related Diseases, and Coping.* 3rd ed. Henry Holt and Company; 2004.
9. Zahavi, A. and A. Zahavi, *The Handicap Principle: A Missing Piece of Darwin's Puzzle.* 1997: Oxford University Press.
10. Ben-Zion D. *Sefer Toldot HaHaganah.* vol 1-3. Sefer Toldot HaHaganah (ספר תולדות ההגנה). Ma'arachot Publishing House; 1956-1972.
11. Kalman M. *Hero Shtetls: Jewish Armed Self-Defense From the Pale to Palestine, 1917-1970.* Harvard University; 2017.
12. Rabkin YM. *What Is Modern Israel.* Pluto Press; 2016.
13. Césaire A. *Discourse on Colonialism trans. Joan Pinkham.* Monthly Review Press; 1972 (Originally published in 1950).
14. Coan TG, Merolla JL, Zechmeister EJ, Zizumbo-Colunga D. Emotional Responses Shape the Substance of Information Seeking under Conditions of Threat. *Political Research Quarterly.* 2021;74(4):941-954. doi:10.1177/1065912920949320

15. Eco U. Ur-Fascism. *The New York Review of Books*. June 22, 1995.
16. Fanon F. *The Wretched of the Earth (C. Farrington, Trans.)*. Grove Press; 1963.
17. Kudryavtseva NN. Positive fighting experience, addiction-like state, and relapse: Retrospective analysis of experimental studies. *Aggression and Violent Behavior*. 2020;52:101403.
18. Lantos D, Molenberghs P. The neuroscience of intergroup threat and violence. *Neurosci Biobehav Rev*. Dec 2021;131:77-87. doi:10.1016/j.neubiorev.2021.09.025
19. Litvin Y, Blanchard DC, Pentkowski NS, Blanchard RJ. A pinch or a lesion: a reconceptualization of biting consequences in mice. *Aggress Behav*. Nov-Dec 2007;33(6):545-51. doi:10.1002/ab.20222
20. McEwen BS. In pursuit of resilience: stress, epigenetics, and brain plasticity. *Ann N Y Acad Sci*. Jun 2016;1373(1):56-64. doi:10.1111/nyas.13020
21. Pappé I. *The Ethnic Cleansing of Palestine*. Oneworld Publications; 2006.
22. Rabkin Y, Yadgar Y. On Political Tradition and Ideology: Russian Dimensions of Practical Zionism and Israeli Politics. *Nationalities Papers*. 2024;52(6):1413-1430. doi:10.1017/nps.2023.84
23. Wolfe P. Settler Colonialism and the Elimination of the Native. *Journal of Genocide Research*. 2006;8(4):387-409. doi:10.1080/14623520601056240
24. Alexander, M., *The New Jim Crow: Mass Incarceration in the Age of Colorblindness*. 2010, New York: New Press.
25. Cohen, S., *Visions of Social Control: Crime, Punishment, and Classification*. 1985, Cambridge: Polity Press.
26. Foucault, M., *Discipline and Punish: The Birth of the Prison*. 1977, New York: Pantheon Books.
27. Walmsley, R., *World Prison Population List*. 12th ed. 2018, London: Institute for Criminal Policy Research, Birkbeck, University of London.
28. Pfaff DW. *The Altruistic Brain: How We are Naturally Good*. Oxford University Press; 2015:ix, 295 pages.
29. Bandura A. Moral Disengagement in the Perpetration of Inhumanities. *Personality and Social Psychology Review*. 1999;3(3):193-209.
30. Pinker S. *The Better Angels of our Nature: Why Violence Has Declined*. Penguin Books; 2012:xxviii, 802 p.

Part III - The Machinations of Theft: A Model of Settler Expansion

As shown in **Part I**, war is a modern, cultural construct which arose from sedentary life, resource hoarding, and the resulting inequalities, not "human nature." **Part II** revealed how the Zionist foundational construct, predating the formation of the state of Israel, adopted the language of fear and defense, though its actions were consistently offensive, aimed at power and control, displacing Palestinians, and expropriating their land and resources.

Next, this knowledge will be used to construct a model of how settler colonial society in general, and Zionist society in particular, mired in land and resource theft, has evolved. It examines how fear is deliberately manufactured and conditioned by the ruling class through various means, including religion, to sustain an appetite for aggression; how the language and tactics of defense are used to mask offensive aims and practices; and how this process produces the brutal oppression, dispossession, and genocide of oppressed communities, including the Indigenous Palestinian people.

The dynamics explored throughout this book can be understood through a Wired to Steal (W2S) model, (**Figure III.1**), a framework which explains how systems of domination are sustained through the interaction of structural power and human psychology.

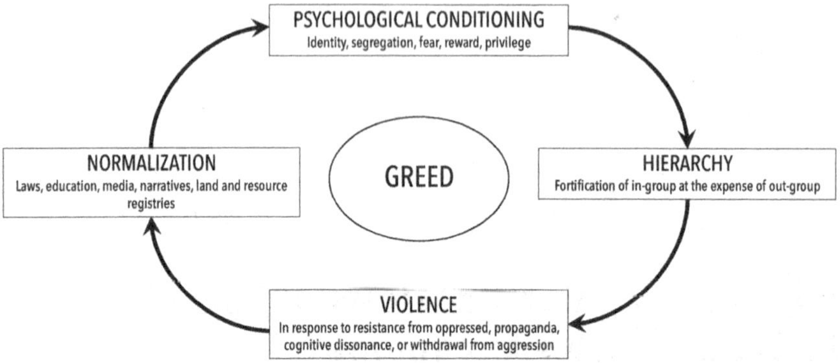

Figure III.1. The Wired to Steal model. The Wired to Steal model depicts a self-reinforcing cycle through which systems of domination reproduce themselves. Greed drives the pursuit of power and control over land and resources. Societies are shaped through psychological conditioning, mobilizing fear, identity and selective privilege and rewards, which produce hierarchical social orders. These hierarchies are maintained through violence and coercion. Over time, inequality and oppression become normalized through institutions, laws and dominant narratives. This normalization reinforces the conditions that allow greed to persist and grow, completing a positive feedback loop that perpetuates the system across generations.

At its core, the W2S model posits that ruling class greed, a drive for extraction and accumulation that emerged alongside sedentary societies, surplus production, animal domestication, agriculture, pastoralism, and was later amplified by the industrial revolution, drives offensive aggression in the form of land, labor, and resource theft. Those dispossessed naturally respond with defensive aggression to protect their lives, families, communities, and resources.

Because most humans possess empathic capacities and are generally reluctant to support or participate in offensive aggression for the benefit of a privileged few, theft and conquest are rarely sustainable on their own. Ruling classes therefore manufacture collective identities that divide populations into in-groups and out-groups and employ propaganda to reframe offensive aggression as legitimate defense. The European conquest of the "New World" illustrates this clearly: the pursuit of wealth came first and the narratives followed. Racial hierarchies, manufactured identities, religious doctrines, and ideological justifications were engineered to justify and perpetuate conquest.

Colonial propaganda suppresses empathy through at least five mutually reinforcing mechanisms: dehumanization, which lowers the threshold for violence by portraying the out-group as less than fully human; threat inversion, which recasts the defensive aggression of the dispossessed as the original act of aggression while presenting the aggressor as a victim acting in self-defense; divine mandate, which removes moral agency by framing violence as sacred duty; historical erasure, which denies the existence, history, and culture of the victimized population; and fear conditioning, which activates defensive neural circuitry, bypassing reason and empathy and making violence appear necessary for survival.

The in-group receives material rewards, status, social belonging, privilege, and access to the spoils of dispossession, while the out-group is excluded, exploited, and targeted for removal. Individuals who uphold the hierarchy are rewarded through material gain, social rewards and belonging, privilege, and the neurological pleasure associated with humiliating or dominating an out-group, a phenomenon known as intergroup schadenfreude. Repeated positive reward across these domains, combined with intermittent negative reinforcement, creates a conditioned appetite for violence that persists and often escalates beyond the original material incentive. Military service, periodic wars, and other institutions ensure that this reinforcement schedule is distributed throughout society rather than confined to those already inclined toward violence.

These processes exploit well-studied neural and endocrine systems, including fear circuitry associated with the amygdala, reward pathways mediated by dopamine, and social bonding mechanisms involving oxytocin. Over time, the resulting hierarchies of oppression become embedded within political, economic, educational, religious, and cultural institutions, reproduced across generations, and intensified in response to resistance. In this way, societies become wired to steal: emotionally, behaviorally, and neurologically conditioned to normalize theft, justify offensive aggression as defense, and view violence, dispossession, and domination as necessary for survival, order, identity, and belonging.

1. The behavioral roots of violence

> In the colonies, the settler only feels safe when the native is annihilated or neutralized.
>
> ~ Frantz Fanon, *The Wretched of the Earth* (p. 41.)

To understand how the Zionist ruling class has seized land and resources while consolidating power, it is necessary to examine how it cultivates a culture in which offensive expansion is framed as existential defense. By promoting fear and insecurity, and decontextualizing resistance by the oppressed, the ruling class encourages the lower classes to adopt a posture of lethal "defensive" aggression, mobilizing them to carry out policies of dispossession and violence which ultimately serve ruling class interests in territorial control and accumulation.

As such, to understand the behavioral causes of this violence, we must first examine its underlying driver, fear, and the science of fear learning, known as fear conditioning or aversive learning. To date, scholarship into settler colonialism has largely confined itself to documenting this fear, without probing its underlying dynamics and their political implications. This book seeks to fill that gap, offering a rigorous, scientific explanation for the phenomenon.

a. Learned fear

Fear evolved as an adaptive emotional mechanism, enabling animals to respond swiftly and effectively to threats. In life-or-death situations, trial and error is too slow, so evolution favored innate, hardwired defensive behaviors to common dangers, producing consistent, species-wide responses with striking cross-species similarities (see **Part II**). Yet while these fixed responses ensure quick reactions to predators, rivals, and environmental hazards, survival often depends on the ability to learn from experience, adapt to novel threats, and modify behavior accordingly.

To survive long-term, an animal must first contend with immediate danger, then rapidly link related cues and contexts to the threat, a process called "aversive learning," which guides future defense. By anticipating danger through conditioned cues, organisms can prepare proactively rather than reactively. In essence, aversive learning integrates innate instincts with learned responses to enhance survival in new and often perilous environments (see **Figure III.2**).

Aversive learning blends classical and operant forms of conditioning. Classical (Pavlovian) conditioning, named after Russian scientist Ivan Pavlov (1849–1936), links neutral cues to biologically significant events. In operant conditioning, when a behavior is followed by a reward (reinforcement), it is more likely to be repeated; when followed by a punishment, it is less likely to occur. Operant models, most readily associated with B.F. Skinner (1904–1990), involve behaviors learned through consequences like pressing a lever for a reward, and escaping or avoiding aversive events. Positive reinforcement adds a pleasant stimulus, a reward, while negative reinforcement removes an unpleasant one. Over time, behaviors are modified depending on how consistently they are reinforced or punished.

Classical fear conditioning is a method for studying how fear responses are learned. In this paradigm, a neutral cue, such as a tone or a light, called the "conditioned stimulus" (CS), is repeatedly paired with an aversive event, like a loud noise or mild electric shock, known as the "unconditioned stimulus" (US). The aversive event naturally provokes a reflexive defensive reaction, such as startle, freezing, or increased autonomic arousal, called the "unconditioned response" (UR). After repeated pairings, the neutral cue alone becomes associated with the aversive event and elicits the same defensive reaction, now called the "conditioned response" (CR).

This mechanism of rapid learning helps the animal anticipate and avoid potential harm, or in other words, the CS comes to predict the US, eliciting a CR, which is typically a defensive behavior.

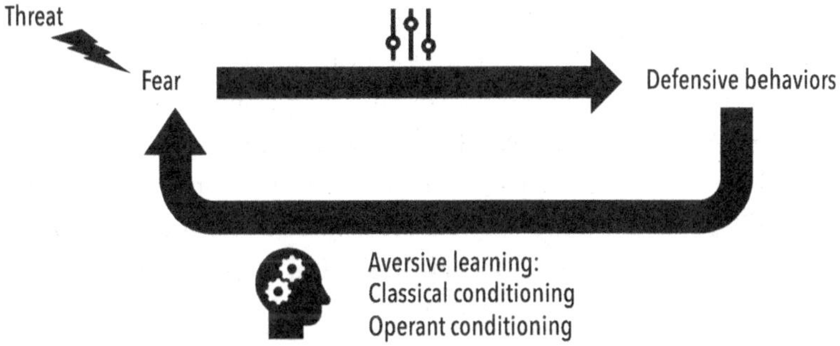

Figure III. 2. Aversive learning (classical plus operant conditioning) modifies fear-evoked defensive behaviors in response to threat.

The operant escape model centers on terminating a negative stimulus, while the operant avoidance model focuses on preventing it altogether. According to the two-factor theory, fear is first acquired through classical conditioning, then a behavior that reduces fear is reinforced, making it more likely to recur.

Innate species-specific defensive reactions, such as freezing or fleeing, often override learned behaviors and are influenced by evolutionary pressures.

Building on these foundational mechanisms of fear formation and expression, we can now explore three different fear processes that contribute to both adaptive behaviors and maladaptive patterns seen in fear and anxiety-related behaviors and associated disorders, as well as how they can be shaped by trauma and potentially manipulated, amplified, or generalized to serve broader political agendas.

Fear reconsolidation is a process in which reactivated fear memories become temporarily malleable and can be modified before being stored again. During this window, the fear association can be either weakened or strengthened, depending on the nature of the experience that follows reactivation. If the memory is reinforced with additional aversive stimuli or no new information, the fear may intensify. Conversely, exposure to safety cues or therapeutic interventions can reduce its intensity, making reconsolidation a key target for both the worsening and treatment of fear-related conditions.

Fear extinction is a process through which fear conditioning is reduced or eliminated. This is typically achieved by repeatedly presenting the CS (e.g., a sound or image previously associated with an aversive event like a shock) without the US (e.g., an electric shock). Over time, the individual learns the CS no longer predicts the US, leading to a decrease in the CR. Notably, extinction does not erase the original fear memory; it merely inhibits its expression, which can sometimes result in the fear response returning under certain conditions, such as reinstatement or spontaneous recovery.

Fear reinstatement refers to the return of a previously diminished or extinguished conditioned fear response following re-exposure to the original aversive stimulus (the US) alone, which was initially paired with a neutral cue (CS). This occurs even after extinction training, where the conditioned stimulus was repeatedly presented without the aversive stimulus to reduce the fear response. Reinstatement indicates that the original fear memory is not erased by extinction but remains latent and can be reactivated under specific conditions.

b. Basics on the neurobiology of fear: the amygdala and prefrontal cortex

To deepen our understanding of fear, it is useful to examine its neural circuitry, with a particular focus on two brain regions: the amygdala and prefrontal cortex (PFC), which govern how fear memories are formed, regulated, and expressed in both healthy and disordered states (**Figure III.3**).

The amygdala, an almond-shaped structure in the medial temporal lobe, is a relatively ancient part of the human brain, shared with vertebrates as far back as jawed fish such as sharks. Serving as the brain's central hub for processing and storing the emotional significance of stimuli, particularly those related to threats, it plays a key role in processing fear and regulating its expression, significantly through classical fear conditioning, which involves changes in the circuitry between sensory and motor pathways. Even when the threat is no longer present, as in a process of fear extinction, the amygdala initially remains active, gradually decreasing its response as the CS is repeatedly presented without harm, though the original fear memory often persists and can be reinstated.

While the amygdala instills fear, the PFC plays a critical role in regulating, interpreting, and extinguishing it. During extinction, the PFC exerts an inhibitory influence over the amygdala, signaling that the once-threatening stimulus is no longer dangerous. This regulatory function is essential, allowing individuals to adapt and respond appropriately rather than remaining trapped in outdated fear responses.

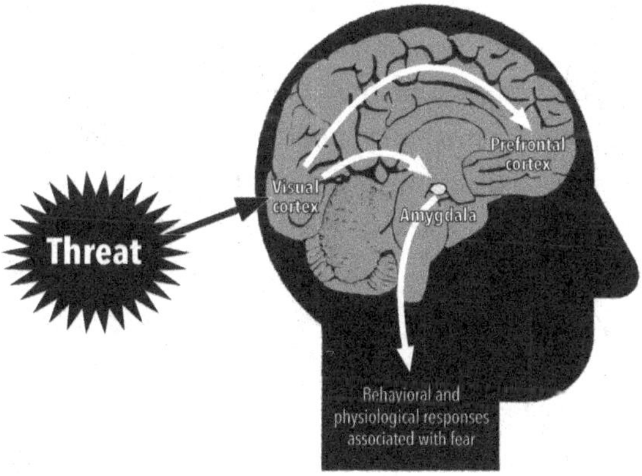

Figure III.3. Brain circuitry involved in behavioral and cognitive aspects of fear

As stated, in fear reinstatement a previously extinguished CR can return after a stressor or unsignaled presentation of the US. This involves reactivation of the amygdala, which rapidly reinstates the original fear memory. The PFC's regulatory control is often reduced during reinstatement, allowing amygdala-driven fear responses to re-emerge.

Fear reconsolidation occurs when a retrieved fear memory becomes temporarily labile and susceptible to modification before it is restabilized. The amygdala is essential for this process, as it re-encodes the memory. The PFC can influence whether the reactivated memory is updated, weakened, or even strengthened, depending on context and timing. Thus, the amygdala imprints fear into memory for rapid threat detection, while the PFC regulates and adapts these responses. Their interplay shapes how fear is learned, unlearned, reinstated, or altered, making them central to both the persistence and resolution of fear.

These systems are dramatically affected by pathology associated with trauma and chronic stress. For example, in individuals with post-traumatic stress disorder (PTSD), these regulatory systems are disrupted. The amygdala tends to be hyperactive, resulting in exaggerated fear responses and heightened emotional memory encoding. Conversely, the PFC is often hypoactive, impairing its ability to inhibit amygdala activity and extinguish fear. This imbalance contributes to persistent and intrusive fear memories, difficulty with extinction learning, and heightened susceptibility to fear reinstatement.

Importantly, it remains unclear whether individuals with hyperactive amygdalas and hypoactive prefrontal cortices are predisposed to trauma or whether trauma induces these pathological changes. Evidence supports both possibilities. Additionally, fear reconsolidation may become maladaptive in PTSD, potentially strengthening rather than modifying traumatic memories after reactivation. Together, these neural dysfunctions help explain the chronic and relapsing nature of trauma-related fear in PTSD. Indeed, traumatized war veterans exhibit changes in the brain where the amygdala becomes primed and the PFC is compromised, rendering them prone to find fear in everything.

c. Manipulation of fear by Zionists

Similar to other settler colonial movements, Zionism appealed to traumatized, often disenfranchised people in Europe, who endured frequent violence, promising the establishment of a European-style settler colony justified by divine will. Its leaders learned to manipulate fear and galvanize consequent defensive behaviors to rally support for offensive, expansionist, and violent policies and suppression of dissent.

This manipulation proved effective, as the neural mechanisms underlying fear are readily activated in individuals with a history of trauma. Fear conditioning can be reinstated in traumatized individuals and collectives through re-exposure to, or recall of, the original fear-inducing stimulus or simply by exposing them to other stressors. Importantly, fear does not necessarily refer to threats to physical survival; it can also reflect anxiety over the potential survival of privileges sustained by a segregated, colonial structure. These include exclusive access to land and resources.

Fear conditioning within the Jewish Zionist collective has been systematically engineered, reinstated, and reconsolidated through several mechanisms. First, the consistent trauma as a result of colonial violence, Palestinian resistance to it, and continual wars against Arab neighbors. The isolation and decontextualization of acts of resistance are then labeled as "antisemitism," and/or "terrorism." Second, by invoking past traumas of Jewish people such as the Holocaust, stressing the central role of the conflation of Judaism, a religion, with Zionism, a modern European settler movement. Finally, by fearmongering and redirecting public attention toward perceived existential dangers, like the Iranian nuclear program.

Until the Iranian threat was manipulated in such a way, it was mostly the abuse of the memory of the Holocaust. The method was very simple: associating the Palestinian resistance to the settler colonial project with European antisemitism in general and Nazism in particular, in addition to the familiar patterns of depicting the Indigenous people as inferior or primitive, it introduced a distinctive feature: the Nazification of the Palestinians, framing them as existential enemies in the image of Nazism itself, a concept analyzed by the historian Idith Zertal.

This manipulation began during the 1948 ethnic cleansing operations in Palestine, when *politruks*, the political officers of the Haganah, a role originated by the Soviet army, encouraged troops on the eve of military operations to view the Palestinians as the new Nazis. It received an additional boost after the Palestine Liberation Organization (PLO) began its guerrilla warfare against Israel in the mid-1960s, which intensified after the occupation of the West Bank and the Gaza Strip in 1967.

The Palestinian resistance was characterized by two modes of action: resistance on small or large scales. The former was an almost daily occurrence in the occupied territories and largely spontaneous, the latter was more deliberate and took the form of two uprisings, intifadas, in 1987 and 2000. The second mode of action included both smaller operations and larger, more daring operations of attacking settlements or army bases (and for a while, hijacking airplanes, which became the hallmark of the left-wing fronts within the PLO).

The appearance of political Islamic resistance groups in the late 1980s did not change these tactics very much. The focus until 1967 was of the liberation of Palestine as a whole and the return of the refugees. From the early 1970s, most Palestinian factions were resigned to the idea of a two-state solution, and hence the armed struggle was focused on ending the occupation of the West Bank and the Gaza Strip.

The mode of action was inspired by third world resistance movements, and hence the wish was to create a hinterland for the resistance (first in Jordan, which kicked out the PLO in 1970) and then in the south of Lebanon, where the PLO was able to build more permanent presence.

Political Islamic groups maintain a military presence in South Lebanon and have developed guerrilla operations in the West Bank, where the PLO largely abandoned armed struggle after the 1993 Oslo Accords, though its younger generation formed the Al-Aqsa Martyrs' Brigade in 2000 to continue the fight. The Israeli withdrawal from the Gaza Strip in 2005 allowed the main political group, Hamas, to build a proper military organization as part of its wish to first lift the siege Israel imposed on the Strip since the Hamas takeover, and to continue to the overall ending of the occupation, although the rhetoric is of an armed struggle for the liberation of Palestine as a whole.

This Palestinian mode of resistance contributed to the Israeli manipulation of fear among Jews in Israel and in the world by ignoring the origin of the violence, the Zionist project, and focusing on its symptoms, the actions described above. Whether these actions were carried out by secular forces or Islamist forces, in the official Israeli discourse they were part of a new Nazism, fused with Islamism, that meant to inflict another Holocaust on the Jewish people.

This is why Menachem Begin likened Arafat, who was stranded in his bunker during the Israeli siege of Beirut in 1982, to Hitler in his Berlin bunker in the final days of Nazism. It is also why Benjamin Netanyahu, with the support of Israeli academia, revived a controversial chapter of Palestinian history: the story of Hajj Amin al-Husayni, the embattled Palestinian leader who sought the help of Italy and Germany against the British, who were intent on executing him for his resistance to their policies in Palestine. In a brazen act of historical revisionism, Netanyahu told the British prime minister, Theresa May, that it was Amin al-Husayni who conceived the idea of the Nazi Final Solution.

The manipulation of fear has been mainly necessary to justify the escalation in satisfying the classical logic of a settler colonial project: the elimination of the native, whether it was done through ethnic cleaning in 1948, incremental ethnic cleaning since 1967, incremental genocide in the Gaza Strip since 2009, and explicit genocidal policies since 2023. Akin to other settler-colonial projects, Zionism consistently dehumanizes the native population.

d. Segregation and disgust

One of the most effective ways to reduce fear of "the other," i.e., fear extinction, is through social integration between in-groups and out-groups. From the outset of the Zionist project, segregation/apartheid has been a foundational principle of settlement, elevating fear and hostility toward the Indigenous Palestinian population while actively preventing extinction of fear. This ongoing separation, enforced through apartheid policies, sustains an ever-escalating process of fear and dehumanization that renders re-exposure, reconciliation, and empathy virtually impossible. The void created is then filled with propaganda and misinformation about the out-group.

Indeed, segregation of Palestinian people was suggested even before organized Zionist settlement of Palestine by British MP Laurence Oliphant (1829–1888), demonstrating a continuity in settler mindset and strategy. In his *The Land of Gilead: With Excursions in the Lebanon* (1880), he said:

> The Arabs have very little claim to our sympathy. They have laid waste this country, ruined its villages, and plundered its inhabitants, until it has been reduced to its present condition … the same system might be pursued which we have adopted with success in Canada with our North American Indian tribes, who are confined to their "reserves," and live peaceably upon them in the midst of the settled agricultural population.

The emotion of disgust plays a central role in dehumanization, making it easier to discriminate against and abuse others. Disgust originally evolved as a biological response to potential sources of disease and contamination, such as spoiled food, animals with the potential to serve as vectors for disease, or bodily fluids. Over time, this response was extended into the social and moral realms, where it shapes how we judge others. People often perceive out-groups as dirty or impure, and this perception activates the same neural circuits in the brain that process physical disgust, particularly in a brain region called the insula. Interestingly, according to Donald Pfaff in *The Altruistic Brain* (2014), the insula also plays a central role in the neural circuitry of empathy. This dual function suggests dehumanization operates precisely here: recruiting the insula's disgust response to block the self-other blurring that would otherwise activate altruism toward the out-group, while leaving that capacity intact for in-group members.

This mechanism helps explain why propaganda frequently uses language that portrays enemies as vermin or contagion, framing them as less than human and morally contaminating. Such dehumanization makes it psychologically easier to deny empathy and justify segregation and eliminatory aggression against those outside one's group. While this tendency is deeply rooted in biology, it is not inevitable and can be countered through conscious effort, desegregation, exposure to out-groups, and a focus on shared humanity.

As discussed in **Part II**, segregation creates multiple parallel societies, each with its own internal hierarchies. Within these groups, nonlethal forms of intragroup offensive aggression help establish and maintain social order. At the same time, each segregated society defines its spatial boundaries through territoriality and responds to perceived intrusions with inter-group defensive aggression, which can be lethal. In this way, segregation not only entrenches division, making fear extinction and future reconciliation impossible, it also inherently predisposes groups to violent conflict. In such a manner, Palestinian resistance/self-defense against colonialism is framed as decontextualized "terrorism" (**Figure III.4**).

Yet how does fear transform into a profound psychological and societal addiction to offensive aggression, encouraging the theft of land and

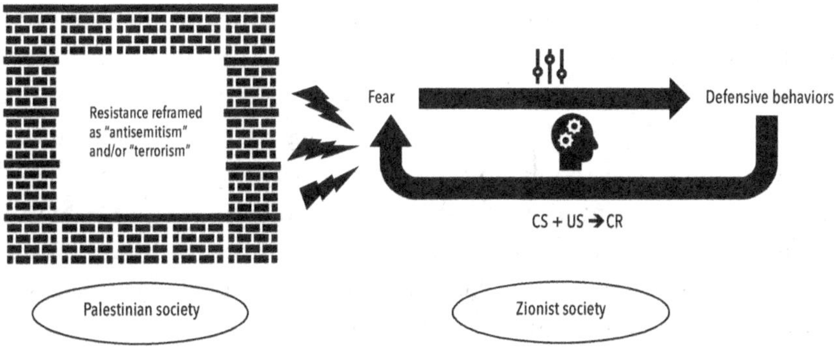

Figure III.4. **Segregation - fear model**. Palestinian resistance against segregation and oppression is weaponized to promote fear conditioning, reinstatement, and reconsolidation in Zionist society, which justifies tactics associated with defensive aggression. Segregation thwarts fear extinction and promotes inter-group territorial violence. CS - conditioned stimulus; US - unconditioned stimulus; CR - conditioned response

resources, binding the population ever more tightly to the interests of the ruling class?

e. Wired to steal: a neurobehavioral model of Zionist aggression

Wired to Steal (W2S), a behavioral model of settler colonial violence, argues colonial violence is behaviorally organized, rather than merely ideological or historical: a system rooted in resource theft, maintained through conditioning and reproduced across generations through structural, social and neurological mechanisms.

In the context of rising antisemitic violence in Europe, the emergence of Zionist self-defense groups can be understood through the lens of classical and operant conditioning as the beginning of a psychological and behavioral process which ultimately evolved into territorial aggression.

Antisemitic attacks acted as USs, provoking URs associated with fear, such as defensive behaviors like freezing, avoidance (through entrenchment/self-segregation), flight (through migration), and defensive threat and attack. Over time, environmental cues or contexts associated with such violence became CSs, eliciting anticipatory fear responses as CRs, conditioning which ruling class actors would later exploit, pairing these same cues with manufactured threat narratives to sustain and intensify fear beyond its original defensive function.

Among those who were able and willing to fight, this dynamic fueled operant conditioning of self-defense (defensive aggression) as a coping mechanism through: (i) negative reinforcement, in which behavior is strengthened by avoiding or removing an unpleasant stimulus and; (ii) positive reinforcement through reward, whether emotional, social, or material. Together, these processes laid the groundwork for a profound behavioral shift: defensive aggression in response to fear developed from a reactive survival tactic into a conditioned, emotionally rewarding and potentially addictive pattern.

This behavioral shift, however, did not occur in a vacuum. The transition from defensive to offensive aggression, from survival to settler colonialism, was directed by a ruling class whose primary driver was greed, not trauma. The conditioning of the population served this project. Manufactured fear narratives, selective reward for aggression, and the systematic dehumanization of Palestinians were deliberate instruments deployed by those who stood to benefit materially from territorial expansion. The traumatized population provided the moral infrastructure and accompanying narratives; the ruling class provided the design.

Here, it is instructive to revisit the animal research from **Part II** on how offensive aggression shapes and upholds social hierarchies. During aggressive encounters in hierarchical social structures, dominants experience reward associated with increased levels of testosterone, while subordinates experience social defeat, raising stress hormones (glucocorticoids) that reinforce the hierarchy by encoding memories of defeat and encouraging submissive behavior toward dominants.

Low social status is associated with increased stress, fear, and irritability due to these heightened glucocorticoid levels; hormones that can damage health if chronically elevated. However, individuals can reduce their glucocorticoid levels and alleviate stress (negative reinforcement) by directing aggression toward those lower in the hierarchy. This cascading pattern of aggression sustains a hierarchy regulated by reward on the one hand and stress hormones and negative reinforcement on the other, leaving the lowest-ranking members, who lack any outlet, with persistently high glucocorticoid levels, harming their health and driving a continual search for aggression as release.

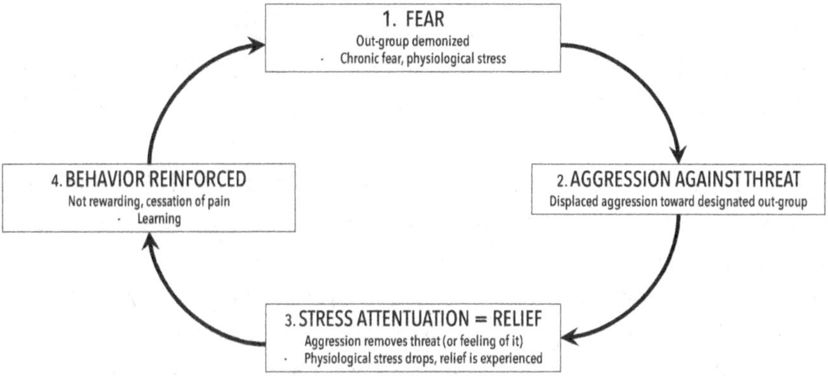

Figure III.5. Negative reinforcement of aggression.

These studies can illuminate the biological roots of the dynamics of oppression across a wide range of stratified, capitalistic, classist human societies, including in the Global South as analyzed by Frantz Fanon. These include the marginalization of BIPOC communities in ghettoized urban centers, the entrenched poverty of Brazil's favelas, the systematic subjugation of Palestinians and other Indigenous peoples under settler colonial regimes, and more.

Moreover, Jaak Panksepp's research reveals that aggression activates the brain's reward circuits, making it intrinsically pleasurable and reinforcing (positive reinforcement). Miczek et al. demonstrate that aggressive mice perform operant tasks for access to attack subordinate intruders, paralleling rodent models of drug self-administration. Robert and Caroline Blanchard add that chronic stress and repeated aggression sensitize associated neural pathways, promoting compulsive aggression akin to addiction. Their research supports a model in which stress and aggression form a feedback loop in which stress increases aggression, aggression activates reward pathways, and repeated aggression reinforces the neural circuits, potentially leading to an addictive cycle of violence. This model parallels mechanisms in substance addiction, where drugs sensitize reward circuits and reinforce drug-seeking behavior. For more on the addictive nature of aggression see work by Sam A. Golden at the National Institute on Drug Abuse in Baltimore, Maryland.

Complementing this, Bessel van der Kolk shows trauma survivors often reenact aggression to recreate familiar emotional states and manage unresolved pain, a process of fear reconsolidation. When used to cope with unresolved trauma or chronic stress, aggression can function like an addiction, activating the brain's dopamine system and providing a rewarding sense of control or emotional release.

PTSD, aggression and addiction are tightly intertwined through shared neurological and behavioral pathways. Trauma dysregulates the nervous system, heightening emotional sensitivity and impairing impulse control, which leaves individuals in a heightened state of fear and reactivity. This makes them prone to aggressive outbursts as a means of reducing fear and stress, while also driving self-medication through drugs, alcohol, or other temporary escapes from intrusive memories, anxiety, or emotional numbness. Addiction further impairs impulse control and worsens both aggression and trauma, creating a vicious trauma-aggression cycle (**Figure III.6**), making recovery increasingly difficult without integrated intervention. Notably, trauma, addiction, and related behaviors and disorders can be transmitted across generations through a variety of mechanisms.

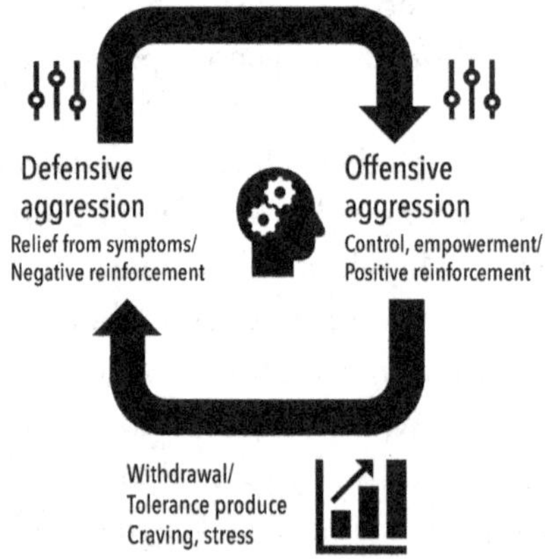

Figure III.6. The trauma-aggression cycle. Trauma and aggression (defensive and offensive forms) interact to form an addictive cycle.

This stress response is driven by overactive brain regions like the amygdala and insula, amplifying fear, pain, and the dehumanization associated with disgust, alongside a compromised PFC that struggles to regulate behavior under chronic strain.

For trauma survivors, especially those exposed to violence and thus powerlessness early in life, aggression may become a default strategy for emotional regulation, offering relief from fear and a sense of power and control in the face of vulnerability. However, like many addictions, repeated aggression leads to tolerance, requiring more intense expressions for the same relieving effect, while its absence may trigger withdrawal-like symptoms such as irritability, impulsiveness, restlessness, and/or agitation.

Fortifying these mechanisms, Mina Cikara's group at Harvard has shown individuals experience reward from targeting out-group members (schadenfreude), suggesting abusive behaviors can become addictive. Collectively, this dynamic may help account for the more extreme expressions of genocidal violence characteristic of colonial systems, including Zionism, which can exceed instrumental necessity, while the escalatory trajectory itself is rooted in the structure of the system.

Fear persists in a self-reinforcing cycle, as fear-based narratives of a so-called "existential threat," rooted in segregation and echoed through collective memory, combine with religious justifications grounded in a manifest destiny ideology. Within this framework, aggressive responses are consistently rewarded and normalized. Thus, over time, they are intensified in nature and frequency. The result is a hardened belief that expansion, lethal aggression, and dispossession are not simply justified, but the only conceivable responses to a conflict constructed as eternal and unsolvable.

Integrating the model of aversive learning (**Figure III.2**) with that of segregation-fear (**Figure III.4**), and the trauma-aggression cycle (**Figure III.6**) yields a comprehensive theoretical framework for understanding Zionist settler colonial aggression, dispossession and genocide on a neurobehavioral level (**Figure III.7**).

This dynamic is especially potent in environments that valorize domination, such as colonial, classist, racialized, patriarchal, or militarized cultures, where aggression is both intrinsically rewarding and materially reinforced through acquisition of land, resources, and/or financial gain. Fear can be employed to enforce obedience and recruit new members into the trauma-aggression cycle, which rewards offensive aggression with social inclusion/identity, a sense of security, elevated status, and material gain, often through the

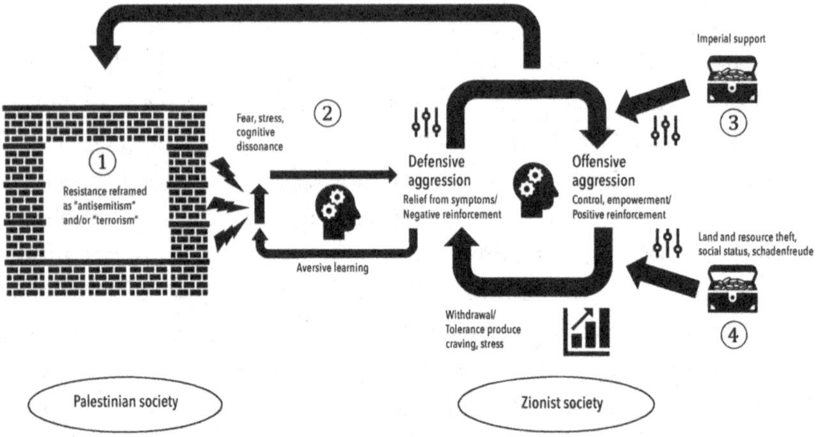

Figure III.7. Wired to steal: a neurobehavioral model of Zionist aggression and theft. (1) Acts of Palestinian resistance to Zionist policies of apartheid, dispossession, and genocide produce trauma, which is weaponized to condition and reinstate fear. (2) Trauma, fear, and cognitive dissonance (more later) trigger chronic stress, which is relieved via defensive aggression, i.e., negative reinforcement. (3) Aggression is rewarded externally by imperial and other powers and (4) internally through land and resource theft from Palestinian society, which in turn fuel and perpetuate the cycle as positive reinforcement. The escalation of this cycle leads to full-scale genocide.

seizure of Indigenous land and resources. Further, periodic bouts of trauma and fear conditioning negatively reinforce patterns of aggression, segregation and dehumanization that would otherwise naturally erode via integration, allowing empathy and reconciliation to emerge.

Repeated positive reward and negative reinforcement, delivered on intermittent schedules, produce a conditioned appetite for violence that persists and escalates. This is the same mechanism that makes slot machines highly addictive: variable-ratio reinforcement schedules are the most powerful conditioning systems known and the most resistant to extinction. The intermittent schedule also explains cases of gratuitous violence that do not appear to be directly rewarded at the time they occur.

This cycle can be somewhat curtailed by internal and external pressures, defining its intensity and speed. On the other hand, no pressure, i.e., impunity for genocidal aggression, can lead to catastrophic genocide and whole-scale land theft, as is evident in Gaza, the West Bank, and Lebanon currently (more in **Part IV**).

2. Transition from Jewish trauma to Zionist aggression

This context illuminates the process which instrumentalized a quest for security and dignity among Jewish communities traumatized by the violence of pogroms and disillusioned by the Enlightenment's unfulfilled promise of equality and emancipation.

For Jewish people in Europe in the late nineteenth century, defensive aggression became a reinforced coping mechanism. However, a major problem persisted: as a targeted, othered group within the white European social hierarchy, Jews endured high levels of racism, violence, and stress yet lacked an outlet to displace their aggression. The Zionist solution was to hijack Jewish fear and identify a weaker outgroup to which aggression could be redirected as a means of creating a new, segregated settler colonial hierarchy. In an era of rising romantic nationalism and white supremacy, Zionism gained appeal by designating Indigenous Palestinians as dehumanized victims onto whom racist aggression could be displaced. Thus, the Zionist project with its syncretic narratives, identity constructs, and manufactured hierarchy hinged on the scapegoating of an Indigenous population.

In European patriarchal culture, reclaiming dignity has frequently been linked to a man's capacity to defend his honor, even at the cost of his life. Assimilated Jews sought to redeem collective honor by embracing intrinsically rewarding Gentile ideals of conquest and physical strength. A striking example is Ferdinand Lassalle (1825–1864), an assimilated Jew who declined to back down from a fatal duel. This act symbolized a broader modern trend to defend Jewish honor, an impulse that may have marked an early emergence of a trauma-aggression cycle and its perceived rewards (**Figure III.6**). In Germany, dueling scars served as social currency (i.e., positive rewards) within elite student fraternities, which largely excluded Jews; young Jews would provoke antisemites into fights, using physical risk-taking to assert Jewish honor. At German universities, this militancy among Jewish students grew; Zionist outlets like *Die Welt* proudly reported on young Viennese Zionists physically confronting their tormentors.

Herzl himself viewed dueling as a noble practice for refining character and educating future leaders and proposed legalizing it in the Jewish state. He envisioned a new kind of Jew, free, proud, and strong, liberated from the psychological burdens of segregated, minority life. To build this identity, he borrowed heavily from white supremacist European nationalism: patriotic songs, heroic myths like the Maccabees, a focus on dignity, and military-style British education.

The idea of the Maccabees also held great appeal for early Zionists in Britain. In 1891, they founded the Maccabean Club, an organization dedicated to supporting the nascent Jewish settlements in Palestine, including through the purchase of land on their behalf. They sent a delegation to Palestine that enacted rituals closely resembling those of Christian evangelical pilgrims, thereby underscoring the messianic dimension of the colonization project.

In the early days of the emerging Zionist identity, Jewish groups formed sports teams often romantically named after historic Jewish heroes, embodying a nostalgic yearning for strength and self-determination. A prominent example is the well-known Viennese team *Hakoach Vienna* (Hebrew for "the Strength of Vienna"), which symbolized this craving for power and control. In this vision, physical strength and nation-building were inseparable, and the future Jewish state required a "new Jew" who could stand equal, both physically and mentally, to his powerful European neighbors.

Building on these notions of honor and dignity and denied equality by European nations, Zionists used Jewish trauma as moral and religious justification to adopt the colonial playbook of those same forces: to secure status by establishing a settler presence elsewhere, where Indigenous populations could be displaced, disenfranchised, and erased. While Palestine could not be "discovered" in the way the Americas or Australia were, Zionist rhetoric subjected Indigenous Palestinians to the same racist white supremacist colonial logic of dehumanization; they were either totally ignored as nonentities in an empty land or cast as backward primitives and illegitimate usurpers. Even the early settlers who, in their initial stages in the new country, depended on local Palestinians for survival through accommodation and agricultural know how, still described those Palestinians as aliens and usurpers.

In this, Zionist ideology reveals one of its defining features: projection, attributing to the colonized the very dehumanizing acts of dispossession and violence enacted by the colonizer. The victim becomes the oppressor, the addict becomes the pusher, the landless becomes land thief and landlord, all serviced by a manufactured identity.

a. Jewish identity, Zionist syncretism, and colonial mimicry

> This new culture had to be syncretistic. Syncretism is not only, as the dictionary says, "the combination of different forms of belief or practice"; such a combination must tolerate contradictions. Each of the original messages contains a sliver of wisdom, and whenever they seem to say different or incompatible things it is only because all are alluding, allegorically, to the same primeval truth. As a consequence, there can be no advancement of learning. Truth has been already spelled out once and for all, and we can only keep interpreting its obscure message. One has only to look at the syllabus of every fascist movement to find the major traditionalist thinkers.
>
> – Umberto Eco, "Ur-Fascism" (1995)

The ultimate propaganda goal of any nationalistic apparatus is to fuse the perception of "self" with that of "nation" into a cohesive identity loyal to the ruling class. Critique of the state then becomes an existential threat which elicits defensive responses aimed at ensuring the survival of both personal and collective constructs.

Settler colonial regimes have routinely invented and imposed named identities to naturalize domination and bind settlers to the violence of conquest. Long before 1948, Zionists embraced the colonial doctrine of "Might makes right," or as a popular Israeli saying goes, "What doesn't work with force, works with greater force." The tensions between the Haganah and Irgun demonstrate this dynamic (**Part II**).

In the United States, the "frontiersman" or "pioneer" emerged as a heroic symbol of white expansion, masking Indigenous genocide as national destiny. In South Africa, the Dutch-descended "Afrikaner" was reimagined as a divinely chosen people, their identity forged through conquest and institutionalized in apartheid. French Algeria produced the "pied-noir," literally "black foot," a settler identity that claimed nativity to the land while asserting supremacy over Algerians. In Latin America, the "criollo" (colonial-born Spaniard) positioned itself above Indigenous and African peoples, justifying continued dominance after independence. These names were not mere labels; they were ideological propaganda tools designed to sanctify and perpetuate land theft, erase Indigenous inhabitants, and align settlers with colonial power.

Like other settler colonial movements, Zionism offered a romanticized vision of heroism and violence through the invention of a new identity: the "New Jew," "New Hebrew," or "Sabra," a locally born, militarized settler loyal to a fledgling ruling class intent on building a new hierarchical, subservient society. Quite ironically yet consistent with the white supremacist nature of Zionism, the "new Jew," as depicted in staged photographs, poetry, fiction, drawings, and pamphlets, embodied a distinctly Aryan ideal. This romantic nationalist figure was cast as a white male European, with his whiteness starkly highlighted against the "black" backdrop of the local "savages."

Amid widespread marginalization and land restrictions in Europe, Zionism appealed to some Jews by promising safety, social cohesion, and empowerment through land and resource acquisition. Backed by a powerful propaganda apparatus, it offered those alienated by antisemitism a sense of belonging, privileged status, and modern national pride.

Rather than confronting the systems which oppressed them, many European Jews believed Zionism offered an alternative path to emancipation, one embedded with the contradiction of "If you can't beat them, join them." Akin to Stockholm syndrome patients, who develop positive feelings, loyalty, or empathy toward their captors or abusers as a survival mechanism, Jewish Zionists embraced the very colonial, antisemitic mindset that conducted their oppression, seeing themselves as a group of colonists with their own version of manifest destiny. Further, it reflects a broader dynamic within capitalism, in which those who rise into the bourgeoisie come to identify with the ruling class rather than the working class, often reproducing the same structures of domination and becoming agents of oppression themselves.

The phenomenon of post-traumatic domination illustrates how historically oppressed groups, shaped by collective trauma, may reproduce systems of power and control as a means of reclaiming agency and security. The dynamic of glucocorticoid reduction, i.e., negative reinforcement (**Figure III.5**), through aggression toward subordinates as a mechanism common in hierarchy formation may underlie the tendency to identify with and serve ruling-class goals.

As mentioned, Frantz Fanon highlights this dynamic in *The Wretched of the Earth*, noting how the colonized often internalize and enact violence to resist subjugation, sometimes replicating oppressive, albeit rewarding structures. Edward Said observes a similar pattern in *The Question of Palestine*, describing how victims can become perpetrators by adopting colonial modes of domination. Psychologist Judith Herman's work on trauma further explains how unresolved trauma can drive groups toward aggression and control as a coping mechanism. Together, these perspectives illuminate how trauma can transform into a force that fuels domination rather than liberation.

Zionism, particularly in its early European formulation, can also be understood through a related concept, Homi Bhabha's theory of colonial mimicry, a process by which the colonized adopt the language, structures, and ideologies of the colonizer in order to gain legitimacy. As Bhabha writes, mimicry is "the desire for a reformed, recognizable Other, as a subject of a difference that is almost the same, but not quite." (p. 122).

Zionists sought to recast the historically persecuted Jewish identity in the image of the Western nation-state, aspiring to be modern, militarized, and civilizationally "Western," in effect, to become "almost the same" as the European colonial powers that had long marginalized Jews.

In the words of Max Nordau at the Zionist conference in 1919: "We shall have to be the guards of the Suez Canal. We shall have to be the sentinels of your way to India via the Near East."

The desire to escape historical vulnerability was transmuted into a project of domination, where power was claimed not in spite of colonialism but through perfecting its logic. In this sense, Zionism emerges as colonialism's most loyal example; a syncretic, aggressive political construct and identity forged through disavowal of the past and a dangerous fidelity to the structures of empire.

b. Berdichevsky, Ruppin, and eugenics

This manufactured colonial identity was constructed by several early Zionist thinkers. One of the earliest ones was Micha Berdichevsky (1865–1921), a Jewish writer, philosopher, and critic of traditional Judaism who became significant for his advocacy of a radical cultural and moral transformation of the Jewish people to align with nationalist and settler colonial ideals.

Berdichevsky, a Nietzschean thinker who admired strength, will, and myth, saw Jewish exile as a source of weakness and glorified war and death over survival and pious submission to divine will. Berdichevsky argues that "national morality" is grounded in the "harsh morality" of conquest, expansion of borders, the destruction of the weak, and settlement in their place," not in traditional ethics (Ba-derekh, Volume 2, 1922, p. 77).

Adopting racist and white supremacist stereotypes promoted by antisemites, he sought to legitimize them by depicting exile as the root of Jewish weakness through selective readings of Jewish texts. His theories signaled a broader departure from the image of Jews as a people guided by moral values, a congregation of the righteous. Instead, Zionists were encouraged to embrace the very traits antisemites had imputed to them, using Jewish scripture, the Talmud, and rabbinical literature to justify this shift. Their goal was to craft a new image of Jews as a white, European people, possessing the same virtues and flaws as other nations, no longer set apart by any special sanctity.

Berdichevsky was also likely the first Jewish writer to recast the grim Masada myth, in which Jewish rebels committed mass suicide in 73 CE to avoid Roman capture, as a heroic narrative of martyrdom and resistance, reshaping it to align with Zionist ideals of militant nationalism. This ideological shift reflected a shared premise between antisemites and Zionists: that Jewish people constituted a biological race in an unfortunate, unnatural, and pathetic condition, destined to be segregated and confined within a racialized, apartheid utopia.

These characterizations follow the overall concepts of "race," as constructed by pseudo-scientists who sought to justify slavery, colonialism, and white supremacy through supposedly "scientific" means in Europe and the settler colony of the United States in the eighteenth and nineteenth centuries. These thinkers, many of whom were physicians, anthropologists, or naturalists, used flawed methodologies, biased observations, and fabricated data to assert that humanity could be divided into distinct biological categories, or "races," each with inherent traits and abilities.

As one of the ultimate manifestations of the dangers of manufactured racialized thinking, Nazi ideology in twentieth-century Germany embraced and radicalized these racial theories to justify their ideology of white Aryan supremacy. Drawing on American Jim Crow eugenics, racial hierarchy, and biological determinism, they defined Jewish identity as a racial, not religious, threat that "infected" society, displacing, projecting, and distracting from actual white supremacist genocidal colonialism. Influenced by figures like Madison Grant and US sterilization laws, Nazi policies framed genocide as a form of racial hygiene. These distorted "scientific" ideas became central to laws like the Nuremberg Laws and ultimately the Holocaust, turning racial theory into state policy and mass murder.

Zionism drew from the same pseudoscientific milieu, once again revealing the troubling convergence of Zionist ideology and antisemitism.

Arthur Ruppin (1876–1943), another prominent ideologue and architect of early Zionism, was profoundly shaped by Darwinism, eugenics, and racial theories. Ruppin had completed a doctoral thesis on eugenics in Germany and later turned to physical anthropology, conducting racialized studies that involved measuring the skulls and noses of Jews from various backgrounds, as well as collecting and comparing their fingerprints. He subscribed to the belief Jews were a distinct white race, descended from Indo-Europeans, not from Semites.

Often recognized as "the father of Jewish settlement in Palestine" or "the sociologist of the Zionist movement," Ruppin played a pivotal role in the movement's development. Ruppin, described by labor movement leader Berl Katzenelson as the chief "colonizer" of the emerging Zionist community (Katzenelson 1968, 30), played a central role in nearly every major national initiative in Palestine between 1908 and 1942, whether economic, legal, diplomatic, or educational.

From the outset, he was deeply involved in shaping and directing these efforts, driven by a clear vision: to construct a modern Hebrew social order/hierarchy as the foundation for a model Zionist state. After moving to Palestine in 1908, Ruppin maintained close ties with German racial theorists, including Hans Günther (1891–1968), a prominent proponent of Nazi racial ideology, whom he visited shortly after Hitler came to power. By that time, Ruppin had already been appointed professor of sociology at the Hebrew University in Jerusalem.

His role combined scientific racism, social engineering, and colonial planning in service of constructing a new "Jewish" national identity rooted in white supremacy, land, and labor. Ruppin envisioned a radical transformation of Jewish identity, one that would break from the diasporic, religious past and emerge as a modern, national, and biologically regenerated collective.

> Jewry only has a justification for its existence if it can exist as a nation and has in itself the power to acquire the basis for the survival of a nation—a territory. Otherwise, it deserves to die out. Zionism or assimilation—tertium non datum [a third is not given].
> ~ Ruppin; Arthur Ruppin, *Die Juden der Gegenwart* (Berlin: Jüdischer Verlag, 1904).

Similar to Berdichevsky, Ruppin believed centuries of exile had led to physical and moral decay among Jews, a decline that could only be reversed through a Zionist project grounded in biological and racial "revitalization." Influenced by contemporary eugenic thought, he promoted the selection of the "fit" and the elimination of what he considered degenerative traits, seeking to cultivate a healthy, vigorous national body. Ruppin's key racial-scientific work, *Die Juden der Gegenwart* (1904/1911) and later writings, applied US/ European concepts of racial hierarchy to Jewish communities. He classified Jews into "Alpine," "Mediterranean" and "Near-Eastern" types and emphasized the necessity of preserving racial "purity" among settlers in Palestine.

Ruppin envisioned this regeneration unfolding in Palestine where agricultural labor would transcend mere economic activity, becoming a biological and spiritual catalyst for national rebirth. He imagined the Jewish farmer as a new kind of Jew: attached to the land, physically robust, and supposedly racially closer to the ancient Hebrews. The soil of Palestine would act as a purifying force, transforming the so-called decadent, physically inferior, over-intellectualized diasporic Jew into a productive, grounded national subject.

Central to this vision was a decisive break from what Ruppin regarded as the degraded elements of diaspora Judaism. He dismissed Orthodox religiosity, secular urban intellectualism, and particularly the traditions of Sephardic and Oriental Jews, whom he viewed through a white supremacist, racialized lens as inferior.

> It is perhaps owing to this severe process of selection that the Ashkenazim are to-day superior in activity, intelligence and scientific capacity to the Sephardim and Arabian Jews, in spite of their common ancestry.
> ~ Ruppin; *Die Juden der Gegenwart* (Berlin: Jüdischer Verlag, 1904)

Zionism, in his framework, offered both a practical refuge and a means of redefining what it meant to be a Jew. Through racial rejuvenation, agricultural rootedness, and national unity, Jews would cease to be a problem in Europe and instead become a sovereign people on their own land, akin to other revered settler societies. In this way, Ruppin's vision fused biology, white supremacist/antisemitic ideology, and colonization into a project of identity-making, one that sought to leave behind the diasporic past and invent a new Jew for the Zionist future.

In *The Invention of the Jewish People*, Shlomo Sand challenges Ruppin and the dominant Zionist narrative that Jews constitute a unified, biologically continuous nation descending from ancient Israel. He contends this notion is a modern nationalist construct, not a historical reality, shaped in the nineteenth and twentieth centuries to legitimize Zionist claims to Palestine. Sand argues that Jewish identity was historically religious rather than ethnic or racial, and the idea of a single Jewish people tied by blood, land, and language mirrors European nationalist models. He disputes the myth of exile and return, proposing instead that Judaism spread through conversion across regions like North Africa and Eastern Europe. By exposing the political motives behind the invention of Jewish nationhood, Sand reframes Jewish identity as a fluid, historically contingent phenomenon and critically undermines the foundational myths of Zionism.

c. Religion and propaganda

Led by Christian and Jewish proponents, nineteenth-century Zionists faced a formidable challenge. They sought to misrepresent a colonial endeavor involving seizure of land and resources, segregation, dehumanization, and genocide of an Indigenous populace in order to entice a globally dispersed Jewish population adhering to a pacifist belief in "divine justice." Additionally, they needed to present a plan which appealed to colonial powers (Ottoman and British) and appeared morally acceptable to millions in the Western world and beyond.

To accomplish this, the early leaders crafted a persuasive, syncretic narrative which deliberately distorted history in favor of effective propaganda.

As mentioned in **Part II 6a**, colonial propaganda, and the Zionist version is no exception, promotes the interests of the ruling class through at least five recurring mechanisms: dehumanization, through religion, racism, economic rationalization (the claim that Indigenous peoples were not making productive use of the land), civilizational and developmental reasoning (the claim that Indigenous peoples were at a lower stage of human development and required European tutelage), or the portrayal of native resistance as savage aggression, which lowers the threshold for violence; threat inversion, which recasts the dispossessed as aggressors; divine mandate, which removes moral agency; historical erasure, which denies the out-group's existence and culture; and fear conditioning, which activates defensive neural circuitry, making violence seem necessary.

Their first move, aided by Christian Zionists and other antisemitic groups, was to convince Jewish people that integration into European nations was a doomed prospect.

The phrase "A land without a people for a people without a land" is often attributed to Israel Zangwill, who popularized it in Zionist speeches around 1901–1902. However, the earliest known use of this exact formulation appears in the writings of Reverend Alexander Keith, a Scottish minister and Christian Restorationist, in 1843.

> Therefore, are they wanderers throughout the world, who have nowhere found a place on which the sole of their foot could rest—a people without a country; even as their own land, as subsequently to be shown, is in a great measure a country without a people.
> ~ Keith, *The Land of Israel According to the Covenant with Abraham, with Isaac, and with Jacob.* Edinburgh: (William Whyte and Co., 1843)

Accompanying this narrative was a familiar colonial settler sleight of hand: "discovering" an "empty land," ("in a great measure," in Keith's words) aside from a few so-called "uncivilized, savage nomads/marauders/barbarians," and settling it with rifles in one hand and scripture in the other. Indeed, Zionist leaders knew very well that Palestine was not empty and were fully aware of the consequences of trying to take it over.

Zionists weaponized Jewish religious texts to justify the unjustifiable, sacralize the indefensible, and advance an antisemitic illusion promoting avarice and theft. Clothed as Jewish manifest destiny, this deception was rooted in Christian restorationist fantasies and modern European colonial white supremacy and directly contradicts the explicit Jewish prohibition against resettlement in *Eretz Yisrael* prior to the arrival of the true Messiah. Exploiting historical trauma, Zionist leaders stoked Jewish insecurities through fearmongering, while offering promises of social cohesion and material incentives as both a panacea and a lure for prospective settlers.

This fabricated narrative perpetuates a long-standing imperialist tradition, intrinsic to Spanish, Portuguese, British, French, Dutch, Afrikaner, Belgian, and North American Puritan colonization, where religion is deployed as a justification for conquest, ethnic cleansing, genocide, and enslavement.

In *The Bible and Colonialism: A Moral Critique*, Michael Prior argues that biblical conquest narratives, especially those in Deuteronomy and Joshua, have been systematically used to justify settler colonial projects beyond Zionism. He highlights the Spanish conquest of the Americas, in which scripture framed Indigenous resistance as sinful and legitimized mass violence; the Afrikaner colonization of South Africa, where settlers saw themselves as a chosen people claiming a Promised Land; and British imperialism in Africa and the Pacific, in which biblical language was used to sanctify land theft and racial hierarchies. In each case, Prior contends the Bible was hijacked for political purposes and contains inherently violent themes which have enabled dispossession and genocide under the guise of divine will.

Notably, the alignment of Zionism with European imperialism and white supremacy has been explicitly identified by global leaders and revolutionary thinkers, including Kwame Ture, Angela Davis, Edward Said, leaders of the Black Panther Party, James Baldwin, Refaat Alareer, Kwame Nkrumah, Ghassan Kanafani, Malcolm X, and others.

Many of Zionism's most fervent proponents, including Israel's founding figures, were secular, white European, mostly Russian Jews, who regarded traditional Judaism as outdated, weak, pathetic, and culpable for European antisemitism. They claimed Zionism marked a return to a purer, prouder, pre-exilic Judaism, one fused with the so-called homeland. In this reimagining, Judaism ceases to be a religion and becomes an exclusivist, white supremacist, eliminationist settler ideology, defined by territorial ambition and sanctioned by the logic of European colonialism.

Early Zionists syncretized many aspects of European fascism, white supremacy, colonialism, and messianic evangelism, with its long and sordid history of working with antisemites, imperialists, and fascists, in order to promote capitalist and expansionist agendas. In fact, Zionists and other antisemites have worked toward the mutual interest of global apartheid by concentrating Jews in Israel: the former to create an exclusivist colony on stolen land while combating the "demographic threat" posed by Indigenous Palestinians and the latter as a means of scapegoating and expelling an unwanted population.

Historically, Zionists have contributed to, at times actively fomenting, antisemitism and consequent fear among Jewish populations. For example, Avi Shlaim presents evidence on how Zionist agents bombed synagogues in Baghdad between 1951 and 1952 to accelerate Jewish emigration to Israel. This is one of many instances, including examples in recent years, where Jewish communities were targeted by agents of "the Jewish state" under the guise of "antisemitic hate."

d. Conflation of Zionism and Judaism

The colonial tactic of conflating theft with religion, in the Zionist case, Zionism with Judaism, does more than provide justification for land theft; it arms propagandists with a powerful weapon: fear.

By falsely claiming to represent Judaism and Jewish people, co-opting Jewish trauma and the ever-present fear of antisemitism, whether real or manufactured, they legitimize access to the rhetoric and tools of "self-defense," including preemptive lethal violence, framed as a desperate fight for survival "by any means necessary." Thus, the role of religion when coopted by a settler regime is to raise the bar of 'permissible' violence as a tool of dispossession.

The conflation of Zionism and Judaism is sustained through ideological manipulation that relies on strategic deployment of fear; fear of antisemitism, fear of annihilation, and fear of the dehumanized Palestinian/Arab/Indigenous/Muslim "other," which Zionist narratives exploit, similar to narratives of other colonial projects, to silence dissent, justify domination, and fuel the addiction to aggression (see **Figure III.7**).

Promoting fear and with self-defense as its raison d'être, this conflation endangers Jews worldwide while shielding colonial violence behind the veneer of religious identity. In doing so, Zionist propagandists have hijacked Judaism to advance an antisemitic fantasy: a global apartheid order with Israel at its core.

Through the conflation of Zionism with Judaism, the Zionist project employs a two-pronged propaganda strategy, targeting both external and domestic audiences. This serves to achieve two main objectives: cultivating support and neutralizing opposition.

To cultivate internal cohesion, subservience, and support, Zionism developed a comprehensive system of indoctrination and fearmongering embedded in nearly every aspect of Israeli life, from the education system to mandatory conscription into the IDF, which functions as the sacred central pillar of national identity in Israeli society. Ritual ideological conditioning continues well beyond military service, shaping both civic life and cultural narratives.

It is worth revisiting the true meaning of "defense" within the "Israel Defense Forces." As with its precursor, the Haganah and HaShomer, the term does not signify universal protection of Jewish people aimed at ensuring survival; rather, its goal has been to defend Zionist interests, privileges, and segregated colonial enclaves. In practice, "defense," as detailed in **Part II** of this volume, serves as a propagandistic veil for a military whose core function has always been fortressing, occupation, and offensive aggression/expansion.

The conflation of Zionism and Judaism also serves Western imperial forces as a convenient distraction from their exploitation and racism. To secure external support, Zionist leaders have consistently appealed to the hegemons and ruling classes of the Global North, from the Ottomans and British to the European bloc and the Americans, by framing a Zionist entity in Palestine, now Israel, as a defender and promoter of their strategic interests, while safeguarding the so-called rights of Jewish people.

Positioned as a loyal client or vassal state, Israel has served as a vanguard for Western militarism in the Middle East. War and destabilization in the region fuel a lucrative market for weapons and surveillance technologies often marketed as "defensive," while also ensuring the subservience of corrupt Arab regimes to imperial control over trade routes and natural resources, especially oil.

Western imperialists encouraged Zionist crimes against Palestinians, delivering impunity to Israel while displacing any accountability from past, present, or future racist abuses of Jews in the US and Europe. Serving this agenda, Israeli propaganda presents the Nazi Holocaust as an unparalleled genocide, granting Jews special victim status. This narrative justifies privileges, discounts, and allowances for Israel as the "Jewish state" constructed to ensure the safety of Jews, at the expense of Indigenous Palestinians.

Notably, Zionist revisionism often neglects and downplays white colonial genocides and other crimes against humanity globally and Nazi crimes against non-Jewish oppressed groups, including communists, socialists, Roma, disabled individuals, LGBTQI+, and African Germans, assisting white Western narratives which dissociate Nazism from its anti-communist, reactionary, and capitalistic core. Israel then provides moral cover and pretense for ongoing Western colonial atrocities globally as the "most moral army in the world."

Far before 1948 and followed since by Israeli governments, this trope has been employed by Zionists as a talking point in order to sabotage and scapegoat critique of their criminal policies. Cynical manipulation of the legitimate guilt and shame over the history of anti-Jewish persecution has not only shielded their colonial agenda but also fueled global antisemitism, ultimately reinforcing the same reactionary, Western, and white supremacist forces with which they align. For this purpose, Israel consistently strengthens its supposed association to Judaism (by promulgating legislation such as the Nation State Law) in order to promote this fallacious antisemitic apartheid framework.

Western support also facilitates migration of Jewish people, Aliyah, from the West to fortress the Israeli vassal state, their so-called homeland. This policy both drains other nations of their Jewish populations, encouraged by the Zionist narrative that casts them as having "dual loyalty," and ensures a steady flow of settlers (preferably white) to counter the so-called Palestinian demographic threat by colonizing newly seized land.

Beyond securing support for violent land theft both domestically and in Western capitals, conflating Zionism with Judaism serves to delegitimize Palestinian resistance and dissociate it from its global anticolonial allies (see earlier re Nazification of Palestinians). Zionists undermine opposition by equating anti-Zionism, an anti-racist, universalist, anti-colonial tradition with Jewish roots dating back to the nineteenth century, with antisemitism, a much older, reactionary form of racism historically used by ruling elites, including Western white supremacists, to deflect criticism and scapegoat and disenfranchise Jewish people.

By equating criticism of Zionism or Israel's treatment of Palestinians with antisemitism, legitimate political dissent is reframed cynically and erroneously as racism. This tactic sows division, weaponizes identity politics as opposed to a class-based analysis, and obstructs the formation of broad, intersectional, anti-racist coalitions, fracturing natural alliances among those resisting capitalist, white supremacist, patriarchal systems, and ultimately serving Zionist and Western imperialist interests.

Finally, the conflation obstructs anticolonial struggle by reframing a political struggle to steal land and resources by imperialist-backed settlers from an occupied Indigenous people as an ancient religious "conflict" between equals at best, or, at worst, as a battle between a Jewish David and an Arab Goliath, the "people of Israel" versus the "Amalekites," the "civilized" versus the "barbarians/terrorists." This decontextualized framing reverses the true balance of power and entrenches Palestinian victimization by portraying the conflict as intractable, resolvable only through violence, mirroring the worldview of "deep rooters" who claim warfare is intrinsic to human nature (see **Part I**), rather than the approach of "shallow rooters," which views war as a cultural construct.

e. The Identity-based model of belief

It is unsurprising that many Jews in the nineteenth century facing horrific abuse, trauma, and disenfranchisement found Zionist propaganda enticing, particularly concerning promises of safety and inclusion in a social hierarchy.

Consistent with and complementary to the mechanisms of identity production detailed in W2S, the Identity-Based Model of Belief details how social identity, especially partisan identity, is maintained, dominating individual beliefs and behavior. Individuals often conform their perspectives to those of their group, valuing group identity over factual accuracy. Further, they frequently spread negative misinformation about those outside their group, often deriving pleasure from their misfortunes (*schadenfreude*).

This model underscores the tension between identity and truth in how misinformation spreads. Research shows that perceiving others as part of one's group activates the brain's reward system, reinforcing loyalty and preference. Partisan identity, like all identities, includes cognitive elements (self-perception, shared norms and beliefs) and motivational drivers (belonging, distinctiveness, status). When identity goals outweigh accuracy goals, individuals adopt group views over facts and in-group norms often determine what kinds of misinformation are acceptable to share.

These dynamics foster cohesion yet make partisans more likely to believe and spread false claims. When enough people do so, it undermines a shared reality, making it harder for society to reach consensus on basic facts.

The Identity-Based Model of Belief can help decipher how for more than eight decades, Zionists have consistently prioritized false partisan beliefs to defend their shared, manufactured identity. This has been used as a tool to instill fear in the colonized Indigenous population, justify genocidal policies, and provide a legal cover for criminal actions, all while rejecting any form of accountability grounded in facts or working-class solidarity with Palestinians.

Further, apartheid and periodic wars of aggression have served to entrench misinformation and violence in subsequent generations; like the US, the Israeli state deliberately conditions each generation through violence in order to maintain complicity reinforced by negative and positive reinforcement.

Importantly, class oppression is far more significant than identity-based divisions, which are often used to distract from ruling-class exploitation. In Western or Western-adjacent societies such as Zionist Israel, whiteness is used to placate the working class with the illusion of superiority. This false sense of privilege tricks workers into acting against their own interests, believing they benefit from rewards reserved for the ruling class, while weakening solidarity with a multiracial workers' movement that embraces all marginalized groups.

This dynamic is why Zionist institutions like the Histadrut went as far as excluding Palestinians, reinforcing segregation rather than fostering true class unity.

f. Zionism as racism

The roots of Zionist segregationist/exclusivist policies, as well as its propaganda, particularly the conflation of Zionism and Judaism, can be traced back to its foundations.

Early Zionism comprised several distinct ideological branches. Secular Political Zionism, led by figures like Theodor Herzl (1860–1904) and Leon Pinsker (1821–1891), focused on establishing a Jewish state primarily as a political solution to antisemitism, often with pragmatic views on the homeland's location and limited reliance on biblical claims. Cultural Zionism, championed by Ahad Ha'am (1856–1927) and Moses Hess (1812–1875), emphasized the revival of Jewish cultural and spiritual identity, viewing Palestine as a vital cultural center rather than merely a political entity. Labor/Socialist Zionism, associated with David Ben-Gurion (1886–1973) and Berl Katznelson (1887–1944), combined Zionism with socialist ideals, prioritizing Jewish labor and collective community-building, often promoting coexistence while largely overlooking Palestinian nationalism. Religious or Messianic Zionism, represented by Rabbi Abraham Isaac Kook (1865–1935) and others, interpreted Zionism as a divine process of redemption rooted in biblical promises, asserting a sacred claim to the land. Finally, Secular Revisionist Zionism, led by Vladimir Ze'ev Jabotinsky (1880–1940), stressed Jewish self-defense, European-style offensive settler colonialism, and sovereignty with a nationalist agenda, generally downplaying religious justification. These diverse streams shaped the complex ideological foundation of the Zionist movement.

Although distinct, all branches of Zionism shared a common thread: a lack of genuine integration efforts with the Indigenous Palestinian people and employing, from early on, the discourse of transfer (see Nur Masalha's book *Expulsion of the Palestinians: The Concept of "Transfer" in Zionist Political Thought* and **Part II** of this volume).

Each pursued a racist, exclusivist agenda, aiming to establish a segregated Zionist colony for Jewish people in Palestine. Further, Zionists of all sorts believed in a process of "voluntary transfer" of native Palestinians, away from Palestine and to neighboring Arab countries. Notably, the "voluntary" aspect pertained to the willingness of Arab nations to accept them, rather than their own wish to depart.

This reveals Zionism's core paradox (see **Table 1** below): how can an eliminatory colonial project be presented as consistent with Enlightenment ideals and gain acceptance, both domestically and internationally, as morally and ethically sound?

The roots of this paradox can be traced back to early thinkers such as Theodor Herzl. Herzl was a secular, bourgeois liberal, a nationalist and a colonialist, who believed in the separation of church/synagogue and state and distrusted leftists and revolutionaries. Herzl valued Enlightenment ideas like reason, individual rights, and civil equality. Disillusioned with efforts to integrate into European society, he rejected liberal universalism and instead advocated for Jewish statehood, viewing assimilation as a futile and misguided pursuit. Similar to antisemites at the time, Herzl subscribed to the racist, antisemitic notion of global apartheid, in which Black people should live in black countries, white people in white countries, and Jewish people in a Jewish state, yet he was initially not wedded to Palestine (though it was his preference) as the solution and considered other target places, including Argentina, Australia, and Uganda.

In spite of his veneer of Enlightened ideals, Herzl was no different with respect to his colonialist approach to the Indigenous Palestinian people:

> We must expropriate gently the private property on the estates assigned to us. We shall try to spirit the penniless population across the border by procuring employment for it in the transit countries, while denying it employment in our own country. The property owners will come over to our side.
> ~ Theodor Herzl's personal diary, dated June 12, 1895

Herzl directly approached Cecil Rhodes (1853–1902) in 1902 to solicit support for the Zionist project of establishing a Jewish homeland in Palestine. Rhodes was a British imperialist, businessman, and politician who played a central role in expanding British rule in southern Africa. Herzl wrote to Rhodes as if the Zionist project were part of the British colonial mission, stating:

> You are being invited to help make history. It doesn't involve Africa, but a piece of Asia Minor; not Englishmen but Jews ...

> How, then, do I happen to turn to you? Because it is something colonial.
> ~ Herzl, Letter from Herzl to Rhodes, 1902

Rhodes did not directly participate in Zionism, yet his racist, imperialist ideology and colonial strategies significantly influenced Zionist thought and practice, especially settler colonial Zionism in Palestine. He believed in the racial and cultural supremacy of the Anglo-Saxon world and was an explicit white supremacist who saw British imperial expansion as a moral mission. He believed that Anglo-Saxons were destined to rule the world and that non-European peoples were inferior and should be subjugated for their own "benefit."

> The native is to be treated as a child and denied the franchise. We must adopt a system of despotism in our relations with the barbarians of South Africa.
> ~ Cecil Rhodes, Speech to the Cape Colony's House of Assembly in Cape Town (June 1887)

Even Berl Katznelson (1887–1944), a founding ideologue of Labor Zionism and close ally of David Ben-Gurion, also known as "the moral conscience of the movement," unequivocally supported transfer of the Indigenous Palestinian population outside of the future "Jewish state." At the twentieth Zionist conference in August 1937, during debates surrounding the Peel Commission's partition plan, which included a proposal for the transfer of Palestinians from the area designated for a Jewish state, he said:

> The matter of population transfer has provoked a debate among us: Is it permitted or forbidden? My conscience is absolutely clear in this respect. A remote neighbour is better than a close enemy. They will not lose from being transferred and we most certainly will not lose from it.

Unsurprisingly, the most honest settler colonial strand of Zionism at the time, Revisionist Zionism, led by Jabotinsky, openly embraced the fascist-inflected ideology of blood and soil, discarding any pretense of adherence to

Enlightenment ideals such as universal rights, equality, or rational progress and revealing Zionism's true reactionary core.

> Zionist colonization must either stop, or else proceed regardless of the will of the native population … This colonization … can proceed and develop only under the protection of a power independent of the native population—behind an iron wall …"
> - Vladimir Zeev Jabotinsky, *The Iron Wall* (1923)

Table III.1. Zionist branches and their narratives

ZIONIST BRANCH	CORE PARADOX	STRATEGY FOR RESOLUTION	RESULTING NARRATIVE
Secular Political Zionism	Justifying settlement in an inhabited land as a liberal/ nationalist project	Claimed Palestine was "empty" or underdeveloped. Framed Jews as a stateless nation. Used civilizing mission rhetoric.	Zionism = national liberation, not colonialism. Justice for Jews.
Cultural Zionism	Reconciling Jewish cultural revival with Enlightenment ethics and native presence	Emphasized moral/spiritual renewal, not conquest. Downplayed or ignored Arab nationalism. Claimed Jewish culture would uplift the region	Zionism = moral and humanistic project. Palestinians rendered culturally invisible.
Labor/ Socialist Zionism	How to reconcile socialist universalism with ethnonational exclusivity	Advocated "Hebrew labor" as redemptive. Framed exclusion as practical necessity. Viewed Arabs as outside the working-class ideal	Zionism = egalitarian utopia for Jews. Colonial aspects rationalized as temporary or necessary.
Religious/ Messianic Zionism	Biblical entitlement vs. Enlightenment secular ethics	Claimed divine right trumps human law. Framed settlement as part of messianic redemption. Viewed Palestinians as spiritually irrelevant	Zionism = sacred destiny. Universal ethics subordinate to biblical covenant.
Secular Revisionist Zionism	Justifying militarism and territorial expansion under liberal moral claims	Asserted moral right through historical trauma. Promoted "Iron Wall" doctrine (strength first, peace later). Recast nationalism as justice.	Zionism = defensive and offensive nationalism. Power and sovereignty are moral imperatives for survival.

The central paradox of Zionism remains unresolved and has only deepened since the establishment of the State of Israel, which for the past seventy-eight years has been marked by persistent addiction to belligerence, apartheid, dispossession, and genocidal violence in service of theft. The ever-increasing challenge of reconciling a genocidal project with so-called Western human rights has led to the development of a strategic, government-backed system, funded by billions of dollars, euros, and shekels, which operates with increasing sophistication and reach.

The term *hasbara* ("advocacy" in Hebrew) refers to the state's coordinated propaganda and public diplomacy efforts aimed at shaping international opinion in favor of Israel. Rooted in a strategy of narrative control, *hasbara* operates through a network of governmental bodies, most notably the Ministry of Foreign Affairs, the Ministry of Diaspora Affairs, and the Prime Minister's Office, as well as military intelligence units like Unit 8200. These are supported by non-governmental organizations and well-funded advocacy groups such as AIPAC, StandWithUs, and the Jewish Agency.

Hasbara campaigns span traditional media, social platforms, campus outreach, and coordinated online trolling or bot networks, often under the guise of combating antisemitism or promoting "truth" about Israel. Heavily funded by both state resources and private donations, especially from wealthy diaspora supporters, *hasbara* works to suppress criticism of Israeli policy, normalize occupation, and deflect accusations of apartheid, genocide, war crimes, and crimes against humanity.

g. Liberal Zionism: a façade for occupation and genocide

> Zionism is the most just and moral national liberation movement in the 20th century.
>
> – Amos Oz (*Haaretz* interview, 2006)

> Even if he is in no way guilty as an individual … he shares a collective responsibility by the fact of membership in a national oppressor group.
>
> – Albert Memmi, *The Colonizer and the Colonized* (1957)

Liberal Zionism, emerging in the mid-twentieth century and gaining prominence after Israel's 1967 occupation, is an ideological current that attempts to resolve the central paradox of Zionism by framing itself as a moral and democratic alternative to more overtly nationalist or religious forms of Zionism. It insists Israel can remain both Jewish and democratic by preserving a Jewish majority while granting civil rights to minorities and supports a two-state solution, the ultimate segregation, as an ethical resolution to the "Israeli Palestinian conflict."

Exemplified by the Israeli "peace camp," liberal Zionists have long championed a so-called peace process centered on a two-state solution which partitions historic Palestine along the 1967 borders. Framed as a path to resolution, this process has served as a political smokescreen, endlessly drawn out while enabling Israel to continue its apartheid, slow-rolling genocide, and ethnic cleansing with impunity. As bulldozers raze Palestinian homes and settlements expand, the root problem, Zionist colonial theft, is obscured. This framework ignores the core realities of military occupation, systemic inequality, and white supremacist domination, reducing a settler-colonial project to a misguided dispute between two equal sides.

Liberal Zionists and their political parties champion civil liberties for the privileged yet refuse to confront the white supremacist core of Zionism, a project they uphold and whose adherents, themselves included, have terrorized Indigenous Palestinians for more than a century. Liberal Zionist media, NGOs, and academic institutions often portray the explicitly violent manifestations of Zionism as expressions of an "extreme" form of Zionism, scapegoating figures like Prime Minister Netanyahu or Israel's Minister of National Security, Itamar Ben-Gvir, as anomalies, rather than acknowledging them as natural products of a colonial eliminationist project. According to them, removing Netanyahu, or any explicit ultra-fascist Zionist politician, would allow Zionism to revert to an acceptable trajectory in line with democracy and human rights.

A key aspect of the liberal Zionist narrative is the presentation of Israeli and Palestinian narratives as "parallel truths," portraying both peoples as victims with legitimate claims requiring lengthy negotiations and concessions. This revisionist narrative duplicitously equates Israeli settler colonial aggressors, who are backed by the global US hegemon and its allies, with their

Indigenous Palestinian targets. This false equivalency underpins the embrace of the "two-state solution," which would formalize existing Palestinian bantustans under the guise of guarding Israeli "security" interests.

Liberal Zionism portrays the occupation, settlement expansion, and systemic inequalities as aberrations from genuine Zionist principles rather than inherent characteristics. Simultaneously, it disregards and sanitizes the Zionist movement's clear settler colonial past, despite explicit declarations from many of its key figures. This approach allows liberal Zionism to present itself as self-critical and geared towards reform. It embraces language of peace, coexistence, and human rights, often invoking the legacy of Jewish suffering, to justify Jewish sovereignty while denying full recognition of Palestinian national rights.

To reconcile Zionism with liberal norms and in line with Zionism's secular roots, liberal Zionists reject the settler colonial framing of Israel, instead presenting it as a national liberation movement for a historically persecuted people. They appeal to Enlightenment ideals by casting Jewish self-determination as parallel to other anti-colonial struggles, while marginalizing the foundational dispossession of Palestinians as a tragic necessity or historical accident while villainizing and decontextualizing their resistance as "terrorism."

In doing so, liberal Zionism offers a duplicitous narrative that postures as having moral clarity without fundamentally challenging the ethnonational structure of the Israeli state. This strategy has proved effective in maintaining international legitimacy, especially in Western liberal circles and appeasing a thriving secular bourgeoisie in Israel, yet it increasingly faces criticism for masking structural injustices under the guise of reform.

As Albert Memmi states, some colonized people are relatively more privileged than others, but the colonizer knows "that the most favored colonized will never be anything but colonized people" and "certain rights will forever be refused them." Liberal Zionists are what he called "the leftist colonizer." These are settlers who remain within the ideological framework of colonialism (or in this case, of settler colonialism) and, in his words, either willingly or reluctantly are still "part of the oppressing group and will be forced to share its destiny."

Liberal Zionists present Zionism as a full-spectrum political project to propagate the illusion of a humane, democratic society grounded in Western capitalist individualism, in which equal opportunity allegedly exists for all under the "start-up nation" brand. They further co-opt elements of Judaism and liberalism, repurposing them into weaponized, identity-based appeals and propaganda tools, such as pinkwashing and greenwashing, to mask and legitimize ongoing colonial expansion.

Liberal Zionism plays a critical role in propagandizing for the Zionist project by masking colonial violence in the language of democracy, moderation, and civil rights. Institutions like *Haaretz*, Israel's longest-running newspaper and a self-described bastion of liberal Zionism, exemplify this dynamic. While presenting itself as a voice of the Israeli left, though subject to censorship by the Israeli military, *Haaretz* frequently acts as a stenographer for political and military agendas while mainly confining its civil liberties advocacy to the privileged Zionist class. Anti-Zionist voices are systematically excluded, and the paper maintains alignment with state policy by reinforcing the notion that Israel must remain a cognitively dissonant "Jewish and democratic state," echoing government narratives that attempt to reframe genocide as justifiable security.

In academia, Israeli universities and legal scholars serve the Zionist agenda by collaborating with the military, legitimizing collective punishment, and exporting weaponry and counterinsurgency tactics developed through the occupation. Prominent liberal Zionist figures, from politicians like Isaac Herzog and Yair Golan to a range of intellectuals regularly featured on the editorial pages of *Haaretz*, reinforce these narratives by invoking false equivalence, speaking of "guilt on both sides," and obscuring the asymmetry of power and violence inherent to Zionist colonialism. In doing so, liberal Zionism functions not as a check on Israeli state violence but as its most palatable and persuasive global advocate.

Liberal Zionists frequently weaponize concepts like empathy and dialogue to promote an imperialist agenda, sugar-coating settler colonial domination in the language of reconciliation and mutual understanding. Under the guise of peacebuilding, they advance an "empathetic" framework that centers "practicality" and deems demands for historical truth and accountability as unnecessary, futile or even divisive. This depoliticized and decontextualized empathy, applied equally to Palestinian victims and their Zionist oppressors, reinforces the existing power imbalance by erasing the structural asymmetry of occupation. Rather than challenging injustice, it functions as a moral anesthetic, discouraging resistance while preserving white supremacy and Western imperial interests.

Such narratives flourished during the Oslo years, when initiatives for "coexistence" encouraged Palestinians and Israelis to sit in dialogue without ever addressing the root causes of violence: land theft, ethnic cleansing, and apartheid. These efforts amounted to little more than public relations exercises. Participants would return to their segregated realities: Israelis to lives of privilege and security, Palestinians to military checkpoints, demolitions, and disenfranchisement. Far from promoting justice, liberal Zionist "empathy" obscures war crimes by framing them as defensive necessities against so-called irrational or antisemitic Palestinian "terrorist" aggression. In doing so, it legitimizes a system of ethnic domination while silencing Palestinian demands for liberation.

To break this cycle, alternative frameworks like the Boycott, Divestment, and Sanctions (BDS) movement offer a radically different vision rooted in accountability, historical truth, and equal rights. Called for by Palestinian civil society in 2005, BDS explicitly rejects hollow dialogue and normalization of oppression through coexistence schemes that ignore the core injustices of Zionism. Instead, it advocates dismantling of apartheid structures and the recognition of Palestinian rights in full, including the right of return of all Palestinian refugees and their descendants. This moral and strategic clarity contrasts sharply with liberal Zionism's deliberate ambiguity.

h. Cognitive dissonance and normalization of atrocity in Israeli society

The result of the continuous, relentless Zionist propaganda campaign is a distorted worldview that clashes with lived reality, one that normalizes inequality, entrenches systems of oppression, and recasts privilege as victimhood. This dissonance between propaganda and reality creates a stress-invoking psychological fracture, demanding constant mental acrobatics and relief (**Table III.2**). To maintain belief in Zionism's moral legitimacy while witnessing its violent realities, supporters often experience a deep cognitive dissonance that ultimately fuels defensive aggression (**Figure III.7**). Understanding how it functions is key to unpacking the ideological hold of Zionist narratives fueling theft.

First introduced by Leon Festinger in his seminal 1957 book, *A Theory of Cognitive Dissonance*, cognitive dissonance refers to the psychological discomfort people experience when their beliefs or identity conflict with reality. Rather than resolve the contradiction by changing their worldview, individuals often rationalize injustice to preserve a sense of moral coherence. In ideological constructs like Zionism, this dissonance allows supporters to justify violence as defense, apartheid as democracy and, colonial domination as coexistence. Rather than stemming from ignorance, it is a coping mechanism for maintaining belief in the face of moral and logical contradiction.

Table III.2. Israeli propaganda and associated cognitive dissonance

#	PROPAGANDA CLAIM	CONTRADICTION	RESULTING COGNITIVE DISSONANCE
1	*"Israel is both Jewish and democratic."*	White supremacy which co-opts religion to structure a privileged hierarchy and exclude out-groups, predominantly Palestinians.	Forces belief in liberal democracy while defending apartheid structures.
2	*"The IDF is the most moral army in the world."*	Documented war crimes, crimes against humanity, genocide, and ethnic cleansing contradict this.	Requires admiration for restraint amid evidence of brutality.
3	*"We made the desert bloom."*	Erases past and existing Palestinian agriculture and land use.	Frames colonization as environmental heroism.
4	*"Both sides are to blame."*	Ignores colonial asymmetry and military occupation.	Promotes false equivalence between oppressor and oppressed.
5	*"The peace process proves our good faith."*	Settlement expansion continues during peace talks.	Frames Israel as seeking peace while it entrenches occupation.
6	*"We're defending ourselves."*	A powerful state targets a stateless, besieged population.	Inverts roles, casts the occupier as the victim.
7	*"Aliyah is a return to our ancestral homeland."*	European Jews are welcomed; Palestinians are barred from return.	Justifies exclusion under the guise of spiritual belonging.
8	*"We had no choice but to remove them."*	Ethnic cleansing and forced displacement are deliberate.	Portrays mass violence as defensive, reluctant necessity.
9	*"Arab citizens have full rights in Israel."*	Discriminatory laws and second-class status persist.	Masks legal inequality with token representation.
10	*"Criticism of Israel is antisemitic."*	Political critique is distinct from bigotry.	Silences dissent by weaponizing historical trauma.

Notably, capitalism in general is based on cognitive dissonance: it sanctions violence and worker exploitation in the name of "productivity" while presenting itself as a "democratic," merit-based system, even as it entrenches inequality, expansionism, patriarchy, and racism. Vladimir Lenin's statement "Imperialism is the highest stage of capitalism," is relevant here.

At its core, cognitive dissonance arises from an inherent human drive for consistency. People strive for coherence in their thoughts and actions, and when this coherence is disrupted, a state of psychological stress emerges. This tension is not merely a logical contradiction; it is an aversive feeling that individuals are motivated to alleviate. The intensity of cognitive dissonance depends on how important the conflicting beliefs are and how wide the gap between them. For example, someone who deeply cares about animal rights yet regularly eats meat will likely experience stronger dissonance than a person who supports animal welfare yet occasionally wears leather. The greater the conflict between values and actions, the more emotional discomfort arises, prompting efforts to reduce that tension through justification or behavioral change.

Individuals primarily cope with cognitive dissonance through three strategies: (i) changing one of the conflicting cognitions: directly altering the behavior or belief to align with the conflicting belief, attitude, or fact (e.g., a smoker quitting or convincing themselves smoking is not too harmful). However, changing established behaviors or deeply held beliefs can be difficult. (ii) adding new cognitions (rationalization/justification) to outweigh the old ones: introducing new thoughts that justify the inconsistency, thereby reducing the discomfort, e.g., a smoker focusing on other healthy habits to balance out the smoking. The smoker, unable or unwilling to quit, might focus on arguments that minimize the dangers of smoking ("My grandfather smoked his whole life and lived to be 101") or emphasize the benefits ("Smoking calms me down after a long day"), and; (iii) rationalizing or justifying the contradiction by decreasing the importance of the dissonant cognitions. The smoker might decide health is not as important as immediate pleasure, or the risks of smoking are exaggerated. By downplaying the significance of the conflicting elements, the individual can reduce the perceived tension.

Normalization of criminality and violence is such a tool for reducing cognitive dissonance, thereby making atrocity more common and acceptable by reducing resistance to it (more in **Part IV**). As illustrated in the Wired to Steal model (**Figure III.1**), normalization functions as a central mechanism which sustains and reinforces the oppressive dynamic.

The implications of cognitive dissonance are far-reaching. Understanding this psychological mechanism can help explain seemingly irrational behaviors and provide insights into how attitudes are formed and changed. In *Behave*, Robert Sapolsky explores how human beings first act in contradiction to their stated beliefs, and only afterward rationalize those actions to maintain a coherent self-image. Sapolsky explains our decisions, especially moral ones, are often made emotionally and subconsciously, with reason arriving only afterward to justify them.

At the neural level, Sapolsky highlights the interplay between the amygdala and PFC, both central to fear processing as discussed earlier, as well as the insula, a key region that generates visceral emotional experiences like guilt, disgust, and empathy, all of which are essential for moral judgment and social behavior. The insula likely contributes to the emotional discomfort people experience when their beliefs and actions clash. This discomfort motivates the psychological processes, such as rationalization or belief adjustment, which aim to reduce dissonance.

Moral or emotionally charged decisions typically activate the amygdala first, triggering visceral, intuitive reactions. Only afterward does the PFC engage, constructing rational narratives to explain or justify those emotionally driven responses. The rewards of aggression described earlier may further reinforce the entrenchment of dissonant dynamics. This sequence helps explain why people can hold on to contradictory beliefs or excuse harmful behavior while still perceiving themselves as ethical. This point is directly addressed by Umberto Eco in his essay "Ur-Fascism":

> The enemy is both too strong and too weak. Fascist governments are condemned to lose wars because they are constitutionally incapable of objectively evaluating the force of the enemy. The enemy is portrayed as at the same time too strong and too weak. By a continuous shifting of rhetorical focus, the enemies are at the same time subhuman and superhuman.
> ~ Umberto Eco, "Ur-Fascism" (Point 10; 1995).

The involvement of the amygdala highlights the inherently threatening nature of cognitive dissonance, helping to explain why it often triggers defensive responses such as avoidance, flight, and/ or defensive aggression. When individuals are confronted with contradictions in their deeply held beliefs, such as the moral inconsistencies within Zionism, the dissonance can feel like a psychological threat. As a result, they may respond defensively, often escalating from avoidance and flight to denial or deflection to outright hostility. In some cases, this escalates into full-scale defensive aggression that, whether expressed through verbal attacks or physical violence, often takes the form of fighting dirty, abandoning principle, or its semblance in favor of humiliation, punishment, or domination, all serving the interests of the dominant, more powerful colonizers.

Escalation, externalization, and projection are useful as they convert the doubt, fear, and disgust inherent to cognitive dissonance into urgency and aggression, portraying reflection and ethical nuance as unnecessary and weak. Fear speeds decision-making, allowing those perceived as strongmen to assume authority and suspend morality, claiming that "survival" dictates every choice until the dust settles. This is precisely how the moral boundaries of a society widen to include and normalize atrocity.

Sapolsky illustrates how people compartmentalize these contradictions through cultural narratives, identity-driven frameworks, and selective moral focus. In politically or morally polarized contexts, individuals rely on these psychological and neurological processes to maintain group loyalty and personal integrity, even when their actions conflict with professed values. In this way, belief-behavior conflict is managed by reinterpretation; enabled by the brain's natural tendency to seek internal consistency, generating justifications that protect one's identity/self-image and moral certainty.

To understand how these dynamics interact with violent settler-colonialist reality of dispossession to shape life in Israel/Palestine, we must now turn to the structure and manifestation of modern occupation, how it transitions from slow-rolling to expedited genocide and land theft, how it is justified, and how it is resisted.

i. Occupation 101: the status quo of settler expansionism

The ultimate result of Zionist propaganda and settler violence is occupation and bouts of land theft following either accelerated (the Nakba, the genocide post October 7th, 2023) or incremental forms of genocide and land theft, i.e., a status quo of occupation.

Yet, once the underlying dynamics detailed in the W2S model (**Figure III.1**) are understood, the process reveals itself as alarmingly simple, repetitive, and predictable. Moreover, each wave of genocidal violence accelerates the normalization of atrocity, setting dangerous precedents that embolden the Zionist movement while profoundly and negatively affecting other criminal regimes, particularly though not exclusively in the West.

Israeli standard operating procedures can be reduced to a concerted effort at seizing territory, murdering and expelling Palestinian people, and consolidating apartheid, while attempting to refrain from evoking outrage perceived as harmful to its interests, i.e., refraining from activating cognitive dissonance above a certain unacceptable threshold, in line with the socially acceptable boundaries of society (more in **Part IV**). The norms and taboos governing this fragile balance are dictated by Israeli public opinion and the "international community."

The so-called status quo of occupation in Palestine, particularly since the 2006 election of Hamas and their 2007 takeover of the Gaza Strip, which is marked by daily violence, surveillance, and dispossession, is periodically disrupted by Israeli provocations or escalations. These include Ariel Sharon's incendiary visit to the Al-Aqsa Mosque compound in 2000, the ongoing construction of the separation wall, the relocation of the US embassy to Jerusalem in 2018, and repeated raids on Al-Aqsa during Ramadan, particularly in 2021, 2022, and 2023. They also include home demolitions in East Jerusalem neighborhoods like Sheikh Jarrah and Silwan, targeted assassinations, and large-scale bombings in Gaza, as seen in 2008–09, 2014, 2021, and 2023–present.

In response, Palestinians protest, both within the Occupied Palestinian Territories and inside the 1948 borders. These protests, whether peaceful or involving resistance, are met with overwhelming Israeli force. The military response includes the targeting of protestors, political leaders, and both violent and nonviolent activists, often through mass arrests without trial, torture by the Shin Bet, and lethal crackdowns. As Palestinian resistance escalates, the Israeli right demands retribution, fueling further militarization. This culminates in full-scale operations, commonly referred to as "mowing the lawn," which begin with aerial assaults and sometimes expand to ground invasions. These operations result in mass Palestinian casualties and displacement, with Israeli casualties typically far fewer in comparison. Mounting international pressure eventually forces Israel to halt its assault, yet the violence concludes only with a return to a new "status quo," marked by more arrests, expulsions, land grabs, and a further entrenchment of apartheid (**Figure III.8**). Importantly, the escalation from incremental genocide ("status quo") to its escalated version can be instigated by either an Israeli provocation or an act of Palestinian resistance, and its limitations are determined by the extremity of the Israeli government and the impunity it's given by its imperial sponsors.

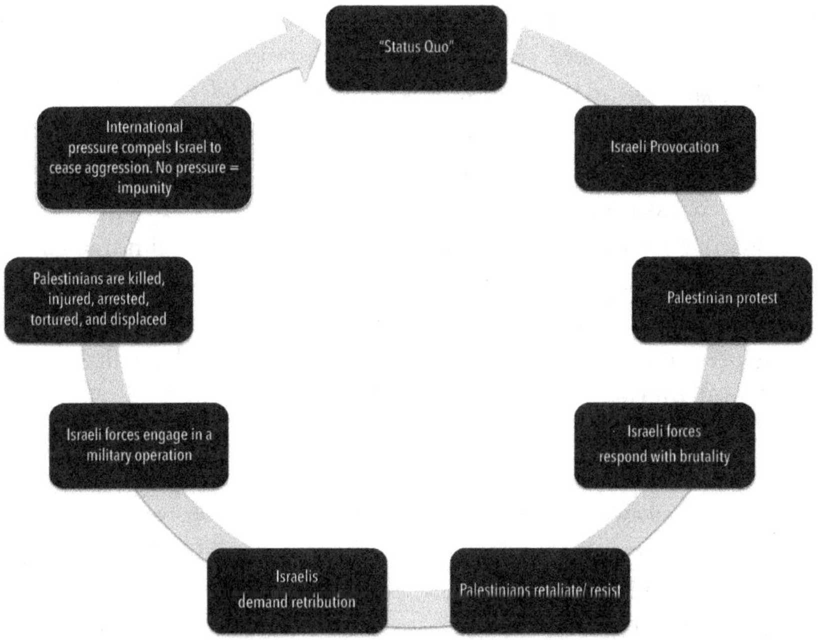

Figure III.8. Israeli Occupation 101.
A deadly cycle of incremental dispossession and genocide.

The consistent expansion of the boundaries of violence and dispossession depend on a host of factors and shift with political expediency, serving the interests of those in power who systematically work to normalize Zionist criminality within Israeli society and external to it. Further, the tolerance to and withdrawal from aggression increases Zionist brutality and fuels increasing levels of Palestinian resistance (e.g., the Second Intifada) in response.

The Palestinian resistance on October 7, 2023, marked a pivotal moment, an opening exploited by Zionist strategists to push the boundaries of what the international community had long treated as untouchable. In its aftermath, Israel entrenched its "self-defense" narrative amid what numerous governments, human rights organizations, and even the International Court of Justice have identified as acts of genocide, war crimes, and crimes against humanity.

Is there a limit to such an expansion of boundaries? Both Ilan Pappé in his book *Israel on the Brink* and Lorenzzo Veracini in a recent article "Genocide in Gaza and the End of Settler Colonialism," each in a different way, surmise this stage is not only unprecedently destructive towards the Palestinians but is also self-destructive to the Zionist project itself.

It would be interesting to follow in the future Veracini's conclusion about the application of the settler colonial paradigm to Israel/Palestine. Veracini asks us to consider whether the kind of genocide we witnessed since October 2023 fits the genocidal features of setter colonialism. For him, the current genocide constitutes "a fateful shift" from the established Israel settler colonial policies. In his mind, this genocide was "a catastrophic departure" from the past that constitutes a "point of no return", a catastrophe that will befall not only the Palestinians but also the settler colonial project itself.

Further Reading

1. Litvin Y, Arakawa H, Blanchard DC , Blanchard RJ. Aversive Conditioning. In: M. D. Binder, N. Hirokawa and U. Windhorst editors. Encyclopedia of Neuroscience Springer; 2009. p. 456-60.
2. LeDoux JE , Pine DS. Using Neuroscience to Help Understand Fear and Anxiety: A Two-System Framework. Am J Psychiatry 2016;173:1083-93.
3. Schiller D, Kanen JW, LeDoux JE, Monfils MH , Phelps EA. Extinction during reconsolidation of threat memory diminishes prefrontal cortex involvement. Proc Natl Acad Sci U S A 2013;110:20040-5.
4. Sapolsky RM. *Why Zebras Don't Get Ulcers: The Acclaimed Guide to Stress, Stress-Related Diseases, and Coping.* New York, NY: Henry Holt and Company; 2004.

5. Panksepp J. *Affective Neuroscience: The Foundations of Human and Animal Emotions.* New York: Oxford University Press; 1998.
6. Miczek KA, de Almeida RM, Kravitz EA, Rissman EF, de Boer SF, Raine A. Neurobiology of escalated aggression and violence. J Neurosci 2007;27:11803-6.
7. Blanchard DC, Litvin Y, Pentkowski NS, Blanchard RJ. Defense and aggression. In: G. G. Berntson and J. T. Cacioppo editors. *Handbook of Neuroscience for the Behavioral Sciences.* John Wiley and Sons, Inc.; 2009. p. 958-74.
8. Blanchard RJ, McKittrick CR, Blanchard DC. Animal models of social stress: effects on behavior and brain neurochemical systems. Physiol Behav 2001;73:261-71.
9. Golden SA, Jin M, Shaham Y. Animal Models of (or for) Aggression Reward, Addiction, and Relapse: Behavior and Circuits. J Neurosci. May 22 2019;39(21):3996-4008. doi:10.1523/jneurosci.0151-19.2019
10. van der Kolk B. *The Body Keeps the Score: Brain, Mind, and Body in the Healing of Trauma.* New York: Viking; 2015.
11. Shapira A. *Land and Power: The Zionist Resort to Force 1881-1948.* Stanford University Press; 1999.
12. Fanon F. *The Wretched of the Earth* (C. Farrington, Trans.). New York: Grove Press; 1963.
13. Said EW. *The Question of Palestine.* Times Books; 1979.
14. Herman J. *Trauma and Recovery.* Basic Books; 1992.
15. Bloom E. Arthur Ruppin and the Production of the Modern Hebrew Culture. The Lester & Sally Entin Faculty of Humanities The Shirley & Leslie Porter School of Cultural Studies Tel Aviv: Tel Aviv University; 2008.
16. Sand S. *The Invention of the Jewish People.* Verso; 2009.
17. Pappé I. *Ten Myths about Israel.* London: Verso Books; 2017.
18. Prior M. *The Bible and Colonialism: A Moral Critique.* Sheffield: Sheffield Academic Press; 1997.
19. Rabkin YM. *What Is Modern Israel.* London: Pluto Press; 2016.
20. Shlaim A. *Three Worlds: Memoirs of an Arab Jew.* One World Publications; 2023.
21. Masalha N. *Expulsion of the Palestinians: the Concept of "Transfer" in Zionist Political Thought, 1882-1948.* Washington, D.C.: Institute for Palestine Studies; 1992.

22. Lloyd D. Settler Colonialism and the State of Exception: The Example of Palestine/Israel. Settler Colonial Studies 2012;2:59-80.
23. Cavanagh E. A global phenomenon: special issue of settler colonial studies. Settler Colonial Studies 2011;1:1-13.
24. Memmi A. *The Colonizer and the Colonized*; 1957.
25. Honig-Parnass T. *Liberal Zionism and the Struggle for Palestine.* Haymarket Books; 2011.
26. Festinger L. *A Theory of Cognitive Dissonance.* Stanford, CA: Stanford University Press; 1957.
27. Sapolsky RM. *Behave: The Biology of Humans at Our Best and Worst.* New York: Penguin Press; 2017.
28. Eco U. Ur-Fascism. *The New York Review of Books* 1995.
29. Pappé I. *Israel on the Brink: And the Eight Revolutions That Could Lead to Decolonization and Coexistence.* Beacon Press; 2025.
30. Veracini L. Genocide in Gaza and the End of Settler Colonialism. *The Journal of Imperial and Commonwealth History*. 2025;53(4):953-68.

Part IV - October 7th and the Normalization of Genocide

> We shall live at last as free men on our own soil, and in our own sovereign State. In that State, we shall have the right to impose our law and our civilization upon the country, to spread our spirit and influence throughout the world.
>
> ~ Theodor Herzl, *The Jewish State* (1896)

As detailed in **Parts I–III** of this book, settler colonial theft and genocide operates through a cycle of interconnected tactics, summarized in the Wired to Steal (W2S) model. Driven by greed of a ruling class, fear is weaponized into segregation and defensive violence, framed as protection or survival and used to kill, destroy, steal, and deflect accountability. Fear becomes a gateway to, and a node of, an addictive cycle driven by defensive and offensive aggression, a response both stress-relieving (negative reinforcement) and externally rewarded (positive reinforcement), which the ruling class actively fosters to tighten control, expand territory, and entrench its dominance.

Periodic waves of fear and stress sustain segregation and dehumanization, impeding the natural erosion of such patterns and blocking the empathy and reconciliation that integration fosters. Resultant theft of land and resources is applauded and cloaked by claims of "divine right," legitimizing and normalizing escalating ongoing violence and brutality.

These elements work together to expand societal norms and taboos in ways that dehumanize "the other" and justify their elimination to enable their dispossession. Akin to an ever-escalating addiction cycle, settler colonists require increasing doses of aggression to address tolerance and alleviate withdrawal symptoms associated with fear, stress, cognitive dissonance, impulsivity, and reward-system dysregulation. The escalation of this cycle leads to full-scale genocide with humiliation (*schadenfreude*) serving as an immediate reward, in addition to that of theft of resources.

To elucidate these dynamics and demonstrate that the events beginning on October 7, 2023, represent an extension of colonial dynamics rather than a departure from them, this analysis reviews the pivotal events, behaviors, and propaganda leading up to that date.

1. Trial balloons as antecedents for genocide

Society is a collective of people bound by shared rules and held together by taboos at its extremes. Societal boundaries reflect the ruling mindset, shaped by the interests of the ruling class and accepted by the majority of the population. These boundaries are typically codified by laws and the practices of enforcement. For example, the United States Constitution defines the rights and restrictions, and it is the evolving interpretation and enforcement of these by which people are either included or excluded from the American collective.

Within societies there are constant tugs of war between forces that reside on its extremes. The fundamental goal of these forces is to stretch or shrink the acceptable boundaries of the society in directions that serve particular agendas: ideological, economical, or otherwise.

Taboos incorporated in a society become deeply embedded within the human psyche. Thus, the process of undermining them with the purpose of reshaping a society is gradual and includes resistance on the one hand and persistence on the other.

The process of breaking taboos and redefining societal boundaries begins with political experimentation: trial balloons. When such an experiment is successful, it becomes a precedent that serves to shatter a taboo. Furthermore, if experiments and the resulting precedents they set are not met with sufficient resistance, the extreme boundaries of the ethical fabric stretch, shifting the society as a whole in a particular direction that can be either regressive or progressive.

Rosa Parks is known as an icon of the civil rights movement. In an act of civil disobedience, on December 1st, 1955, Parks refused to relinquish her bus seat to a white passenger. Her courageous experiment served to galvanize many in the struggle against racial segregation. Parks's case became a precedent, which created a new, progressive ethic in American society. Yet Parks was not the first to protest segregation on buses, so what made her act successful?

An experiment can set a precedent only within a broader context of a society that is primed for that particular change. In addition, an experiment must withstand a variety of challenges to its integrity. In the Parks case, American society was ready for desegregation. Also, she was viewed by the National Association for the Advancement of Colored People (NAACP) as a good candidate to see through the court proceedings in Montgomery, Alabama. Collectively, her experiment set a precedent, which significantly helped serve to shatter a taboo.

On Saturday, October 7, 2023, a shift occurred in the Israeli-Palestinian narrative. What was a normalized, often gradual incremental genocide, peppered by savage episodes of "mowing the lawn" (see **Figure III.8**), concealed by liberal Zionist propaganda and conditionally backed by a benefactor in Washington, transformed into an overt, unapologetic mass murder of Palestinians with total imperial impunity, captured vividly on video for the world to witness.

Though the genocide of Palestinian people has persisted since well before 1948, this latest phase of explicit brutality can be traced to several pivotal trial balloons in which Israel's genocidal policies were enacted, broadcast for all to see.

a. Abdel Fattah al-Sharif

> The colonized is elevated above his jungle status in proportion to his adoption of the mother country's cultural standards. He becomes whiter as he renounces his blackness, his jungle.
>
> ~ Frantz Fanon, *Black Skin, White Masks* (p. 9)

On Thursday, March 24, 2016, an Israeli soldier, Elor Azaria, was filmed executing Abdel Fattah al-Sharif, a wounded twenty-one-year-old Palestinian man alleged to have carried out a stabbing attack against Israeli soldiers in the

Tel Rumeida neighborhood of Hebron. The videographer responsible for the filming was Imad Abu Shamsiya, a Palestinian shoemaker, who later received death threats and intimidation from Zionist settlers.

Though the incident was part of a wave of extrajudicial killings of Palestinians carried out by Israeli soldiers, this particular case was different. Here, the film unambiguously showed the wounded Palestinian man did not present a danger to his surroundings. Quite shockingly, not only did the film implicate the executioner; it also showed his military comrades, including medical personnel, as completely unfazed by the incident. Further, the soldier received a wave of Israeli public support that Israeli politicians seized on as an opportunity to further erode Israeli society in a bid to serve their political and ideological interests.

Under international law, summary executions, killings carried out without a fair trial, are strictly prohibited under all circumstances. This prohibition is enshrined in international human rights law and international humanitarian law (IHL). The International Covenant on Civil and Political Rights (ICCPR), in Article 6(1), guarantees the right to life and states that "no one shall be arbitrarily deprived of his life." Article 14 of the ICCPR further guarantees the right to a fair and public hearing by a competent, independent, and impartial tribunal. These protections are "non-derogable," meaning they remain in force even during public emergencies or armed conflict. Under IHL, Common Article 3 of the Geneva Conventions (1949), which applies in both international and non-international armed conflicts, explicitly prohibits "the passing of sentences and the carrying out of executions without previous judgment pronounced by a regularly constituted court, affording all the judicial guarantees which are recognized as indispensable by civilized peoples." This is reiterated in Article 75 of Additional Protocol I (1977) and Article 6 of Additional Protocol II (1977), both of which reaffirm the necessity of judicial guarantees before any execution can take place. Furthermore, summary or arbitrary executions may constitute war crimes or crimes against humanity under the Rome Statute of the International Criminal Court, particularly Articles 7 and 8.

In Israel, Azaria's filmed execution served as a trial balloon, testing how the Israeli mainstream would react to an uncensored video depicting the cold-blooded murder of a Palestinian. The disastrous precedent set was by no means the beginning of an open season on Palestinians. That had been ongoing since at least the First Intifada. What changed was the shift from de facto to de jure. Before Azaria's case, extrajudicial killings were not broadcasted so openly, testing a transition from a "don't ask, don't tell" policy to shameless endorsement of and even pride in murder of Palestinian people.

Cold-blooded executions of Palestinians became openly sanctioned by the Israeli mainstream and political class, further eroding the already fragile rule of law. Israeli politicians declared Palestinians fair game, with broad public support. It marked a watershed moment for Israeli society: the incident ended without a serious conviction for the soldier (who received a mere slap on the wrist), no accountability for his commanders, and no independent investigation into the lax rules of engagement. As such, a dangerous, notorious, and graphic precedent was set, raising the bar of "permissible" violence that could be inflicted on Palestinian people. The precedent solidified the complete dehumanization of Palestinians and paved the way for enhanced ethnic cleansing and genocide en route toward the messianic fantasy of Greater Israel.

Months later, in January 2017, Elor Azaria was convicted of manslaughter, yet he became a modern Israeli hero, hailed by many as "the child of all of us." His conviction was the exception rather than the rule, as the army routinely shields soldiers from accountability for killing or injuring Palestinians. Reflecting this impunity, a poll conducted soon after the verdict found that an overwhelming 70 percent of Israelis supported pardoning Azaria. Significantly, key figures of the Israeli government unified in their call for pardoning Azaria, using it to galvanize political power and support. The judges involved in the case were threatened on social media to the point where they were assigned a security detail by the military.

The Azaria case was also a milestone because it further exposed the widespread and mainstream appeal of genocidal violence in Israeli society, not only among the original European Zionist elites from ethnically cleansed, exclusively Jewish communities but also within Arab Jewish (Mizrahi) communities. Azaria, born to a low-income Mizrahi family in Ramle, a working-class city in central Israel that was not fully ethnically cleansed and still houses both Jewish Zionists and Palestinians, embodied the deep entrenchment of white supremacist Zionism within socioeconomically marginalized communities.

Zionism showed little interest in Arab Jews before the Holocaust. They were brought into Palestine through a campaign of manipulation and deceit, aided by more extreme strains of Arab nationalism that emerged in response to the Zionist project. Upon arrival, they were pushed to the geographical and social margins of society. Their "absorption" was framed through modernization theories, guided by S.N. Eisenstadt, the leading modernization theorist of the time and the chief government advisor who preached "de-Arabization," essentially how to erase their Arab identity and make them into Europeans. The easiest way to gain acceptance from Ashkenazi Jews was to display clear anti-Arab sentiment: first toward oneself (losing the accent, Hebraicizing one's name, changing the food one ate, etc.), and then by aligning with right-wing parties.

The next generations, educated and socialized through welfare and schooling systems dominated by orthodox Mizrahi rabbis and leaders, inherited a mix of racism and theocratic visions of statehood. The present generation of Arab Jews has largely allied itself with settlers in the West Bank, fueling the "State of Judea," which is swallowing the State of Israel.

Frantz Fanon's concept of the "epidermalization of inferiority" in *Black Skin, White Masks* illuminates how marginalized Mizrahi communities internalize and reproduce the white supremacist Zionist ideology imposed upon them. Colonized subjects come to see themselves through the colonizer's dehumanizing lens, adopting their values and norms in a process of psychological alienation and mimicry. This internalized colonialism helps explain the deep entrenchment of oppressive Zionist structures even (and especially) within those communities that suffer from socioeconomic marginalization and exclusion.

Consistent with Fanon, and the role of negative reinforcement emphasized in W2S, this case starkly reveals how displacement of aggression fuels hierarchical systems like white supremacist Zionism, with marginalized Mizrahi communities channeling their frustrations into violence against Palestinians, the quintessential "other" whose brutalization both defines and unites the Zionist settler collective.

b. Shireen Abu Akleh

On May 11, 2022, Shireen Abu Akleh, a prominent Palestinian-American journalist for *Al Jazeera*, was shot and killed by Israeli forces while covering an Israeli military raid in Jenin, in the occupied West Bank. Abu Akleh was wearing a clearly marked "PRESS" vest and helmet at the time she was shot. Multiple eyewitnesses, journalists, and independent investigations concluded that the lethal shot came from an Israeli soldier, and that there were no active crossfires with Palestinian militants in the immediate vicinity. Israel initially claimed Abu Akleh was killed in crossfire yet later conceded there was a "high probability" she was shot by an Israeli soldier, while refusing to hold anyone criminally accountable. Her killing sparked international outrage and widespread demands for an independent investigation. Further inflaming global condemnation, Israeli police violently attacked mourners and pallbearers at her funeral in East Jerusalem, an assault captured on video and broadly denounced.

Although the case drew some international attention, it failed to provoke significant pushback either within Israeli Zionist society or from the outside, despite clear international laws guaranteeing the safety of journalists.

Article 79 of Additional Protocol I (1977) to the Geneva Conventions explicitly states that "journalists engaged in dangerous professional missions in areas of armed conflict shall be considered as civilians" and must be protected as such, "provided they take no action adversely affecting their status as civilians." This protection is grounded in the broader civilian protections found in Article 51 of Additional Protocol I and Article 3 common to the four Geneva Conventions (1949). These legal safeguards are part of customary international humanitarian law, applicable to both international and non-international armed conflicts. Further, under the Rome Statute of the International Criminal Court (1998), deliberately targeting civilians, including journalists, constitutes a war crime under Article 8(2)(b)(i) and Article 8(2)(e)(i), and can amount to crimes against humanity under Article 7 when part of a widespread or systematic attack. The UN Security Council, in Resolution 2222 (2015), reaffirmed these protections, condemning violence against journalists and calling on member states to end impunity for such attacks.

Palestinian journalists had been shot before; as Rebecca L. Stein notes in *Screen Shots*, nine were killed between 2000 and 2005. Had Shireen not been an American citizen and a beloved fixture in Palestinian households, her killing, alas, might not have marked such a watershed moment. As such, this case tested international response to whether the rights of Palestinian journalists, even popular ones with American citizenship, could be targeted.

Abu Akleh's targeted assassination was not only an attack on a Palestinian journalist. It was also an assault on an alternative truth to Zionist propaganda that forces Zionists into cognitive dissonance and compels a painful reckoning for all who support the colonial project. As such, the event revealed not only the Israeli regime's willingness to kill the truth but also its imperial benefactor's willingness to bury it.

These two events, the summary execution of Abdel Fattah al-Sharif and the murder of Shireen Abu Akleh, perhaps more than any other in recent times, marked critical turning points, eroded any remaining constraints on the use of force (i.e., its normalization), and paved the way for the wholesale disregard of humanitarian law, culminating in the expanded genocide, ethnic cleansing, war crimes, and crimes against humanity committed against the Palestinian people beginning October 7th. The events that unfolded from that date onward form the focus of the next segment in which we apply the W2S frameworks explored so far to unpack the mechanisms, psychological, ideological, and strategic, that have shaped this ongoing catastrophe. The ensuing violence erupted within an Israeli Zionist society ideologically primed, socially conditioned, and politically willing.

2. October 7th and Hannibal

On October 7, 2023, Hamas fighters breached the Gaza prison fence, launching a coordinated attack on at least seven Israeli military installations located within (or surrounded by) twenty residential communities. A total of 1,139 people were killed, including 695 Israeli civilians, 71 foreign nationals, and 373 members of the security forces. Approximately 3,400 others were injured and around 251 people, including civilians, soldiers, children, the elderly, and foreign nationals, were abducted by Hamas and other militants from southern Israel.

The Israeli military responded to the attack in a frenzy, firing indiscriminately on breached localities, slaying Israeli civilians alongside Hamas fighters in a tactic dubbed "the Hannibal Directive" (also known as the Hannibal Protocol), a highly controversial IDF military policy. It took the Israeli forces nearly a day to recapture all lost territory and secure the Gaza perimeter.

The Hannibal Directive's declared aim is to prevent Israeli soldiers from being captured by militants and subsequently used as pawns for prisoner swaps, even if it necessitates lethal force that could endanger hostages, including civilians. After initially denying the use of the Hannibal Directive on October 7th, Israeli officials, including Defense Minister Yoav Gallant, have admitted to its employment. On October 7th, this directive epitomized defensive aggression/attack: lethal, indiscriminate, and borne out of panic of a Zionist ruling class prioritizing its own survival over the lives of those it purports to protect. Sources estimate that between fourteen and nearly 100 Israelis may have been killed by Israeli forces under the Hannibal Directive on October 7, 2023, with the UN Commission of Inquiry confirming at least fourteen likely cases and investigative reporting by *Haaretz* and independent analyses suggesting the number could be significantly higher.

Since, Israel's assault on Gaza has created a devastating humanitarian catastrophe. According to the Gaza Ministry of Health, as of writing this book in June 2026, the officially confirmed death toll is over 73,000 Palestinians, including at least 21,000 children; a conservative estimate due to severe restrictions imposed by Israel, which limit independent verification and prevent journalists and humanitarian workers from accessing the territory (OCHA 2024; UNRWA 2024).

The true death toll may be much higher: an analysis published in *The Lancet* estimates that when indirect deaths from hunger, disease, and lack of medical care are included, fatalities may exceed 186,000. The wide discrepancy reflects initial chaotic reporting, unverified cases, unrecovered bodies buried under rubble, and Israel's ongoing blockade, which has hindered transparent documentation and forensic investigation. Over 173,000 Palestinians have been reported injured, many suffering severe, life-altering injuries including burns, spinal damage, and amputations. The World Health Organization (WHO) reports that at least 6,000 amputees require long-term rehabilitation, with children comprising a significant portion. Around 90–95 percent of Gaza's population has been displaced, many of them multiple times, compounding the scale of this humanitarian disaster and overwhelming the collapsed health care infrastructure.

Massive destruction of homes, schools, universities, hospitals, and infrastructure has left the territory in ruins, with widespread hunger, disease, and acute malnutrition compounding the crisis. Gaza's health, water, and sanitation systems have collapsed under relentless bombardment and siege, while repeated attacks on aid convoys and civilians have deepened the suffering. The devastation marks one of the most severe humanitarian disasters of the modern era.

3. The context of Gaza's blockade and Israel's imperial impunity

To properly contextualize the October 7th attacks, it is essential to trace back to (at the bare minimum) 2006, when Hamas won the legislative elections (called for by the George W. Bush administration) and consequently Gaza was sealed off from the world under a blockade imposed by Israel and Egypt, an extreme act of segregation. The siege followed Hamas's takeover from the Palestinian Authority (PA) after a failed US/Israeli-backed coup and intense internal fighting. Framed as a measure to isolate Hamas, the blockade restricted movement by land, air, and sea, severely limiting the flow of people, goods, and essential supplies.

Under international law, a blockade is considered a method of warfare and, when targeting civilians, may constitute an act of war. This is explicitly stated in the San Remo Manual on International Law Applicable to Armed Conflicts at Sea (1994), which defines a blockade as a method of warfare and a hostile act. Similarly, the Hague Convention XIII (1907) treats blockades as wartime measures. When imposed on an occupied population, as in Gaza, a blockade falls under the scope of Geneva Convention IV, which prohibits collective punishment and starvation of civilians, both common consequences of prolonged blockades. If a blockade targets civilians or deprives them of essentials, it likely violates international humanitarian law.

The purpose of a siege during warfare is to cut off an enemy stronghold from essential supplies and reinforcements, aiming to weaken and force its surrender without direct assault. While justified by Israeli officials as a defensive security measure to prevent weapons smuggling and attacks on Israeli civilians, the blockade has predominantly targeted civilians, severely restricting vital supplies such as medical equipment, fuel, and construction materials and fueling a deep and ongoing humanitarian crisis. It has been an integral part of Israel's offense against the Palestinian people.

Gaza has also faced severe food restrictions under the blockade, with profound consequences documented by agencies such as the United Nations

Office for the Coordination of Humanitarian Affairs (OCHA) and the World Food Programme (WFP). In early 2006, Dov Weisglass, a senior adviser to Israeli Prime Minister Ehud Olmert, said: "The idea is to put the Palestinians on a diet, but not to make them die of hunger." This statement, which preceded the formal blockade, reflected early planning for economic pressure before it became fully institutionalized in 2007.

While staple foods like flour, rice, and cooking oil were generally allowed, many processed and fresh foods faced strict limitations, reducing dietary diversity and nutritional quality. The World Health Organization highlighted how these restrictions, combined with damage to food storage and refrigeration infrastructure, have led to spoilage and limited access to fresh produce. OCHA has reported frequent fluctuations and occasional complete closures of border crossings exacerbate shortages, causing price spikes and widespread food insecurity. Humanitarian organizations like Oxfam and Human Rights Watch have condemned the blockade's impact on Gaza's food supply, warning these restrictions contribute to chronic malnutrition and hunger, particularly among vulnerable groups like children. Furthermore, limits on agricultural inputs hinder local food production, deepening dependency on constrained imports. Despite some humanitarian food aid allowed under strict controls, bureaucratic delays and security vetting by Israeli authorities hamper effective relief, as detailed in multiple UN and Non-Governmental Organizations (NGO) reports.

In May 2010, the International Committee of the Red Cross explicitly described Israel's blockade as "collective punishment" in violation of the Fourth Geneva Convention. A September 25, 2009, United Nations fact-finding report (the Goldstone Report) concluded the blockade violated international law by severely restricting civilian access to food, fuel, and medical supplies. Most recently, on June 24, 2025, the UN Human Rights Office stated that the "weaponization of food" in Gaza, through restricted access to aid, "constitutes a war crime." Collectively, these findings underscore that Gaza's blockade is not merely a policy but a prolonged act of war with devastating humanitarian consequences.

This immoral blockade, ongoing for nearly two decades with occasional adjustments, has been widely normalized in Israeli society and Zionist/imperialist circles as a legitimate act of self-defense, framed by Zionists as though Israel had "withdrawn" from the Strip and bears no responsibility for its peoples. The sustained segregation, isolation, and dehumanization created the volatile, criminal environment leading to the events of October 7th.

Yet governments, particularly in the Global North, ignored this stark violation of international law and clear policy of deliberate collective punishment intrinsic to Israel's incremental genocide of Palestinian people. Even verbally, governments of the West expressed concern rather than abject rejection of the policies, let alone were willing to take an effective measure to tame Israel and stop the cruelty on the ground.

The indifference in quite a few cases was tantamount to compliance as the West continued to supply the arms employed in Israeli military assaults on the Gaza Strip in 2008/9, 2012, and 2014. Further, the United States used its veto power multiple times in the security council to prevent any UN condemnation from becoming operative.

The twin pillars of Israeli impunity are the orientalist foundations of Western politics and the influence of the pro-Israel lobby. The first is rooted in white supremacist, Islamophobic, and Arabophobic attitudes among Western elites, which present Israel as culturally aligned with the West, an extension of Europe, and a bastion against what they portray as Arab and Islamic "barbarism." The second stems from Zionist lobbying efforts that began in the early twentieth century, systematically cultivating political elites and making their careers closely tied to their position on Israel. At the same time, the prominence of political Islamic groups within the Palestinian resistance movement made it easier to associate Hamas in particular with the American notion of "the war on terror" in the wake of the 9/11 attack. Hence, without much deliberation, Western security services and governments adopted Israeli attitudes toward Palestinian factions, apart from the Palestinian Authority, as terrorist organizations, consequently accepting the Israeli retaliation to this resistance as "self-defense," and as a response that might have been excessive at times, but never illegitimate or illegal.

The mass influx of refugees into Europe from the Arab world and North Africa since 2011 has enmeshed the anti-immigration and racist impulses of Western establishments with Israel's rejection of the Palestinians, as if the Palestinians themselves were mere immigrants in their own homeland.

In 2016, Israeli Katz, then minister of intelligence, offered Israeli expertise to European governments of how to deal with Muslim immigrants. The following was his particular condemnation of the Belgian approach:

> "The first rule of war is know your enemy, and Europe and the current American government are unwilling to define this war as against Islamist terrorism. If in Belgium they continue eating chocolate and enjoying life, and continue to appear as great democrats and liberals, they won't be aware that some Muslims in their country are organizing terror, they won't be able to fight them."
> - Israeli Army Radio, March 2016

While these words enraged people in Belgium, the security services there and elsewhere in the West collaborate daily with Israeli intelligence, exporting Israeli securitization methods and integrating them into their policies vis-à-vis their Muslim minorities. Since the early 2000s, especially after 9/11, U.S. law enforcement has adopted Israeli policing tactics through training programs by groups like the Anti-Defamation League. These tactics, drawn from Israel's control of Palestinians, include surveillance and riot suppression. Their influence was seen during the 2011 Occupy protests and drew sharp criticism after the uprisings in Ferguson (2014) and nationally in the wake of George Floyd's public execution by police, where policing methods closely resembled those used against Palestinians

This highlights also the connection between Israeli operations on the ground in the Gaza Strip and the military industrial complex around the world, which further adds to the impunity. As several researchers have shown, there is a spike in arms sales from Israel after operations on the ground, as weapons were tested in real time.

Notably, Israel does not enjoy impunity before the UN General Assembly or the UN Human Rights Council, nor before judicial bodies like the International Court of Justice and the International Criminal Court, which have demonstrated a willingness to condemn genocide and issue arrest warrants for Benjamin Netanyahu and his former defense minister, Yoav Gallant. However, the global political balance means most countries do not enforce these decisions, and crucially, the United States has actively undermined both courts, weakening the potential impact of international law on Israel's standing in the world.

4. Atrocity propaganda

During Hamas's unprecedented operation, both Palestinian fighters and Israeli victims shared harrowing footage on social media, flooding the internet with scenes of brutal violence. The assault involved acts of extreme violence, including shootings, stabbings, and possibly executions.

As the attack was unfolding, Israel's public relations apparatus launched a misinformation campaign to deflect attention from the political, intelligence, and military failures that enabled it. Designed to incite fear and fury, the narrative relied on decontextualized, emotionally charged content, securing public support for the mass mobilization of reserve units in order to enable a ground invasion of Gaza.

This was assisted by the long-standing and total segregation of the thoroughly dehumanized Palestinian society in Gaza, which had already erased any meaningful understanding of and empathy for Palestinian life or suffering among mainstream Israelis and Zionists worldwide. The Hamas attack occurred at a moment perfectly suited to framing it as an existential threat, providing a pretext for pursuing the ultimate goal and reward: the total seizure of Gaza's land and resources, emptied of its people, with the carnage creating a smoke screen for escalated violence and dispossession in the West Bank, Syria, Iran, and Lebanon.

Psychological mechanisms like fear in response to the real trauma due to the events of October 7th, fear conditioning, reinstatement, reconsolidation, and cognitive dissonance (**Figure IV.1**) were weaponized to turn fear into compliance and aggression, reinforced by seductive promises of security, vengeance, and rewards through land theft, resource seizure, expulsion, and genocide. This manipulation framed Israel's ensuing campaign of mass violence and dispossession as necessary and righteous self-defense, echoing classic settler colonial narratives amplified by biblical references. In doing so, it laid the ideological and emotional groundwork for a return to an accelerated version of genocide and land theft, in service of long-standing Zionist agendas.

The campaign was marked by concocted sensational claims of babies "beheaded en masse," "burned" and "hung on a clothesline," alongside false accounts of mass rape reminiscent of narratives common in the Jim Crow–era American South. Israel also revived the long standing "Pallywood" trope, falsely claiming Palestinians staged or fabricated scenes of suffering in order to

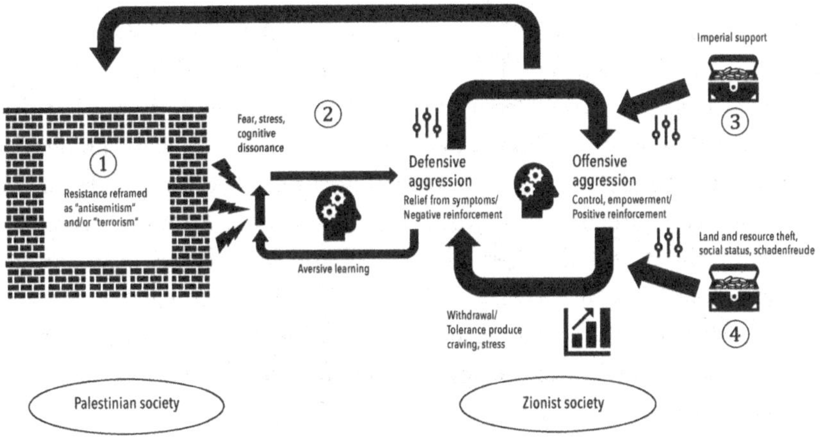

Figure IV.1. Wired for genocide: October 7, 2023 (1) Hamas led an attack meant to break the siege on Gaza; (2) trauma, atrocity propaganda, fear conditioning, reinstatement, and reconsolidation of fear of past atrocities associated with the conflation of Zionism and Judaism, in addition to profound cognitive dissonance, were used to fear-monger and dehumanize the entirety of Palestinian society, (3) paving the way for mass-scale aggression framed as "defensive," i.e., genocide, reinforced by imperial rewards and impunity. The seventeen-year-long blockade thwarts extinction of fear and promotes inter-group territorial violence. (4) Theft of Palestinian land and resources (including looting) in Gaza and the West Bank, as well as territorial land grabs and attacks aimed at domination and control in Lebanon, Syria, and Iran serve as reward for offensive aggression.

discredit documented Israeli atrocities and delegitimize Palestinian accounts of the ongoing genocide. These contrived narratives framed the October 7 attack as an extension of the Nazi Holocaust and the worst massacre of Jews since World War II, reinforcing the false conflation of Zionism with Judaism and weaponizing and reinstating fear of historical trauma to justify Israel's criminal response.

In addition to fostering support from Western allies, Netanyahu activated relationships with billionaires and social media moguls. The owner of the popular X platform Elon Musk's services to Zionism included a visit to Auschwitz and the adoption of far-right, decontextualized interpretations of the October 7th events justifying an acceleration of Zionist genocide of and theft from the Palestinian people. Netanyahu's relationship with Elon Musk culminated in a carefully choreographed visit to Israel, where a crib was conspicuously staged amid the crime scene littered with bullet casings, a theatrical touch to drive Netanyahu's atrocity propaganda home. Musk's continuous promotion of Zionist narratives seemed aimed at rehabilitating his image and ongoing antisemitism, which has often been laced with typical white supremacist attacks on George Soros, historical revisionism, misrepresentation of Hitler, and apologetics for Hitler's ideological heirs in Germany, the xenophobic far-right party Alternative for Germany (AfD).

These sorts of visits by politicians and celebrities are part of a disturbing Israeli practice dubbed "atrocity tourism." Decontextualized art exhibits and mass campaigns further fueled the Israeli narrative.

5. Biblical framing

Shortly after October 7, 2023, numerous evangelical Christian leaders and pro-Israel figures publicly framed the conflict in explicitly biblical and spiritual terms. Many portrayed the war not simply as a geopolitical struggle but as a cosmic battle between good and evil, valorizing Israel as the chosen nation fighting against demonic or ancient adversaries.

Groups like the International Christian Embassy Jerusalem (ICEJ) described Hamas's violence as "rooted in the demonic realm," invoking the "Spirit of Amalek," a biblical symbol of relentless evil, to emphasize the moral urgency of supporting Israel. This language positioned the conflict as a fulfillment of scripture, urging believers worldwide to join Israel's cause as part of a divinely mandated mission.

In his speech on October 28th, 2023, Netanyahu reiterated ICEJ's notion thus: "You must remember what Amalek has done to you, says our Holy Bible. And we do remember." This quotation is from Deuteronomy 25:17, which recalls an attack by the Amalekites on the Israelites during their exodus from Egypt. The verse calls for the Israelites to remember this act and to "blot out the memory of Amalek from under heaven," i.e., Netanyahu used a common Zionist practice, employing a biblical reference and conflating Zionism with Judaism, to convert public shock into genocidal tribalism.

Prominent evangelical voices went further, presenting Israel's survival and military efforts as fulfilling biblical prophecy. They highlighted passages from the Old Testament and apocalyptic literature, suggesting the war was an essential part of God's unfolding plan for the end times. This narrative infused the conflict with a sacred purpose, in which backing Israel was seen as divine will.

By casting the war in spiritual terms, these leaders reinforced a worldview where Israel's struggle is central to a larger cosmic drama of "light versus darkness," framing typical of white supremacist, settler colonial, manifest destiny-driven projects. Again, Netanyahu was not far behind; on October 16, 2023, during the opening of the Knesset's winter assembly, he said, "This is a struggle between the children of light and the children of darkness, between humanity and the law of the jungle," while on October 28th he claimed, "This will be a victory of good over evil, of light over darkness, of life over death."

Further inflaming genocidal fervor, Israeli politicians dehumanized and implicated the entirety of Palestinian society, not just those responsible for the events of October 7th (see **Table IV.1**).

Table IV.1. Dehumanizing rhetoric by Israeli officials promoting collective punishment

OFFICIAL	POSITION	DATE	STATEMENT	DEHUMANIZING ELEMENT
Yoav Gallant	Defense Minister	October 9, 2023	*"We are fighting human animals and we are acting accordingly."*	Compares Palestinians to animals, justifying harsh actions
Itamar Ben-Gvir	National Security Minister	October 11, 2023	*"They are all terrorists. The entire Gaza Strip is a nest of snakes."*	Labels entire population as terrorists and snakes
Bezalel Smotrich	Finance Minister	October 15, 2023	*"There is no such thing as a civilian in Gaza."*	Denies civilian status, erasing Palestinian humanity
Mickey Levy	Knesset Speaker	October 16, 2023	*"We must crush the enemy with unprecedented force, without hesitation or mercy."*	Advocates total destruction, disregards civilian lives
Amihai Eliyahu	Minister of Heritage	November 5, 2023	*"They can go to Ireland or deserts, the monsters in Gaza should find a solution by themselves."*	Calls Palestinians "monsters," demonizing entire population

6. Normalizing genocide through media

To grasp how genocide unfolds, it's crucial to understand the shifting role of dehumanizing propaganda, which incites hatred, suppresses dissent, and ultimately sustains and justifies mass violence across each phase of a genocidal campaign.

Before violence begins, such rhetoric helps suppress dissent, normalizes extreme and violent ideas, and emboldens those already inclined toward aggression. By portraying targeted groups as subhuman, disgusting, and dangerous, propaganda legitimizes deadly actions, making them appear acceptable despite being illegal and morally abhorrent. Once violence starts, perpetrators often experience emotional and physical distress; here, dehumanizing narratives become essential in reframing these acts as morally justified, helping individuals overcome initial resistance and ensuring continued participation.

As Aliza Luft's research highlights, dehumanization frequently emerges as a consequence of sustained violence rather than its sole cause, facilitating psychological adaptation by dulling empathy and transforming perceptions of victims. Throughout the genocidal campaign, this propaganda also deters opposition by increasing fear of speaking out and shifts social norms to create tacit consent for brutality.

Here, we return to the importance of segregation, which operates as a foundational mechanism in the evolution of genocide by solidifying in-groups and out-groups, amplifying dehumanization and fear, enabling lethal defensive aggression, and obstructing the possibility of fear extinction through empathy. This also makes clear the siege on Gaza and the construction of the West Bank separation wall, like so many Zionist policies, are components of a long-standing eliminationist strategy rooted in the movement's earliest segregated settlements, not isolated security responses.

Throughout the accelerated genocide that started on October 7th, 2023, Israeli as well as other Western media outlets have played a central role in normalization efforts by repeating debunked atrocity propaganda ("mass rape," "40 beheaded babies") and presenting crimes against humanity as matters of legitimate "debate." Across networks, official Israeli spokespeople, Islamophobes, and right-wing extremists have been given uncritical airtime alongside anti-genocide voices under the guise of balance, creating a false equivalence that muddies ethical clarity and prevents legal accountability.

This framing trivializes atrocity, reducing genocide to a debate topic for ratings rather than confronting it as a crime demanding urgent condemnation and justice. Such normalization, as also defined by the Boycott, Divestment and Sanctions (BDS) movement, helps repackage illegal, racist policies as ordinary and "controversial" rather than abhorrent, while diverting attention from the Palestinian struggle for liberation. Media platforms that claim neutrality yet promote these agendas serve as conduits for what Orwell termed "newspeak," distorting language and meaning to manipulate public perception and suppress dissent. Through this process, the Western media landscape has become complicit in sustaining systems of violence and domination under the pretense of open dialogue.

7. The process of erasure and starvation

Although Israeli society had been primed for genocidal violence, some of which had been thoroughly normalized, Israel needed to gauge both its readiness and the international community's tolerance for the mass criminality required to realize the government's goals of complete ethnic cleansing and land theft. Among them was the mass-scale, deliberate targeting and destruction of hospitals, universities, and places of worship, as well as the systematic elimination of key figures in Palestinian civil society, including journalists (e.g., Duaa Sharaf, a prominent Palestinian journalist and radio presenter for Radio Al-Aqsa, was killed in an Israeli air strike on October 26, 2023, along with her young daughter, when their home in Al-Zawaida, central Gaza, was targeted); academics (e.g., Dr. Sufian Tayeh, President of the Islamic University of Gaza and a renowned physicist, who was killed on December 2, 2023, in an Israeli air strike on Jabalya Refugee Camp); medical workers (e.g. Adnan Al-Bursh, a leading Palestinian orthopedic surgeon from Gaza's Al-Shifa Hospital, who died in Israeli custody in April 2024 after months of detention and torture); clerics (e.g., Jamila al-Shanti, a Hamas political leader and former member of the Palestinian Legislative Council, who was killed on October 19, 2023, in an Israeli air strike in Gaza); thought leaders (e.g., Said Al-Zubda, president of the University College of Applied Sciences in Gaza, who was killed on December 31, 2023, in an Israeli air strike targeting his home); writers (e.g., Refaat Alareer, a renowned Palestinian poet, academic, and activist from Gaza, killed in an Israeli air strike on December 6, 2023, along with six family members); and artists (e.g., Dorgham Qareqa, a Palestinian artist and community organizer known for using art as resistance and healing, who was killed in an Israeli air strike in Gaza's Shuja'iyya neighborhood on March 18, 2025, whose presence symbolized resilience, identity, and continuity.)

Importantly, before it carried out mass criminal violations, Israel tested the waters, starting with an event that shattered a long-held taboo, a "trial balloon" (see Part II and **Table IV.2**).

Genocide destroys far more than human lives. It aims to erase an entire people's existence. Beyond mass killing, it dismantles families and communities, erases culture, language, and religion and severs ties to land and history. Survivors are left with deep trauma, often passed down through generations, while political, economic, and social structures are shattered.

Deliberate starvation by Israel served an especially insidious purpose. Beyond repeated forced criminal displacement of the population, it deliberately engineered social atomization, creating extreme deprivation, chaos, and internal conflict through food scarcity and loss of control. This manufactured breakdown then provides a pretext for further genocide, expulsion, theft, and domination.

Here, it is useful to return to concepts introduced in **Part I**, gleaning insights from research on animal behavior. Renowned primatologist Jane Goodall documented a prolonged conflict (1974–1978) between two chimpanzee groups, the Kasakela and the Kahama, in Gombe Stream National Park, Tanzania. This "Gombe Chimpanzee War" saw the Kasakela community systematically attack and eliminate the Kahama group. Goodall's findings were widely reported as support for the idea that warfare and territorial violence are natural elements of human behavior, inherited from our closest primate relatives.

Notably, reactionaries have co-opted these notions on so-called human nature to justify colonialism, falsely depicting Indigenous tribes as inherently violent "savages" to legitimize land theft and genocide.

Anthropologist Brian Ferguson challenged Goodall's interpretation. In an analysis of each case of documented aggression during the "Gombe Chimpanzee War," he argues that the violence observed was not natural or inevitable. Rather, it was the result of external influences, primarily human interference by Goodall, her team, and others. Ferguson points to changes

Table IV.2. International Legal Protections Violated During Israel's Gaza Campaign Post-October 7, 2023.

VIOLATION	LEGAL PROTECTION	FIRST INSTANCE ("TRIAL BALLOON")
Attacks on hospitals & medical personnel	GC IV, Arts 18–19; AP I, Arts 12–15; AP II, Art 11 – Medical facilities and staff are protected unless misused; warnings required before attack	Al-Ahli Hospital bombing in Gaza City, October 17, 2023
Starvation as a method of warfare	AP I, Art 54; GC IV, Arts 23(3), 55–56; AP II, Art 14 – Deliberate starvation of civilians is prohibited	The siege as a prelude. March 2024: Near-total cutoff of food, fuel, medical aid
Collective punish-ment and siege tactics	GC IV, Art 33; AP I, Art 51; AP II, Art 4 – Collective punishment and siege with deprivation are banned	October 9, 2023: Defense Minister's complete siege order
Killing of civilians and children	GC IV, Art 3; AP I, Arts 48-51; AP II, Art 13 – Intentionally targeting civilians and disproportionate attacks prohibited	October 17, 2023: Al-Ahli hit during civilian displacement
Targeting of journalists	GC IV, Art 3; AP I, Art 79; AP II, Art 13 – Journalists are protected civilians; harm is forbidden	October 2023: Multiple strikes on media workers (e.g., Nasser Hospital journalist)
Destruction of schools, universi-ties, worship sites	GC IV, Arts 12-14; AP I, Art 53 – Cultural and civilian infrastructure is protected	October 17, 2023: UNRWA school struck in Al-Maghazi camp
Forced displacement of civilians	GC IV, Art 49; AP I, Art 49; AP II, Art 17 – Deportation or forced displacement prohibited except for medical/safety reasons	October 2023: Mass evacuation orders to Rafah and Khan Yunis
Public calls for genocide	Genocide Convention, Arts II-III – Direct incitement to genocide is illegal	October 2023. Minister Amihai Eliyahu called Gazans "monsters"

GC IV - Geneva Convention IV (1949): Relates to the Protection of Civilian Persons in Time of War. This is the primary Geneva Convention addressing civilian protections during conflict; AP I - Additional Protocol I (1977): Supplement to the Geneva Conventions, applying to international armed conflicts. Expands protections for civilians and regulates the conduct of hostilities; AP II - Additional Protocol II (1977): Applies to non-international (civil) conflicts. Reinforces protections for civilians, including prohibitions on starvation, collective punishment, and attacks on medical facilities; IHL - International Humanitarian Law: The broader body of law governing the conduct of armed conflict, including the Geneva Conventions, Additional Protocols, and related customary international law; Genocide Convention–Convention on the Prevention and Punishment of the Crime of Genocide (1948): Defines genocide and obligates states to prevent and punish acts of genocide.

in provisioning practices (feeding of bananas) by these researchers, which disrupted social dynamics and led to unnatural group fragmentation. He also cites ecological pressures, such as resource scarcity due to nearby human activity, which may have exacerbated tensions.

Ferguson contends these factors, rather than innate aggression, better explain the conflict, emphasizing violence is context-dependent and can be negatively affected by human interference, and not a fixed part of primate and human nature. Thus, he cautions against simplistic evolutionary (and reactionary) narratives that use such cases to justify human violence. In line with these notions, a broad range of social science research links income inequality to higher crime rates in diverse settings.

The same dynamics have unfolded in Gaza, where Israeli and American strategies of siege, blockade, and forced starvation have created the very social fragmentation they later cite as proof of Palestinian dysfunction and innate barbarity.

Starvation is a tool of colonization, weaponized to weaken bodies, fracture bonds, undermine social cohesion, fuel internal aggression, weaken resistance, and turn survival into an isolating struggle. These conditions are neither natural nor inevitable; they are constructed and inflicted deliberately to serve a white supremacist goal: to manufacture potentially lethal chaos within Palestinian society and shift blame for genocide onto the victims themselves.

As internal conflict escalates, Israeli forces can portray Palestinians as irredeemably violent "savages," justifying shooting them at aid stations under the guise of civilizing and evicting them "for their own good." This was reflected by Trump in his immoral plan to turn Gaza into a resort.

This strategy mirrors decades of Zionist colonial tactics: assassination, imprisonment, torture, and psychological warfare, all deployed to reinforce the false narrative that Palestinian anti-colonial resistance is proof of inherent barbarism, rather than a defensive response to European invasion, oppression, and dispossession.

8. Reproductive genocide and psychological torture

Since October 7, 2023, and arguably 1948 (and before), Israel has been engaged in reproductive genocide; a systematic destruction or suppression of the Palestinian peoples' reproductive capacity, through policies, violence (systematic sexual, reproductive, and gender-based) or conditions intended to prevent births, endanger pregnancy, obstruct parenting, or annihilate generational continuity. According to Freeman and Shoman (2025), this has encompassed both direct and indirect acts which undermine the three tenets of reproductive justice: the right to have children, the right not to have children, and the right to parent in safe, sustainable environments.

Israel's genocidal behavior in Gaza and elsewhere in historic Palestine, as well as many documented cases of humiliation and *schadenfreude*, resonates with patterns seen in two well-known, yet notably artificially constructed, experiments into human psychology, cruelty, and the lengths to which people will torture others if provided the context and opportunity: the Stanford Prison Experiment (1971) and the Milgram Experiment (1961).

Conducted by Philip Zimbardo, the Stanford Prison Experiment assigned college students as guards or prisoners in a simulated prison. Planned for two weeks, it was halted after six days as guards became abusive and prisoners showed severe stress, revealing how situational power and roles can drive ordinary people to oppression and sadism.

Led by Stanley Milgram, the Milgram Experiment tested obedience by instructing participants to deliver escalating electric shocks to an actor for wrong answers. Despite hearing simulated screams, 65 percent administered the maximum voltage under authority pressure, entering what Milgram termed an "agentic state," revealing how ordinary people obey orders that conflict with their morals.

Compounding the well-documented physical and sexual torture of Palestinians, the Zionist campaign has deployed a range of psychological tactics aimed at humiliating the Palestinian people and breaking their spirit. These tactics have included dropping demoralizing leaflets from airplanes and drones, broadcasting abusive messages over loudspeakers, and even using recordings of crying babies to lure civilians into the open, where they are then targeted by snipers.

Adding to this dehumanization, Donald Trump suggested turning Gaza into a casino resort, where few Palestinians might be allowed to remain as servants, reducing an entire population's suffering to a grotesque spectacle of exploitation akin to Naomi Klein's concept in *The Shock Doctrine* of disaster capitalism, where crises are exploited for profit and control. Such methods are designed not just to kill, but to terrorize, dehumanize, and break the human spirit, eroding any sense of safety, resistance, or hope.

Shockingly, Israeli actions reveal a chilling level of detachment, cruelty, and a lack of empathy toward the Palestinian "other." Israeli soldiers have documented their own war crimes, flaunting them online for "likes," seemingly using these displays to gain attention, even from potential partners on dating applications, showcasing a disturbing normalization and sexualization of violence.

These can be witnessed in the military through its genocidal campaign, which regularly targets women, children, peacekeepers, journalists, academics, prisoners of war, and medical personnel, among others, and within Israeli society through countless examples since October 7th, 2023, including cases of Israelis mocking Palestinians for their pain and loss.

The disturbing practice of IDF soldiers donning the clothing of Palestinian women in homes they have invaded reveals a ritualized form of conquest, exposing the gendered and racialized violence at the heart of Zionist colonialism. This political phenomenon signifies a celebration of conquest and patriarchal white supremacist colonization, with females of "the other" as a resource to be degraded, controlled, abused, and acquired.

In "Ur-Fascism," Umberto Eco argues that fascism glorifies death as the ultimate heroic act and channels its authoritarian impulse into machismo, misogyny, and intolerance of sexual difference, weaponizing these ideals to enforce conformity and justify violence.

Notably, Klaus Theweleit's *Male Fantasies* is a landmark psychoanalytic and cultural analysis of the proto-fascist male psyche, revealing how misogyny, eroticized violence, and militaristic masculinity fuse in sadistic fantasies of domination and self-preservation. In *Male Fantasies*, Theweleit describes how Freikorps soldiers' violent acts, tearing apart women's bodies and clothing, symbolize both their fear of and fascination with femininity, momentarily confronting and even imagining themselves enveloped in the very softness they seek to annihilate.

The racism and misogyny at the heart of Zionist white supremacy recall the logic of misogynoir: the intersection of racism and misogyny that targets Black women. Though coined for the Black experience, the term helps expose how Zionism weaponizes gender and religion to cast Palestinian women's bodies as demographic threats, erasing their identity while killing them outright. In its place, a Western Zionist femininity is constructed, one that is permitted and encouraged to participate in violent, male-dominated structures like the military. Israel routinely celebrates women's participation in its offensive aggression, most recently highlighting the female pilots involved in bombing Iran as symbols of "civilized" warfare (see Masculinity and war, **Part I**).

In ethnic conflicts, controlling women who maintain national boundaries through reproduction and cultural transmission, represents the ultimate conquest and victory. In yet another example of the effects of cognitive dissonance, Israel, like its Western allies, often projects its own culpability onto its adversaries, hypocritically accusing Palestinian society of misogyny, much like the US did with its "protecting women" narrative in Afghanistan. This phenomenon deepens our understanding of the motivations behind the ongoing genocide and the intersecting forms of oppression at play: patriarchy, white supremacy, capitalism, and violence in the context of Israel's actions against Palestinians.

9. Learned helplessness and deliberate debilitation

> Recently, an Israeli officer called an elderly Gazan, and he said, "you have to evacuate now. We're issuing mass evacuation orders for your area." The old man responded with tears in his eyes, "go ahead, bomb us. We have nowhere to go, we don't even have physical energy to run away." And he started to beg the Israeli officer, literally he started to beg him to bomb them. He said, "Just let us rest. Bomb us now." And when the argument escalated he started begging the officer for food. He said, "if you are going to send planes here anyways just let them drop any food on us so that we can get any energy to move from this area.
>
> ~ Muhammad Shehada, Palestinian journalist on *Democracy Now* (July 1, 2025)

In the context of ongoing Zionist oppression and humiliation of Palestinians, the learned helplessness (LH) model, an experimental paradigm in psychology and neuroscience, offers insight into how prolonged uncontrollable stress fosters depression-like behavior.

In the lab, the LH model uses a triadic design with three animal groups: one exposed to controllable stress, one to identical yet uncontrollable stress, and one left unstressed. In the test phase, all are placed in a setting where escape is possible.

Traditionally, the LH model was thought to show how exposure to inescapable aversive stimuli, whether electric shocks in a laboratory or systemic violence in reality, conditions individuals to stop trying to avoid negative outcomes, even when escape later becomes possible: a behavioral shutdown marked by passivity, diminished motivation, and impaired learning, akin to major depression.

More recent research, however, reveals this passivity is not learned but reflects an innate, unlearned biologically default response, mediated by the neurotransmitter serotonin with a focus on the dorsal raphe nucleus (DRN) in the brain.

Passivity is seen as an unlearned default response to the prolonged aversive events, driven by sensitization of serotonergic neurons in the DRN, which inhibits active escape. When no control is detected, the PFC fails to inhibit the DRN, perpetuating passivity. In contrast, when control is detected, or expected from prior experience, the PFC suppresses DRN activity, preventing passivity and enabling active coping. Thus, learned helplessness reflects a biologically driven state shaped by stress and a lack of perceived control, rather than simply a psychological attitude.

Prior experiences of control produce lasting neural changes, creating "immunization," which fosters resilience to future stress. These findings reframe LH as an innate biological reaction modulated by control, with the PFC–DRN pathway, sometimes called the brain's "hope circuit," central to fostering agency and mitigating stress. This updated understanding also suggests therapies enhancing perceived control may engage these same pathways to build resilience against depression and anxiety.

As a tool, the LH model has been instrumental in advancing our understanding of depression. It has illuminated the role of brain regions like the PFC and DRN and neurotransmitter systems like serotonin and dopamine. Moreover, it remains a staple in the development and testing of new antidepressant treatments. Through decades of refinement, the LH model continues to offer vital insights into how chronic stress shapes behavior and brain function, and how therapeutic interventions might restore a sense of control, agency, and hope.

In addition to behavioral outcomes, human studies often incorporate self-reported measures that capture perceived helplessness, hopelessness, and control. These subjective assessments consistently reveal that exposure to uncontrollable stress elevates feelings of helplessness and diminishes perceived agency.

Palestinians in Gaza have been subjected to deliberate starvation, random attacks, and the targeting of protected, socially foundational groups: women, children, doctors, academics, journalists, artists, and others, along with physical and psychological torture and a total lack of control, contributing to a state of learned helplessness. This offensive traumatization is deliberate; it fosters deep depression and is strategically deployed to break resistance, erode motivation, and ultimately enforce compliance and subjugation, paving the way for genocide, permanent displacement, and theft.

Furthermore, maiming and debilitating Palestinians has been an intentional Israeli colonial practice for its entire history, e.g., during the Great March of Return (2018), and has continued throughout the accelerated genocide that began in October 2023. In her seminal book *Right to Maim,* Jasbir Puar argues that oppressive regimes often rely on producing and managing debility as a state of physiological and social erosion that parallels the psychological dynamics of learned helplessness. In her framework, "maiming" is an intentional tactic that renders populations easily governable, profitable, and permanently weakened. Maiming circumvents the practice of reporting death as the ultimate proof of wrongdoing by the state, while serving the capitalist/colonialist bottom line as well as a posture of benevolence toward disabled individuals. Rana Barakat and Yasmin Snounu further developed this concept and applied it to the case of the Palestinians.

This perspective resonates with concepts detailed in this chapter: the behavioral and neuroendocrine consequences of chronic subordination, the enforcement of hierarchies through fear, and the production of subjects whose diminished capacities are pathologized or erased. Puar's distinction between the celebrated, rehabilitated injured soldier and the invisibilized debilitated civilian, particularly in the context of Israel/Palestine, echoes the very asymmetries of power, worth, and agency underlying social defeat and learned helplessness. Her insights on biopolitics, debility, "homonationalism" (the alignment of LGBTQ+ rights with nationalist, xenophobic or imperialist agendas to justify oppression or exclusion of others), and pinkwashing further illuminate how states manipulate vulnerability, producing the physiological and psychological conditions that sustain domination while providing it plausible deniability.

10. Zionism coming home to roost

> "Being an old farm boy myself, chickens coming home to roost never did make me sad; they've always made me glad."
>
> ~ Malcolm X, December 1, 1963

On October 7th, the carefully constructed Zionist facade of incremental genocide within a liberal/democratic framework collapsed, exposing Israel's genocidal and fascistic core. Zionists in Israel and beyond did not mourn the end of this charade and instead celebrated their newfound freedom to kill and destroy Palestinians without any restraint or pretense, en route to their ultimate fantasy of Greater Israel. This development not only poses a threat of elimination to the Palestinian people, but since the occupation of Palestine, as previously mentioned, has been used as a laboratory for the development and testing of new military technology and strategies, as well as those employed to impose subservience and oppression, it sets the stage for similar violent escalations against oppressed communities in the Global South as well as against BIPOC and immigrant communities within the Global North.

In contravention of international law, Israeli genocidal expansionism knows no limits, as conveyed by its finance minister who called for Israel's borders to extend to Damascus.

Since October 7th, 2023, Israel has launched strikes on Lebanon, Syria, Iran, and Yemen, while senior officials have issued threats against neighboring countries including Turkey, Iraq, and Egypt, reflecting a broader Zionist expansionist vision of "Greater Israel," which extends even to parts of Saudi Arabia. Notably, Israeli strikes in Lebanon were in retaliation to the Hezbollah attack, as were those against Ansar Allah in Yemen. The ones against Syria and Iran were unprovoked.

However, Israeli Zionist tactics have never been confined to Palestine and the Middle East; they have long extended back to its imperial sponsors. In particular, the labeling of opposition as "terrorism," the use of fear to promote, and the framing of theft and offensive aggression against BIPOC communities and the commons as "defense," thereby justifying the use of lethal force, are now unfolding at the very heart of the Western empire: the United States. Here, "Project Esther," developed by the same architects at the Heritage Foundation behind the authoritarian, Christian nationalist "Project 2025," has launched a new crackdown on anticolonial and antiracist resistance, cynically framed as a defense against "antisemitism."

Published on October 7, 2024, to mark the first anniversary of the Hamas attacks on Israel, Project Esther purloins the story of Queen Esther, the Jewish heroine celebrated during Purim for saving Jews of ancient Persia from extermination at the hands of Vizier Haman, with modern-day Zionist narratives of defense and victimhood to depict her as a defender of Jews against activists, academics, and progressive members of Congress in the US who oppose racism, apartheid, and genocide. The strategy paper, supposedly designed to be "a blueprint to counter anti-Semitism in the United States," includes several fundamental aspects of fascistic thought and practice as outlined by Umberto Eco in his *Ur-Fascism*, such as syncretic culture, xenophobia, a cult of heroism, and anti-intellectualism.

Targeted individuals, including numerous Black, Brown, and Jewish elected representatives who voiced any criticism of Israel, including senators Bernie Sanders and Chuck Schumer, are collectively mischaracterized as members of "Hamas Support Organizations (HSO)," part of a "Hamas Support Network" and equated with Purim's villain, Haman. Through this framing, the campaign targets prominent social justice advocates and progressive Democratic Party representatives as enemies of the Jewish people, using the mythology of Queen Esther to justify their persecution and repression.

Project Esther shamelessly states its aims to eliminate anticolonial perspectives from the US education system, limit the dissemination of related information, and restrict advocates' access to American society, the economy, and Congress. It seeks to prosecute alleged legal and criminal violations by

"HSO" members, disrupt their communications, restrict demonstrations, and rally the Jewish community, allies, and the American public against anticolonial resistance movements.

With fearmongering rhetoric draped in patriotism and "American values" and the latest Zionist spin on rebranding offensive aggression as "defense," Project Esther institutionalizes repression of dissent within a fallacious, fascistic theoretical framework, casting itself as the final bulwark against an imaginary threat of "foreign influence" and valiant protector of citizens from brown-skinned heathen hordes who have supposedly promised to infect white American open society with an anticapitalist agenda. Typically, Project Esther ideologues see themselves, much as Zionists do in Israel/Palestine, as superheroes, courageously waging a holy war to preserve "Western values," much to the tune of the Ku Klux Klan's infamous portrayal in *Birth of a Nation*.

Under the guise of combating hate and appealing to a supposedly terrorized and humiliated underclass, Project Esther seeks to frame antiracist opposition to Zionist apartheid and genocide as inherently antisemitic. However, this exposes Zionism itself as white supremacy and a modern embodiment of antisemitic ideology, much like Haman in the myth of Queen Esther, actively targeting Jewish organizations such as Jewish Voice for Peace and the Reform Jewish movement.

Project Esther criticizes what it sees as "complacency" within the American Jewish community, invoking the Zionist-manufactured antisemitic ideal of a "new Jew" who rejects traditional beliefs that interpret oppression and hardship as divine punishment for sins. This vision disparages traditional reliance on defense as passive and weak, promoting instead an assertive, offensive approach to resistance. In line with this view, Zionists adopt the antisemitic notion that Jews have been responsible for their own suffering, advocating for segregation and land acquisition in a new homeland as the ultimate solution.

Notably, fearmongering has long been used by Zionists to encourage Jewish, preferably white, immigration to Israel as a means to restock the Israeli military and combat the Palestinian "demographic threat." By amplifying the partnership between US white supremacy and Zionist expansionism, Project Esther presents a serious threat to anticolonial and justice-oriented intersectional movements across the country, on the one hand, and minorities, including Jews, on the other.

Project Esther promises to continue to speed up the mobilization of Zionists and right-wing antisemites emboldened by Trump's presidency to dismantle resistance to their racist policies through financial and academic audits, "name and shame" campaigns, and "lawfare." While shielding Zionist policies and aligning with US white supremacy, the document, riddled with misinformation about "anti-Israel and anti-Zionist Jew-haters attempting to lay siege to our education system, political processes, and government," reinforces the Trump administration as well as Zionist vigilante groups like the "Jewish Defense League" (JDL) and their natural allies, American neo-Nazis, to stifle free speech and dissent.

Ironically, along with Trump, Zionist vigilante groups, such as Magen Herut Canada and the Jewish Defense League, constitute an emboldened threat on North American university campuses, engaging in intimidation of anti-genocide student protesters under the guise of "Jewish defense." These groups, often with far-right links and fascist roots, use "self-defense" rhetoric to justify offensive aggression, aiming to fracture anti-colonial resistance and support Western imperial expansionism.

The JDL has a long history of racist violence and terrorism. Its members bombed Arab and Soviet properties in the US and assassinated those it labeled "enemies of the Jewish people," focusing on Arab American activists. They were linked to several bombings in 1985, one of which killed West Coast Regional Director of the American-Arab Anti-Discrimination Committee Alex Odeh. In 1994, twenty-nine worshippers were fatally shot in a Hebron mosque during Ramadan, an event known as the Cave of the Patriarchs massacre; and in 2001 a plot targeted US Representative Darrell Issa in his San Clemente, California, district office and at the King Fahad Mosque in Culver City, California.

Another such group, Betar (Brit Yosef Trumpeldor), founded in 1923 by Vladimir Jabotinsky, was the youth movement of Revisionist Zionism (see **Part II**), promoting Jewish nationalism, military training, and allegiance to a future Jewish state built through strength and discipline. Jabotinsky admired aspects of Italian fascism in the 1920s, particularly its emphasis on discipline, nationalism, and the regeneration of a strong state. Though he may have said he ultimately rejected fascist authoritarianism, his Revisionist Zionist movement adopted paramilitary structures and rhetoric influenced by Benito Mussolini's model. In the 1930s, Jabotinsky even sent members of the Betar youth movement to train with Mussolini's naval forces in Italy, seeking to instill military discipline and tactical skill.

Zionist vigilante groups invoke the rhetoric of "self-defense" to justify offensive aggression and colonization, appropriating Jewish victimhood to mask criminality perpetrated by Zionists and the Israeli regime. They weaponize fear to generate compliance and support for their eliminatory agenda, rewarding acts of aggression while framing them as defensive. Relying on deterrence and the dehumanization of Palestinians, they obscure the illegality of offensive violence by portraying it in propaganda as a response to perceived threats. These groups serve a dual purpose: to fracture and discredit intersectional resistance to white supremacy, including anti-Zionism, and to advance US-led imperial expansion at home and abroad, with Israel at the forefront.

Further Reading

1. Fanon F. *Black Skin, White Masks.* Translated by Charles Lam Markmann. Grove Press; 1967.
2. Stein RL. *Screen Shots: State Violence on Camera in Israel and Palestine.* Stanford University Press,; 2021:1 online resource.
3. Pappé I. *Lobbying for Zionism on Both Sides of the Atlantic.* Blackstone Publishing, Inc.; 2024.
4. Luft A. The Moral Career of The Genocide Perpetrator: Cognition, Emotions, and Dehumanization as a Consequence, Not a Cause, of Violence. *Sociological Theory.* 2023;41(4):324-351.
5. Goodall J. *The Chimpanzees of Gombe: Patterns of Behavior.* Belknap Press of Harvard University Press; 1986:673 pages, 8 unnumbered pages of plates.
6. Ferguson RB. *Chimpanzees, War, and History* Oxford University Press; 2023.
7. Cikara M. Intergroup schadenfreude: Motivating participation in collective violence. *Current Opinion in Behavioral Sciences.* 2015;3:12-17. doi:https://doi.org/10.1016/j.cobeha.2014.12.007
8. Zimbardo PG. *The Lucifer Effect: Understanding How Good People Turn Evil.* First edition ed. Random House; 2007:xx, 551 pages.

9. Milgram S. *Obedience to Authority: An Experimental View*. First edition ed. Harper & Row; 1974:xvii, 224 pages.
10. Klein N. *The Shock Doctrine: The Rise of Disaster Capitalism*. Picador ed ed. Picador; 2007:701 pages.
11. Eco U. Ur-Fascism. *The New York Review of Books*. June 22, 1995.
12. Theweleit K. *Male Fantasies, Volume 1: Women, Floods, Bodies, History, trans. Stephen Conway*. University of Minnesota Press; 1987.
13. Freeman, C. and H. Shoman, *No Justice in a Genocide: Sexual and Reproductive Health and Rights in Gaza*. Sex Reprod Health Matters, 2025. **33**(1): p. 2523095.
14. Bailey M, Trudy. On misogynoir: citation, erasure, and plagiarism. *Feminist Media Studies*. 2018;18(4):762-768. doi:https://doi.org/10.1080/14680777.2018.1447395
15. Cho, S., K. Crenshaw, and L. McCall, *Toward a Field of Intersectionality Studies: Theory, Applications, and Praxis*. Signs: Journal of Women in Culture and Society, 2013. **38**(4 (Summer 2013)): p. 785-810.
16. Maier SF, Seligman MEP. Learned helplessness at 50: Insights from neuroscience. *Psychological Review*. 2016;123(4):349-367. doi:https://doi.org/10.1037/rev0000033
17. Seligman MEP. *Helplessness: On Depression, Development, and Death*. A Series of books in psychology. W.H. Freeman; Trade distributor, Scribner; 1975:xv, 250 p.
18. Puar JK. *The Right to Maim: Debility, Capacity, Disability*. Duke University Press; 2017.
19. Snounu Y. Apartheid, Disability, and the Triple Matrix of Maiming in Palestine. *Peace Review*. 2019;31(4):459-470.
20. Barakat R. The right to maim and its implications for Palestine studies. *Journal of Palestine Studies*. 2019;49(1):101-108.

Part V: Wired to Heal: Reclaiming Humanity Amidst Helplessness

"The opposite of war isn't peace, it's creation"
- Jonathan Larson, *Rent,* Act 2, "La Vie Bohème B"

As detailed throughout this volume, settler colonial aggression and expansion are facilitated through segregation and a dynamic interplay of fear, identity and reward, which drive defensive and offensive aggression, respectively, fueled by ruling-class interests in land and resource theft.

The Wired to Steal (W2S) model detailed in Parts III and IV aligns with Césaire's, Fanon's, Freire's, Memmi's, and others' insights, which describe the colonial relationship as resting on the ruthless dehumanization of both colonized and colonizer, though in different ways, with the colonized stripped of humanity and the colonizer abdicating their own.

This construct of greed and psychological conditioning, including fear, domination, identity restructuring, and theft fuels imperialist violence, fractures dissent through divide-and-conquer tactics, and provokes profound rage, grief, and helplessness. Liberation, therefore, is not simply a transfer of power; it is a pedagogical, cultural and neurobehavioral process: a collective un- and relearning, a rewiring of the brain, and a reclamation of humanity, empathy, truth, and accountability through dialogue, solidarity, creativity, collaboration, and worldmaking. Empathy is natural and moral disengagement is conditioned, and therefore reversible. Those who resist can maintain or recover empathy circuits through exposure to the humanity of the out-group, counter-narratives, and alternative social community. Solidarity becomes the neurological antidote to the rewards and privileges the oppressive system installs.

Global capitalism and its colonial projects, led by the United States, Europe and allied states such as Israel, are driving the world toward disaster, including the risks of nuclear war, climate collapse, and the large-scale destruction of human life and the natural world in service of profit.

Yet the histories of anti-colonial resistance, in Palestine and beyond, offer a counterpoint of hope, demonstrating how struggle and solidarity can reclaim a humanity in which liberation of the colonized inevitably frees the colonizers as well. From anti-colonial uprisings in the Global South, to the fight against racism and ruling-class persecution within the imperial core, these histories affirm the need for a collective, intersectional alliance capable of confronting oppression and segregation, reclaiming humanity, and manifesting liberation.

Countering the current trajectory requires a profound cultural transformation led by those subjected to oppression, one that is grounded rather than utopian, grassroots rather than top-down, liberatory rather than punitive and carceral, and adaptive rather than rigid.

Disrupting the coercive mechanisms described in the W2S model, fear, identity manipulation and selective distribution of reward and privilege, requires cultivating the social and intellectual capacities which resist and deconstruct them: sociality, critical education and intersectional solidarity. A cultural revolution aligned with the social nature of the human species and the architecture of our brains: collective rather than individualistic, sustainable rather than predatory, socialist rather than capitalist.

Such a transformation emphasizes the dismantling and abolition of oppressive hierarchical structures through an intersectional lens, advances desegregation and restorative justice, and develops bottom-up, community-centered, emergent strategies for survival and transformation (see work by Mariame Kaba, adrienne maree brown, and Andrea J. Ritchie).

This final part of the book turns to anti-colonial and Indigenous traditions, focusing on modes of resistance to oppression within and outside of the imperial core, with particular attention to the Palestinian collective. It examines their histories, successes and failures, potential future directions, and the neurobehavioral foundations of collective and creative action, framing these practices as pathways toward healing and growth grounded in shared humanity.

1. Anti-colonial struggles

> At the level of the individual, violence is a cleansing force.
> It frees the native from his inferiority complex and from his despair and inaction; it makes him fearless and restores his self-respect.
> ~ Frantz Fanon, *The Wretched of the Earth*, "On Violence" (p. 94)

The trajectory of settler colonial projects, including the Zionist strategy in Palestine, typically begins with invasion and initial contact framed as divine will and/or benign exploration or trade, followed by permanent settlement and expansion. This accompanies and results in the displacement and elimination of Indigenous peoples through violence, forced removals, and assimilation, alongside the establishment of settler governance and legal systems that delegitimize Indigenous sovereignty and cultural practices.

Over time, constructed national myths and propaganda erase, appropriate, or romanticize Indigenous presence, naturalizing settler claims to the land and recasting settlers as its rightful natives. Throughout, resistance persists, yet settler colonialism proceeds relentlessly, perpetuating dispossession through the assumption and normalization of sovereignty, assimilationist reforms, or symbolic reconciliation, while fiercely resisting genuine decolonization.

In rare cases, such as Algeria and Haiti, settler colonial projects were overturned through sustained, large-scale resistance combining armed struggle with mass mobilization. In Haiti, enslaved Africans revolted against French rule, waging a protracted war that culminated in independence in 1804 and the complete expulsion of the settler class. Similarly, in Algeria, decades of organized anti-colonial resistance, culminating in the Algerian War of Independence (1954–1962), forced French settlers and colonial authorities to withdraw. These cases succeeded by dismantling colonial power structures outright rather than reforming them, though they were marked by extraordinary violence and came at immense human cost, underscoring how brutally settler societies resist decolonization.

One of the most impressive, albeit controversial, successes of defeating a thoroughly entrenched settler colonial project is the African National Congress (ANC) toppling of the apartheid regime in South Africa. Therefore, it is not surprising that its mode of reaction and resistance, in large parts, have been adopted both by the Palestinian national movement and the international solidarity movement with it (the BDS campaign, for instance). Yet with one caveat: while there was a significant anti-apartheid white movement within South Africa, there is no significant anti-Zionist Jewish presence in Israel.

In the 1960s, the Algerian model planted hope for an eviction of the settlers, while the South African model orientated the movement towards a fundamental regime change that would include the right of self-determination and democratization and the end result of decolonization.

It is also important not to be trapped by dichotomous definitions of failure and success in Indigenous resistance to settler colonial projects. The Mapuche in southern Chile, the Māori in Aotearoa/New Zealand, the First Nations of Canada, Native Americans in the United States, and Aboriginal peoples in Australia have all sustained long-term struggles for their rights and survival.

Notably, Indigenous scholars point out that since settler colonialism is still at work in many parts of the world where it had first appeared, it stands to reason that the struggle against it continues. The endgame of Indigenous resistance is therefore inconclusive. This fact was recognized by the UN when it issued its declaration for Defending the Rights of Indigenous People (UNDRIP; 2007), which among other issues recognizes the right of the Indigenous people to defend themselves (e.g., the UN frames the resistance of the First Nations in Canada as ongoing resistance, compared to other Indigenous people whose resistance is defined by this declaration as a matter of the past).

In many ways, the timing of the inception of the settler colonial project (in the case of Zionism, a very late appearance in the colonial age) and the level of nationalization and modernization of the Indigenous population (Palestinians were in the process of building a national movement and modernizing their society) chart both the limitations of the settler colonial project as well as help to assess the aspirations of the Indigenous movement. Palestinians are not looking for recognition or compensation; they remain steadfast in their goal of full liberation.

Indeed, Palestinians and their allies have resisted the Zionist project since its inception, well before 1948 (see **Part II**). Next, we briefly survey examples of the diverse forms of their resistance, both within the settler project (in the '48 borders of Palestine and the Occupied Palestinian Territories) and at its imperial core (in the United States), assessing their alignment with the model presented therein. Effective forms of resistance and desegregation strike at the very core of the Zionist project and its benefactors, which is ultimately geared to steal land and resources from the Palestinian people (and others en route to "Greater Israel") and fragment resistance through fallacious and divisive propaganda.

2. Resistance to Zionism

If resistance can both defeat (e.g., Algeria, Haiti, South Africa) and perpetuate aggression (by eliciting fear and subsequent defensive aggression), and the colonial ideology itself cannot be reformed, what, then, is the best path to ending this ongoing injustice?

As **Parts I-IV** of this book illustrate, all Zionists, including those who claim to be "liberal," promote segregation and aggressive expansionism fueled by a genocidal agenda of dispossession and land theft from the Indigenous Palestinian people. Reforming Zionism is simply not possible.

As the events since October 7, 2023, have resoundingly demonstrated, achieving freedom and justice for Palestinians and rectifying their dispossession necessitates dismantling Zionism and its inherent drive for aggression by any means necessary. This can only be accomplished through a process of decolonization on multiple fronts, of which the principled Palestinian call to BDS Israel forms an integral part (**Table V.1**).

Palestinian resistance has combined diverse strategies including grassroots uprisings, armed struggle, political and diplomatic efforts, cultural expression, legal challenges, nonviolent campaigns, and community institution building. These tactics seek to confront occupation, assert rights, preserve identity, and undermine settler colonial control, reflecting a multifaceted movement balancing survival, empowerment, resistance, and international advocacy. **Figure V.1** presents these forms of resistance within the "Wired to Steal" neurobehavioral model of Zionist aggression from **Part III**.

Table V.1. Modes of Palestinian resistance and relationship to Figure V.1

METHOD	HISTORICAL PHASE	MAIN ACTORS	OUTCOMES	IN FIGURE V.1 MODEL OF RESISTANCE
Armed rebellion (riots, attacks)	British Mandate (1920–1939)	Rural militias, Arab Higher Committee	1936–39 Revolt crushed; leadership exiled; set precedent for armed resistance	(2), (5)
General strikes & boycotts	1936–39 Revolt	Urban workers, unions, Arab Higher Committee	Economic pressure; drew British concessions yet ultimately failed	(1), (4), (5)
Political resistance, armed resistance, civil disobedience and popular actions	1939–1948	Political leadership, Armed resistance groups, grassroots and civil society, External actors (Arab states)	Suppression of leadership, failure to prevent partition, weakened political organization, erosion of institutions, rise of *sumud*, military defeats, Nakba (1948), shift in regional dynamics, entrenchment of Zionist control.	(1), (2), (4), (5)
Fedayeen raids (guerrilla)	1950s–1960s	Refugee fighters in Gaza, Jordan, Egypt	Harassment of Israel, limited tactical success; inspired organized armed struggle	(2), (5)
Cultural & intellectual resistance	Post-1948 Nakba– present	Writers (Darwish, Kanafani), educators	Preservation of national identity, global awareness	(1), (3), (4)
Palestinian/ Israeli joint ventures	—	—	Matzpen and the Communist party of Israel	(2), (3), (4)
PLO-led armed struggle	1964–1982 (PLO in Jordan, Lebanon)	PLO, Fatah, PFLP, DFLP	Gained global recognition, UN observer status; provoked harsh reprisals	(2), (5)
Hijackings & international attacks	Late 1960s–1970s	PFLP, Black September	Put Palestine on global agenda, but alienated some allies	(1), (3)
Diplomatic campaigns	1974–present	PLO, Palestinian Authority (PA), Hamas	UN recognition as observer, ICC membership, UN recognition of Zionism as racism (1975), subsequently. Revoked (1991)	(3), (4)
First Intifada: mass civil resistance	1987–1993	Grassroots committees, youth, women's groups	Major disruption of Israeli control; led to Oslo process	(1), (2), (3) (5)
Second Intifada: armed & suicide bombings	2000–2005	Hamas, Islamic Jihad, Al-Aqsa Martyrs Brigades	Heavy losses, loss of international sympathy	(1), (2), (5)

(continued on next page)

Village protests & civil disobedience (including the Great March of Return)	2005–present	Local committees, International Solidarity Movement (ISM), activists	ICJ ruling on Wall, symbolic wins, local awareness, losses	(1), (3), (4), (5)
Legal & international law appeals	2000s–present	PA, human rights NGOs, ICC, first academic BDS call (2002)	Some recognition of Israeli violations, ongoing cases	(1), (4), (5)
BDS movement (boycott, divestment, sanctions)	2005–present	Global activists, PACBI, civil society	Economic, cultural pressure; delegitimizing occupation	(1), (3), (4), (5)
Digital & social media campaigns	2010s–present	Grassroots activists, diaspora youth	Global solidarity, narrative shift	(1), (3), (4)
Armed resistance in Gaza & West Bank	2005–present	Hamas, Islamic Jihad, Lions' Den, others	Asymmetric warfare, heavy civilian toll	(1), (2), (5)

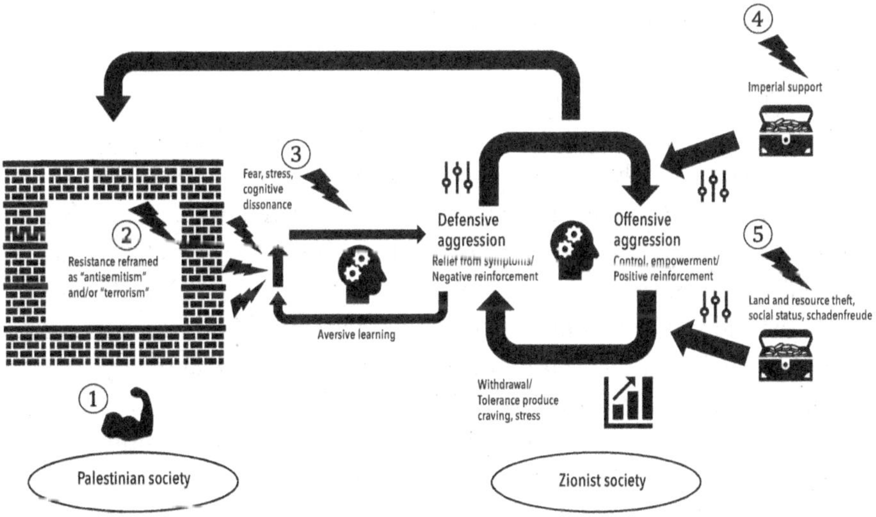

Figure V.1. Palestinian resistance to Zionist settler colonialism within the Wired to Steal model. (1) empowerment of Palestinian society and cultivation of bonds between all oppressed communities/ societies; (2) resistance to segregation by any means necessary; (3) efforts to combat Zionist propaganda; (4) disruption of imperial and other support of Zionist aggression; (5) target land and resource theft, including manpower.

An example of the multifaceted nature of Palestinian resistance came in 1987, when the First Intifada ("uprising" in Arabic) erupted in response to Israel's brutal occupation of the West Bank and Gaza Strip. It included a vast assortment of tactics aimed at challenging the Israeli encroachment on Palestinian freedoms and rights, such as civilian disobedience in the forms of general strikes, boycotts, rejection of taxes, and protest graffiti, as well as throwing stones and Molotov cocktails at Israeli army and police. The Intifada also fostered a spontaneous, nonviolent, women-led collective uprising, which emphasized the importance of an intersectional approach to the Palestinian struggle.

Crucially, on the legality of armed struggle the United Nations General Assembly Resolution 3070 (1973) was clear. It "affirms the legitimacy of the struggle of peoples for independence, territorial integrity, national unity and liberation from colonial and foreign domination and foreign occupation by all available means, particularly armed struggle." And Resolution 37/43 (1982) "reaffirms the legitimacy of the struggle of peoples for independence, territorial integrity, national unity and liberation from colonial and foreign domination and foreign occupation by all available means, including armed struggle."

These resolutions were controversial with support from many states in the Global South, Non-Aligned Movement, and the United Nations General Assembly majority (UNGA), which emphasized the right of self-determination for colonized or occupied peoples and, in the decolonization context, often framed armed struggle as a legitimate last resort when peaceful means were denied. Opponents, unsurprisingly, included the US, Israel, and other states in the Global North, which rejected armed struggle by non-state actors, deeming it "terrorism," and posited that only states can invoke the right of self-defense under Article 51 of the UN Charter.

The Palestinian resistance and the varied results of other anti-settler colonial movements highlight the critical necessity of a broad alliance. This is largely due to the power imbalance where hegemonic forces possess significantly greater wealth and weaponry.

In whatever means of resistance the Palestinian people deem necessary, and beyond the discontinuation of the Israeli war of elimination, a path to liberation would inevitably involve embracing the truth regarding Zionism's history and nature, committing to authentic accountability, eroding and removing external support for Zionist colonization, and recognizing and empathizing with the humanity and suffering of the Palestinian people.

Once resistance facilitates the dismantling of the oppressive framework of Zionism, a path toward desegregation, rehumanization, and reconciliation can emerge through empathy, paving the way for justice and potential coexistence.

3. Palestinians in the driver's seat

One of the most obvious reasons for the failure of the (genuine or cynical) so-called peace attempts was the total disregard for Palestinian aspirations and visions. At every junction of this process, Palestinians were asked to react to proposals of "peace" or "solutions" to "the conflict." Therefore, their natural adoption of an anti-colonialist vocabulary involving decolonization was rejected outright as irrelevant at best or as "fanatical" and even "terroristic" at worst.

Whichever models of reconciliation are discussed above, they are presented with the full recognition that contrary to the past, the paths forward have to be charted by the Palestinian national movement. However, the current disarray and fragmentation within the movement means there is no official or established call for action or specific vision for the future.

The exception is the BDS movement, which provides the solidarity movement with a clear orientation regarding Palestinians and has done so successfully. Despite the challenges facing the national movement at this historical moment, these efforts are compatible with our analysis in this volume on human behavior and its relationship to decolonization and reconciliation.

Yet by looking beyond the current political establishment and drawing on the rich work of a young Palestinian generation, we can identify key points of consensus about the future.

Unlike most of the current Palestinian political institutions (the Palestinian Authority (PA), the Palestinian parties in Israel, and the official positions of Fatah or Hamas), there is a great unity about a vision for the future: one democratic state between the river and the sea. Secondly, there is strong emphasis on restorative and transitional justice, both as an alternative for retribution, and perhaps more importantly, as providing the legal infrastructure for the return of the refugees, the land stolen, and compensation for prisoners and bereaved families.

The best way of presenting these visions is through a number of questions that are posed and answered about the future. The first question to address is what, in practical terms, restorative justice would entail within a future political solution. In the Palestine context and from a mainly Palestinian perspective, its main feature would be the Right of Return for all the Palestinian refugees and their descendants who had been expelled in the 1948 ethnic cleansing and ever since.

Repatriation is a known process in international law. In 2005, Paulo Sérgio Pinheiro, the special United Nations rapporteur, presented a report to the commission of the UN Human Rights. He focused on economic, social and cultural rights, with particular emphasis on housing and property restitution in the context of the return of refugees and that of internally displaced persons. (Hundreds of thousands of Palestinians are internal refugees inside Israel today.)

The principles regard the restitution of housing, land, and property rights and the right of return as "essential to the resolution of conflict and to post-conflict peacebuilding." In fact, it states clearly that the right of return is "a key element of restorative justice, [and as a factor that] contributes to effectively deterring future situations of displacement and building sustainable peace."

Moreover, projects by young Palestinian scholars, coming from the disciplines of urban planning, architecture, and geography, provide us with models (some in 3-D visual presentations, some as mini-models) of imaginary reconstruction of Palestinian villages that had been destroyed in 1948; this is a visual representation of actual decolonization on the ground. Scholars such as Salman Abu Sitta provided us with an assessment of how much of the land taken is today inhabited by Israeli citizens to calculate the full potential of return. His conclusion was that return will not require most Israelis to move.

The second question is the future of the illegal settlements Israel built, mostly in the West Bank, some of them constituting proper urban sprawls, ever since 1967. All the plans for the two-state solution never really determined what would be their future. Decolonization offers a far better and comprehensive approach, based on the history of decolonization of European urban colonial centres. The options range from wholesale destruction to repopulation at a general level, or more targeted decisions concerning individual buildings or neighbourhoods.

The urban settler sprawls of the West Bank are built on the expropriated land of Palestinian villages out of which few would have become themselves metropolises had they not been colonized. Leaving them intact rather than destroying them and opening them for Palestinians and compensating the villages could be one way forward. Decolonization of urban infrastructure would be preferrable to destroying them.

A third question concerns the future status of the millions of Jews who now live in Israel in a decolonized future. Any identification of this collective through the lens of the Zionist ideology will challenge significantly the chances of decolonization. Current literature that grapples with this query stretches from those proposing a binational state (an idea that had already been proposed in the 1920s by a group of Jewish settlers and Palestinians called Brit Shalom) to the negation of the Jewish collective as a national group and instead defining them as an ethnocultural group, very much like the Druze, the Kurds, the Yazidis, etc.).

Closely associated with the issue are two additional questions that the conversation about decolonization can trigger. The first is reestablishing the past connection of Palestine to the Arab world in general and of the Mashreq (the Eastern Mediterranean) in particular, and the second is the future connection between world Jewry and the Jewish community in today's Israel.

At the very core of the Zionist project was an ambition to manufacture a Zionist hierarchy by planting a European Jewish state at the heart of the Arab world at the expense of the Palestinians. This developed into an obsession once the State of Israel was established. In the eyes of founders and Zionist leaders until today, it became, in the words of former prime minister Ehud Barak, "a villa in the Jungle." Both Israel and Europe ignored the geographical, historical, and cultural locations of Israel/Palestine and insisted it was part of Europe.

A similar attempt to ignore geography, history, and culture failed in the case of South Africa. For the sake of both a future Palestine and a future Middle East, the past organic connation between the country to its region must be reestablished as part of the process of decolonization. This enables rethinking about the political structures, particularly the nation state, imposed on the Arab world by the colonial powers after the First World War. In the Mashreq it replaces a mosaic of coexistence between ethnocultural and ethnoreligious communities with a supra state that often represents one group at the expense of others.

The clear definition of the Jewish collective in historical Palestine as an ethnocultural group, rather than a national one, or not exclusively a national one, will also redefine the relationship between the Jews in today's Israel and the Jewish communities around the world. A transformation has already begun among young Jews, including in the US, of dissociating themselves from Israel and Zionism and being able to define their Jewish identity independently, be it cultural rather than a religious identity.

When Zionism appeared on the map, Jews in different countries were citizens who happened to be Jewish, as others happened to subscribe to other religions or no religion at all. Zionism argued the opposite: Jews were aliens in other countries, exiled from their homeland. The reversal will happen with decolonization; American Jews will be American who happen to be Jewish and not part of a so-called national diaspora.

The implications of such an approach are profound. Zionism enabled the West to deal with its own antisemitism through support for a "Jewish state" with its manufactured hierarchies. Decolonization of Palestine, i.e., deconstruction of Zionist hierarchical society, can offer several necessary challenges to the West: How can governments effectively fight antisemitism within a broader struggle against institutional and societal racism, ensuring they avoid hierarchies of racialized groups and confront racism wherever and against whomever it emerges?

Further yet, can Europe look to the decolonization of Palestine as a model and precedent for finally confronting the long-term consequences of its own colonial projects, particularly the expulsions, settler colonization, genocides, and resource plundering that accelerated after the Berlin Conference of 1884, which carved up the African continent? The same lessons could extend to the Americas, Australia, New Zealand, the Pacific Islands, and other regions where the US and Europe, and others continue to uphold colonial practices.

Finally, in the interconnected world we live in, decolonization is not limited locally or even regionally as a process; it affects global developments as much as it is affected by them. Much as the genocide in Gaza (2023–) exposed a crisis of confidence in the Global South about the universality of international justice as being exclusively preserved for non-Western countries and that freedom of speech and truthful media coverage is under attack also in democracies, decolonization can reinstate this confidence.

For policymakers, decolonization in Israel/Palestine is widely seen as a nonstarter, off the table and irrelevant. For decolonization to be accepted as a legitimate paradigm, as it already is within academia and civil society, the nature of global politics must transform, since it requires a political break from conventional and convenient frameworks that preserve privilege and segregation, such as the two-state solution. Such a departure can only be contemplated by courageous politicians willing to risk uncharted territory, motivated by the grassroots and moral rather than careerist considerations.

Politics is often treated as a job rather than a vocation and proposing a bold new approach to a century-old conflict can jeopardize political careers. However, this is not a concern unique to Israel and Palestine. Without such departures from established norms, the global challenges of climate change, poverty, and immigration will not be properly met, and collaboration on a global level is impossible without a universal and consensual international legal system. If the International Criminal Court withstands the pushback, discussions on Israel and Palestine's future could be shaped by a vocabulary reflecting its history and present realities, creating space for both liberation and reconciliation.

The Palestinian resistance and the varied results of other anti-settler colonial movements highlight the critical necessity of a broad alliance. This is largely due to the power imbalance where hegemonic forces possess significantly greater wealth and weaponry than oppressed peoples. Consequently, beyond the study of strategies of anti-colonial struggles in general and Palestinian resistance in particular, it is important to examine other forms of revolt, activism, civil disobedience, protest, and dissent as a lens for understanding and fostering alliance-building.

4. Resistance and decolonization within the imperial core: the Black Panther Party

The Black Panther Party (BPP) offers a valuable blueprint for a multicultural network of revolutionary groups. This network has confronted the constructs of capitalism, imperialism, white supremacy, settler colonialism, and racism, including Zionism, both in the United States and globally. Notably, the BPP was originally named the Black Panther Party for Self Defense, an appropriate use of the term "defense," as opposed to the cynical and propagandistic misuse of the term by the Zionist militia Haganah ("defense" in Hebrew) and the so-called Israel Defense Forces.

The BPP resisted oppression through practical programs, revolutionary ideology, and diverse methodologies applied domestically and internationally. At the heart of its work were "community survival programs," designed to meet urgent needs neglected by the state. These included the Free Breakfast for School Children program, which began in Oakland in 1969 and quickly spread nationally; the Oakland Community School and earlier "Liberation Schools," which reflected key ideas from Lev Vygotsky's social theory of learning (more later in this chapter): knowledge develops through collaboration, culture shapes how people think, and education can function as a collective practice of empowerment rather than a hierarchical transfer of information; free medical clinics such as the Carolyn Downs Family Medical Center in Seattle; and sickle cell anemia testing and education, which forced public health institutions to finally address a disease long ignored. The party also pioneered drug detoxification centers, published *The Black Panther* newspaper to disseminate uncensored news globally, and advocated for community control of police, alongside other services like ambulance programs, childcare, and arts initiatives.

These programs reflected the BPP's broader ideological framework, grounded in challenging systemic racism, capitalism, and imperialism. Central to its worldview was the right to self-defense against police brutality, revolutionary socialism aimed at dismantling oppressive structures, and the unifying slogan "All Power to the People!", which emphasized solidarity across racial and class lines. The Party's Ten-Point Program outlined demands such as community self-determination and an end to police violence, while its education efforts sought to raise political consciousness by linking local oppression to global imperialism. The BPP rejected narratives equating property damage with violence, instead exposing state violence as the true source of harm and reframed "looting" as the reclamation of resources denied to marginalized people. Rage at injustice, the Panthers argued, was inseparable from love for the people and a vision of collective liberation.

Methodologically, the BPP shifted fluidly between armed self-defense, political education, community organizing, and strategic alliances. Early police patrols openly carrying firearms were designed to defend against and deter brutality, while political education classes grounded members in revolutionary theory. The Panthers built multiracial coalitions through efforts like the United Front Against Fascism (UFAF), while also resisting liberal co-optation by insisting on constant protest and critique. They combined grassroots service work with electoral interventions, as seen in their campaign for community-controlled policing. Many former members channeled their commitment into professions like law, medicine, teaching, and social work, sustaining the party's ethos long after its peak.

Internationally, the BPP saw its struggle as inseparable from global liberation movements. It established an International Division in Algiers and chapters across Africa, Europe, and Oceania, while forging ties with revolutionary movements such as SWAPO, the ANC, and Palestinian resistance organizations. Panthers participated in delegations to China and Palestine, shared printing equipment with African liberation groups and created art that circulated worldwide as symbols of solidarity. Their work affirmed that the oppression faced by Black Americans was part of a broader imperialist system, linking their fight to those of oppressed peoples globally. Through this synthesis of local service, revolutionary ideology, direct action, and international solidarity, the BPP built a model of resistance that continues to inspire movements for justice and liberation around the world.

Unsurprisingly and as a direct testament to their effectiveness in undermining US empire, the BPP and its members were severely targeted by the state: assassinated (e.g., Fred Hampton), exiled (e.g., Assata Shakur, Pete and Charlotte O'Neal), incarcerated (e.g., Mumia Abu Jamal), and otherwise abused, framed, and maligned by an unprecedented FBI campaign, a counterintelligence program (COINTELPRO) aimed at surveilling, infiltrating, discrediting, and disrupting domestic political organizations deemed "subversive." FBI Director J. Edgar Hoover went so far as to call Dr. Huey P. Newton, co-founder and Minister of Defense of the BPP, "the most dangerous man in America."

The party explicitly identified the conflict between Zionists and Palestinians as a central anti-colonial struggle, linking it to other white supremacist projects around the world and urging US taxpayers to question their complicity in the continued genocide and apartheid of Palestinian people. For the Panthers, Palestinians endured the same kind of oppression and systemic discrimination faced by Black people in the United States and this shared condition naturally bound their struggles together. This perspective resonated even among their allies, reinforcing the BPP's foundational belief that racism itself was a byproduct of imperialism and capitalism, which functioned as a global force oppressing all colonized peoples.

In practice, this ideological stance translated into active solidarity with Palestinian liberation movements. Through its international division in Algiers, the BPP featured the Palestinian liberation struggle prominently in its publications as early as the 1960s. Dr. Huey P. Newton met with PLO Chairman Yasser Arafat and other Palestinian leaders during a visit in the 1980s, while Minister of Culture Emory Douglas used his artwork to highlight Palestinian resistance both in *The Black Panther* newspaper and in public murals.

At its height, *The Black Panther*, published weekly, boasted a print run of 100,000 copies and reached 400,000 readers worldwide. Its uncensored, factual, hard-hitting, and provocative approach to information garnered global interest. Unlike today with instant internet accessibility, the BPP fostered direct, physical connections with communities through its forty-nine chapters and branches, allowing them to learn firsthand about people's concerns and needs. The BPP also utilized music, via its house band, The Lumpen, to spread its revolutionary agenda.

For the BPP, dismantling the occupation of Palestine and challenging the global exploitation of Black and Brown people were inseparable goals, each essential to the transformation of the world order. Their opposition to Zionism was thus a natural extension of their revolutionary project: to confront the intertwined systems of colonialism, white supremacy, and capitalism wherever they appeared, and to build solidarity among all oppressed peoples resisting them.

In a fascinating development, an Israeli chapter of the Black Panther Party emerged in the early 1970s as part of the broader international expansion of the BPP's anti-colonial and anti-racist struggle. Founded primarily by Mizrahi Jews, i.e., Brown Jews of Middle Eastern and North African descent who faced systemic discrimination within Israeli society, the group adopted the BPP's militant stance against oppression and their focus on social justice. The Israeli Panthers challenged the Ashkenazi-dominated establishment, highlighting issues of poverty, police brutality, and ethnic inequality, while aligning their struggle with global fights against racism and imperialism. Unfortunately, the Israeli Panthers ultimately betrayed the core notions of the BPP and the Palestinian people when they adopted many of Zionism's core racist tenets.

5. Prejudice and desegregation

The relentless campaign by Zionist leaders to dehumanize Palestinians has had two primary goals: first, to portray them as a monstrous, powerful, uncivilized, unworthy threat that must be segregated, conquered and expelled, and/or exploited; second, to reduce them to a pitiable, fragmented state so weak and disorganized that their displacement provokes no moral outrage.

This seemingly contradictory depiction of Palestinians, as both a significant existential threat and weak, pitiable victims, echoes how slavers treated their human "possessions," and how Indigenous peoples were genocided and driven off desirable land after being depicted as primitives. It reiterates Eco's characterization of Ur-fascism in the way antisemites in general and Nazis specifically portrayed Jews in Europe. As discussed in previous parts of this volume, this eliminatory framework serves ruling-class interests of dispossession and domination.

So how then can this form of prejudice be dismantled?

In the classic text *The Nature of Prejudice* (1958), Allport conjectured that:

> Prejudice, when it is reduced, may be reduced by equal status contact between majority and minority groups in the pursuit of common goals. The effect is greatly enhanced if this contact is sanctioned by institutional supports (i.e., by law, custom, or local atmosphere) and provided it is of a sort that leads to the perception of common interests and common humanity between members of the two groups. (p. 281).

As mentioned regarding fear conditioning and its extinction in **Part III**, segregation and consequent lack of contact between groups serves as a means to degrade empathy, boosting campaigns of dehumanization and consequent aggression, similar to the one accelerated by Zionists following the October 7 Hamas attack (**Part IV**). Since then, in-group Israeli support for collective, indiscriminate violence, humiliation, and torture against the Palestinian people has reached unprecedented levels; Israeli military and citizenry have valorized soldiers who raped Palestinian prisoners in the infamous Sde Teiman detention camp in the Negev desert and lack any substantial empathy for Palestinian people suffering through genocide, starvation, and displacement. Israelis celebrate Palestinian deaths in grotesque acts of schadenfreude, endeavoring to witness Gaza's bombing from surrounding hilltops and obstructing aid trucks from alleviating the humanitarian crisis.

This valorization of killers and the deaths they perpetrate is reminiscent of the favorable treatment Elor Azaria received from the broad Israeli public and its politicians after his summary execution of Abdel Fattah al-Sharif (**Part IV**).

The broader W2S model of Zionist settler colonialism, as outlined in **Part III**, clearly demonstrates de-escalation, accountability, equality, and justice are impossible within a system built on segregation, fear, and an addiction to aggression, driven by an insatiable ruling class that exploits religion and racism to fuel their greed and theft. In other words, justice cannot coexist with a society structured around injustice. Dismantling that structure, that is, decolonization, is the only practical solution.

Palestinian resistance, though essential for both physical and psychological survival, is abused by Zionism to sustain its cycle of trauma and fear, reinforcing its addiction to aggression through negative reinforcement. As long as Zionists' belligerence and expansionist land theft remain backed by the US empire and its allies in the West, Israel's brutalization of the Palestinian people is likely to continue through escalating tactics aimed at their submission and elimination.

Here, an evolutionary lens can be applied to examine two distinct outlooks on global ethnic conflicts in general, and the Zionist settler colonial project in particular.

A regressive evolutionary approach aligned with the "deep rooters" (**Part I**) posits that only the strongest survive in multiethnic lands, framing war as "human nature." This fosters fear, division, and aggression, with ruling classes promoting individualistic, racialized, competitive, and exclusivist narratives to justify segregation, wealth appropriation, and corruption. These dynamics are central to settler-colonial ideologies, which create false in-groups and undermine resistance by fostering racial divisions, reframing anti-colonialism as a conflict between "civilized" pioneers and "uncivilized" "savages."

In contrast, a progressive view of evolution, aligned with the "shallow rooters" who see war and aggression as products of learned culture rather than innate biology, highlights the adaptive value of desegregation, mutual interest, inclusion, empathy, accountability, and cooperation, all within a decolonizing framework.

This perspective promotes a cultural shift in which social integration, education, dialogue, and empathy facilitate processes of decolonization, paving the way for coexistence and reconciliation rooted in equality as the foundation of lasting peace. Unlike fear-based cultures that promote inequality, education and de-escalation require upfront investment, both material and emotional, yet ultimately yield far greater returns in social stability, productivity, and collective well-being.

6. Deradicalizing settler society

Zionism in its present form can easily be classified as a right-wing extremist ideology. Hence, the decolonization of Palestine necessarily entails the deradicalization of Israeli Jewish society, drawing on the same frameworks and approaches that Western countries apply to other forms of extremist ideology. This approach focuses on violent groups and their leaders, seeking to understand their socioeconomic background and their individual trajectories in order to build programs that, through education and regulation, and at times coercion, would lead to their deradicalization.

Yet how do we deradicalize an entire society, the majority of which have been socialized into a culture of racism, participates in an occupying army as conscripts or reservists, and broadly accepts or condones eliminatory policies toward Palestinians?

Post-apartheid South Africa still grapples with this challenge, though there are lessons to be learned from the process there so far. Those involved point to a formula that was relatively successful, consisting of advocacy and firm anti-racist policies as part of what is known as transitional justice (represented in the famous truth and reconciliation committees).

The works of Mahmood Mamdani and Raif Zureik offer perspectives on decolonization as a process with the greatest potential for deradicalizing colonial societies.

Briefly, Mamdani sees the nation-state as a major hurdle on the way to decolonization that can be challenged by building a society on the principles of equality of political rights, not only on human rights as the latter do not necessitate a dramatic fundamental shift in the nature of regimes. His work was followed by that of Raif Zureik, who also wished to build a future that does not distinguish between settlers and Indigenous people but rather building a shared future based on equality.

Notably, these works were written before the 7th of October 2023 and the whole idea of the Jewish settler society as a partner in the future becomes more difficult to comprehend since the exposure of Israel as an explicitly genocidal, not just a settler colonial state.

Therefore, its deradicalization as a society needs to be preceded by regional and international recognition of the absence of any internal dynamics of change within the Jewish Israeli society. Such a recognition ought to lead to the imposition of a severe regime of sanctions and pressure, without which no process of deradicalization and indigenization of the settlers would be possible.

The extensive literature on deradicalizing extreme right-wing movements may be most effective as a later-stage intervention, addressing residual pockets of resistance once a genuine process of decolonization is underway. A neurobehavioral approach, however, is crucial at an earlier stage: it helps explain why sustained pressure is necessary and how a century of racist indoctrination has been neurologically and socially embedded within a settler society that must ultimately adapt to life beyond apartheid. It also clarifies why economic compensation of the victims is far from sufficient.

As a necessity, the processes of deradicalization and decolonization must confront the fragmenting force of individualism, inherent within capitalism, and cultivate an alternative collectivist, social culture capable of challenging entrenched ruling-class power. Yet to dismantle oppressive societies and build just ones, it is first necessary to understand the behavioral foundations of human social organization. The final part of this volume is devoted to this task.

7. Individualism and collaboration

> I cannot manage without another, I cannot become myself without another; I must find myself in another by finding another in myself (in mutual reflection and mutual acceptance).

> Justification cannot be self-justification, recognition cannot be self-recognition. I receive my name from others, and it exists for others (self-nomination is imposture).
>
> ~ Mikhail Bakhtin, *Problems of Dostoevsky's Poetics*, trans. R. W. Rotsel and Caryl Emerson (University of Minnesota Press, 1984, pp. 287–288.)

In the age of celebrity role models, epic Twitter rants, and reality TV presidents, money talks loudest and the capitalist cult of the individual reigns supreme. Yet does the idealized image of the self-made man turned Silicon Valley billionaire reflect a natural, healthy, and productive society, or does it represent a deep crisis of our civilization? Are humans, a profoundly social species with enlarged prefrontal cortices, capable of surviving without other humans? Does human innovation come from the inspiration of lone geniuses, or is it a product of a slow process of cooperation within collaborative networks?

The lone genius/rags-to-riches narrative is compelling and lucrative. It boosts book sales, TV ratings, and followers on social media, yet it is largely inaccurate and wholly alienating and unhealthy. Upon close inspection, many individuals revered as lone geniuses have been in reality the public face of a collaborative relationship.

Donald Trump and his followers consistently attempt to capitalize on framing his trajectory as a self-made man, when in fact Trump made his fortune as a real estate developer largely due to the political and economic connections of his father, Fred Trump. George Lucas owes much of the success of the Star Wars trilogy to his ex-wife, Academy Award-winning film editor Marcia Lucas. Apple's creator, Steve Jobs, would not have been nearly as productive without his collaborative partner Steve Wozniak. Warren Buffett's intimate business partnership with Charlie Munger is one of the major reasons for his immense wealth. Tiger Woods was dependent on his caddy, Steve Williams, for far more than schlepping around his golf clubs (for more examples see Joshua Shenk's *Powers of Two: Finding the Essence of Innovation in Creative Pairs*).

Pioneering Soviet psychologist Lev Vygotsky (1896–1934) revolutionized our understanding of human learning and development with his cultural-historical theory, which argues that social interaction and cultural tools fundamentally shape thought and higher mental functions. He viewed human knowledge and thinking as inherently collective rather than individual, emphasizing the dynamic interplay between social and individual processes, particularly language and thought. Vygotsky's influential concept of the Zone of Proximal Development (ZPD) illustrates how skills and concepts emerge initially through interaction with more knowledgeable others: teachers, mentors, and peers, and are later internalized as individual capabilities. In this way, collaboration is not a mere supplement to individual learning; it is its foundation and language, mediated by dialogue, negotiation, and shared meaning.

Vygotsky's work provided a philosophical foundation for later movements toward inclusive and desegregated education. In the Soviet Union of the 1920s and '30s, he championed the integration of children with disabilities into mainstream schools and social life, rejecting their isolation in special institutions. He argued intellectual and social growth depends on access to broader society's cultural tools and interactions and that inclusion requires transforming social attitudes and practices, not merely "fixing" the individual. His vision of inclusive, participatory education continues to inform efforts to combat exclusion along lines of disability, race, and class.

As Vera John-Steiner underscores in her book *Creative Collaboration*, Vygotsky's focus on dialogue and the social origins of cognition challenged earlier individualistic views of development, laying the groundwork for modern approaches to education, inclusion, and collaborative learning. He also highlighted how cultural artifacts such as works of art, mathematical systems, maps, and drawings mediate representational activity, shaping how individuals construct and connect with themselves and others. People learn and develop by creating, appropriating, and internalizing the tools and processes that shape their growth through relationships and joint activity.

John-Steiner illustrates the typical stages of every collaboration as entailing connection, fusion, transformation, conflict, and finally resolution or breakup. She identifies three main types of creative collaboration: (i) distributed, where individuals work independently on different aspects of a shared goal; (ii) complementary, in which collaborators with diverse yet compatible skills actively support and enhance each other's contributions and; (iii) integrative, the most intertwined form, involving deep, sustained interaction that merges ideas and identities to produce wholly new outcomes. Each type highlights different patterns of interaction and shared effort, illustrating how collaboration can vary from loosely connected teamwork to fully blended co-creation.

Another book on collaboration, *Women's Ways of Knowing* by Mary Field Belenky, Blythe McVicker Clinchy, Nancy Rule Goldberger, and Jill Mattuck Tarule, highlights a culture of collaboration as a vital aspect of women's learning and knowledge development and epitomizes Marshall McLuhan's famous idiom, "The medium is the message." The book argues that many women's ways of knowing are relational and connected, emphasizing dialogue, shared experience, and community as central to how they construct meaning and understand the world. Unlike individualistic, patriarchal models of knowing, women often engage in a culture of collaborative, conversational processes that value multiple perspectives and foster mutual support. This collaborative approach encourages listening, empathy, and negotiation, enriching cognitive growth and empowering women to integrate personal and social knowledge.

Notably, ways of knowing and collaborating are shaped by social, cultural, and relational experiences rather than biologically "natural" differences between men and women (see **Part I**; Masculinity and war).

What are the neurobehavioral roots of sociality and how do creativity and collaboration foster desegregation and a collective resistance against ruling-class divide-and-conquer tactics? Here, it is noteworthy to briefly address concepts of individualism and collectivism, and their associated neurobehavioral correlates.

8. The science of sociality, accountability, and creativity

In addition to the significant evidence of innovation stemming from collaboration, scientific research on the biology of human behavior clearly proves the meeting of minds is natural, healthy, and facilitates human creativity, whereas individualism is comparatively unnatural and serves a stratified, vertical societal structure (also see **Part II** (5), Is violence inevitable?).

Here, it is useful to once again examine comparative work on social systems in other animals, with implications for human behavior.

Illuminating work by the late Larry Young at Emory University has shown that pair bonding in monogamous prairie voles is mediated by the brain's oxytocin and vasopressin systems, which interact with the dopamine reward system. By comparing prairie voles (which form lifelong bonds) to promiscuous montane voles, his work demonstrated that higher densities of oxytocin and vasopressin receptors in key brain regions of prairie voles underlie their social attachment, revealing a neurobiological basis for social bonding.

Young's findings imply that the capacity for attachment, trust, and long-term bonding is rooted in ancient neural circuits conserved across mammals. In humans, studies show oxytocin and vasopressin are similarly involved in romantic attachment, parental care, empathy, social recognition, and aggression. Young's work supports the idea that human sociality is biologically grounded in these neurochemical pathways, helping explain both the benefits and vulnerabilities of our social bonds (such as attachment disorders or social dysfunction when these systems are disrupted).

Socializing is not merely a luxury or pleasure; it is crucial for well-being. As work by Bruce McEwen, Robert and Caroline Blanchard, Robert Sapolsky, and others demonstrate, social animals, including humans, exhibit substantial harm to body, brain, and behavior when subjected to repeated social defeat or prolonged exposure to other social stressors, including social isolation.

Indeed, prisoners held in solitary confinement, an extreme form of segregation and isolation, and people who experience chronic abuse or bullying experience severe and lasting negative psychological and physical consequences, some of which involve the same systems implicated by Larry Young in voles. Accordingly, the Center for Constitutional Rights and the United Nations have declared solitary confinement a human rights abuse that can amount to torture, a recognition rooted in our fundamental need for social connection.

Processes of accountability, i.e., recognizing injustice and working toward reconciliation, engage some of the same brain networks implicated in sociality, including the PFC, emotional regions involved in empathy, fear, and disgust (e.g., amygdala and insula) and reward pathways that reinforce prosocial behavior. This makes sense, as accountability requires curtailing of fear and disgust, recognizing and empathizing with others' perspectives, anticipating their judgments, and adjusting behavior accordingly. It can also provide a lens into how capitalism reinforces and profits from settler colonial narratives and culture that manufacture divisions of gender, race, ethnicity, and more, imposed by the ruling class.

a. Universal languages

The need for social connection is reflected in the human brain, much of which is dedicated to interpreting and expressing social and altruistic behaviors. Among these, humans have developed complex communication systems, including thousands of languages, which enable us to form and maintain vital social bonds within our communities.

There exist universal languages that transcend all humans, demonstrating the potential for cross-cultural alliance building with healing relationships across ethnic and other divides. Indeed, in *The Expression of the Emotions in Man and Animals* (1873), Charles Darwin first advocated that human emotions and their nonverbal expressions have evolved from similar expressions in animals, are innate and are conserved across humans.

Paul Ekman (b. 1934) and Wallace V. Friesen (1937–1989) continued the work of Charles Darwin in their studies of isolated tribes in New Guinea. They found that tribesmen who had no contact with the outside world were able to recognize, differentiate, and reproduce facial expressions that correspond to different feelings, proving that emotional output is universal and showing that basic emotions are universal and biologically hardwired rather than purely cultural. In the 1960s and 1970s, they developed the Facial Action Coding System, a comprehensive method for objectively measuring facial muscle movements.

Through cross-cultural studies, they demonstrated that people everywhere recognize the same core emotions, happiness, sadness, anger, fear, disgust, and surprise, through facial expressions, including in isolated populations with no exposure to Western culture. Their research also revealed the role of "microexpressions," brief, involuntary facial expressions that can betray concealed emotions, which became influential in psychology, law enforcement, and lie detection. *Lie to Me,* a TV series that aired from 2009-2011 on Fox TV, starred Tim Roth as a master interpreter of body language and facial expressions, a human lie detector of sorts, is based on Ekman and Friesen's findings.

b. The arts

The arts share many communicative qualities with nonverbal emotional expressions. Prehistoric cave paintings in Europe, Africa, and Asia show an uncanny similarity in their representations of animals, demonstrating the universal nature of visual art. Research in music neuroscience illustrates how up-tempo, major-mode compositions boost arousal and positive mood, enhancing cognitive performance, whereas slow-tempo, minor-mode pieces tend to lower energy and induce sadness. Music's complexity is capable of expressing the most nuanced emotions. Mediated through touch rather than digitization, it retains immediacy and authenticity.

As Manfred Clynes argues in *Sentics: The Touch of the Emotions*, human emotions follow precise, measurable patterns of touch, such as pressure and timing, which can be expressed through music or other physical gestures. By mapping these "sentic forms," he shows how subjective feelings can be directly communicated through performance, dissolving the barriers between self, emotion, and expression, and suggesting a sort of universal language of human feeling.

Language and nonverbal communication through the arts or otherwise enable the formation and development of cooperative relationships that have been crucial for the survival, development, and propagation of the human species. From the onset of civilization, humans have collaborated with each other at work, in the family setting, during religious ceremonies, while engaging in cultural and recreational activities, and as a tool of resistance against oppression.

Successful collaborations have a kind of magic to them, often producing outcomes that far exceed the individual contributions of the participants. The celebrated songwriting partnership of John Lennon and Paul McCartney illustrates this dynamic well: when distinct perspectives and talents interact, the result can be something neither individual could have produced alone. Collaboration, in other words, is not merely additive. It is emergent. When multiple minds interact within a shared structure, new ideas, insights and possibilities arise from the interaction itself, generating outcomes that are greater than the sum of their parts.

German critical theorist Theodor W. Adorno emphasized that creativity at its best is dialectical: it emerges from, struggles with, and transforms its social context, rather than existing as mere personal expression or entertainment. He stressed the ability of the arts to raise consciousness of the violent inequities damaging human lives within late capitalism, in ways that enhance and transcend written language. In his *Aesthetic Theory,* Adorno wrote, "Art respects the masses, by confronting them as that which they could be, rather than conforming to them in their degraded state."

Indeed, art and artists have traditionally been of particular concern for the ruling class, which has recognized it as a means of resistance. In their radical critique of modernity, *Dialectic of Enlightenment* (1947), Max Horkheimer and Adorno outlined how the Enlightenment and the progress of Western civilization have led to our current "culture industry." This culture industry, which is profoundly affected by the machinations of war, perfects the mechanisms for the wholesale destruction of art not beholden to establishment narratives.

In contrast, uncommodified art can appeal to those who do not have the ability, time, resources, or interest to access or afford auction houses, exclusive concert halls or museums. Uncommodified art forms, like the graffiti and street art movements that originated in 1960s New York City and Philadelphia before spreading globally, represented raw, grassroots expression. Consequently, New York's power structure, under mayors Ed Koch and Rudy Giuliani, harshly targeted this art through severe anti-graffiti legislation and police crackdown (reminiscent of COINTELPRO).

Uncommodified art has also been one of the cornerstones of revolutionary, anti-capitalist, communist, anti-colonial movements worldwide, including within the cultural section of the BDS movement. In the words of the BPP's Minister of Culture Emory Douglas:

> My art is intended to connect to an audience, to the masses. It appeals to victims of oppression, with a focus on brothers and sisters in Black communities, but not exclusively … The headlines, captions, artwork and photos reflected the gist of the drawn-out articles and therefore appealed to those who were not able to or going to read them."
>
> – Emory Douglas, *Veteran Black Panther: Links Between Capitalism and Racism Are in Plain Sight,* Interview in *Truthout* by Yoav Litvin, July 20, 2020

9. Creativity and the brain

In *Creativity: The Human Brain in the Age of Innovation*, Elkhonon Goldberg discusses the social dimensions of creativity, emphasizing that innovation is deeply embedded in cultural and social contexts. He argues that creativity is not merely an individual pursuit; instead, it is shaped and driven by its cultural context.

Echoing John-Steiner, Goldberg highlights that even the most original innovations are built upon previously accumulated knowledge and concepts, underscoring the importance of cultural influences in the creative process. Furthermore, Goldberg introduces the concept of "directed mind wandering" (DMW), describing it as an interplay between focused attention and spontaneous thought. This dynamic process allows for the generation of novel ideas and solutions, suggesting creativity involves a balance between deliberate cognitive effort and a freedom to explore new associations.

Goldberg identifies key brain regions and networks supporting creativity, including: (i) the prefrontal cortex (PFC), which affects executive functions and cognitive flexibility; (ii) the default mode network (DMN) involved in spontaneous thought and imagination; (iii) the salience network, which shifts focus between spontaneous and goal-directed thinking and includes the amygdala, among other regions and; (iv) the executive control network (ECN), which helps evaluate and refine ideas. These networks interact dynamically to support various aspects of cognition including creativity, by switching between internally oriented thought (DMN), detecting relevant stimuli and shifting attention (salience network), and exerting focused control and problem-solving (ECN).

Stress, trauma, and associated disorders can disrupt this balance by impairing PFC function, hyperactivating emotional centers like the amygdala and reducing connectivity between networks. This results in diminished cognitive flexibility, increased mental rigidity, and a decreased capacity for creative thinking and collaboration. Goldberg emphasizes that supporting creativity requires managing stress and fostering environments that allow these brain systems to function optimally. These results conform with fear-conditioning mechanisms outlined in **Part III** demonstrating how fear, trauma, and aggression can negatively affect creativity and collective action in both colonized and colonizer populations.

10. An intersectional resistance moving forward

It is not enough to work and create together. Decolonization and construction of alternative, just societies, must factor in the myriad forms of oppression at play and their respective interactions.

Intersectionality, a term coined by Kimberlé W. Crenshaw, complements classic teachings from the Black Radical Tradition, Pan Africanism, Paulo Freire's Critical Pedagogy, feminism, and other liberatory, anti-colonial works.

Intersectionality highlights how structural domination, political marginalization (in feminist and human rights movements), and intertwined identities (e.g., women, Palestinians, Muslims) interact to produce compounded vulnerability and unique forms of oppression, exclusion, and outright violence. It provides a vital, concrete framework for the struggle for justice against oppression with the solidification of inclusive alliances, driving and representing the fundamental structural change necessary to dismantle systems of domination, which include settler colonialism and its Zionist form.

By embracing the interconnectedness of identities and moving beyond a reductive hierarchy of oppressions, intersectionality fosters resilient empathy and conscious understanding across diverse groups who face different yet linked manifestations of ruling-class power instrumentalizing patriarchy, white supremacism, ableism, and other bigotries.

This interconnected lens exposes how colonial and imperial projects thrive by dividing oppressed peoples and how solidarity grounded in shared struggle is essential for resisting these structures.

Intersectionality counteracts the deliberate entanglement and weaponization of racism, capitalism, and imperialism, enabling oppressed communities, whether Indigenous peoples resisting displacement in the Global South, BIPOC communities in the United States, or elsewhere, or Palestinians confronting Zionist occupation, apartheid, and genocide, to see their struggles reflected in and strengthened by one another, thereby forging a transnational solidarity capable of challenging entrenched systems of power worldwide.

Decolonization, in this framework, is both deeply personal and inherently collective. It demands a conscious effort to dismantle colonized, segregated ways of thinking and to recognize how racial, economic, national, or other forms of privilege can perpetuate oppression, even within marginalized communities, through lateral violence. This involves cultivating humility, patience, and accountability, while adopting a structure of shared power to disrupt internalized hierarchies that mirror the very systems being resisted.

Decolonization thus becomes not only the undoing of colonial systems externally by any means necessary, a right to defense outlined in Article 51 of the UN charter, but also the reclamation of thought, identity, and community from within. Central to this process is the creation of spaces that move beyond the limited notion of "safety" to become "sacred, welcoming" spaces: environments where each person's lived experience is honored as part of a collective tapestry of resistance to oppression and existence free of it.

In the context of struggle, storytelling operates as a crucial artistic decolonial practice, functioning as a method of empowerment, a counter to colonial erasure and segregation, and a practice that builds trust and relieves the stress of isolation. Stories transmit Indigenous wisdom, preserve suppressed histories, promote truth in opposition to dehumanizing propaganda, and rebuild fractured communities, allowing narratives of survival and resistance to coalesce into collective truths that challenge colonial frameworks.

Storytelling connects personal experience to structural critique, reframing isolated acts of oppression within a broader historical context of dispossession and resistance. Through decolonization within an intersectional framework, movements can cultivate the solidarity and consciousness necessary to confront and dismantle these intertwined systems.

As this book has argued, such systems endure not simply through force; they function and sustain themselves through a recurring psychological and social cycle. The W2S model describes how ruling interests harness fundamental human drives, especially fear, identity/belonging and selective rewards and privileges, to construct hierarchies which normalize aggression, dispossession and the theft of land and resources. Once established, these structures reinforce themselves, continually reproducing the conditions that sustain domination and completing a cycle in which extraction and inequality feed the very structures that produced them.

In this book, we retell a story that has been told many times, yet through a novel neurobehavioral-historical lens grounded in modern science and complementary to leftist, anti-colonial thought. Through the case of Zionist settler colonialism, we examine the inner mechanics of how such conditioned systems form and persist, while drawing lessons that may resonate across struggles for liberation worldwide and attempting to dispel many of the myths sustained by political rhetoric.

It is our hope that these pages inspire, embolden, and fortify the struggle for freedom and justice for all oppressed peoples, fostering a cultural shift from dispossession and greed toward collaboration, mutual flourishing and collective thriving, in line with our natural wiring as deeply empathic, social beings.

Further Reading

1. brown am. *Emergent Strategy: Shaping Change, Changing Worlds.* AK Press; 2017.
2. Ritchie AJ. *Practicing New Worlds: Abolition and Emergent Strategies.* AK Press; 2023.
3. Newton HP. *War against the Panthers: A Study of Repression in America.* Harlem River Press; 1996:148 p.
4. Shames S, Seale B. *Power to the People: The World of the Black Panthers.* Abrams Books; 2016:254 pages.
5. Allport GW. *The Nature of Prejudice.* Doubleday anchor books, A149. Doubleday; 1958:xxii, 496 p.
6. Bakhtin MM. *Problems of Dostoevsky's Poetics.* University of Minnesota Press; 1984:vii, 249 pages.
7. Mamdani M. *Neither Settler nor Native: The Making and Unmaking of Permanent Minorities.* Harvard University Press; 2020.
8. Zureik E. *Israel's Colonial Project in Palestine: Brutal Pursuit.* Routledge; 20
9. Shenk JW. *Powers of Two: Finding the Essence of Innovation in Creative Pairs.* Eamon Dolan/Houghton Mifflin Harcourt; 2014.
10. Vygotsky LS. *Mind in Society: The Development of Higher Psychological Processes.* 1978:xi, 159 pages.
11. John-Steiner V. *Creative Collaboration.* Oxford University Press; 2000.
12. Belenky MF, Clinchy BM, Goldberger NR, Tarule JM. *Women's Ways of Knowing: The Development of Self, Voice, and Mind.* Basic books; 1997.
13. McGraw LA, Young LJ. The prairie vole: an emerging model organism for understanding the social brain. *Trends Neurosci.* Feb 2010;33(2):103-9. doi:10.1016/j.tins.2009.11.006

14. Blanchard RJ, McKittrick CR, Blanchard DC. Animal models of social stress: effects on behavior and brain neurochemical systems. *Physiol Behav.* Jun 2001;73(3):261-71. doi:10.1016/s0031-9384(01)00449-8
15. McEwen BS. In pursuit of resilience: stress, epigenetics, and brain plasticity. *Ann N Y Acad Sci.* Jun 2016;1373(1):56-64. doi:10.1111/nyas.13020
16. Sapolsky RM. *Why Zebras Don't Get Ulcers: The Acclaimed Guide to Stress, Stress-Related Diseases, and Coping.* 3rd ed. Henry Holt and Company; 2004.
17. Pfaff DW. *The Altruistic Brain: How We are Naturally Good.* Oxford University Press; 2015:ix, 295 pages.
18. Darwin C. *The Expression of the Emotions in Man and Animals.* D. Appleton and Co.; 1873:v p., 1 l., 374 p.
19. Ekman P, V. FW. *Facial Action Coding System: A Technique for the Measurement of Facial Movement.* Consulting Psychologists Press; 1978.
20. Goldberg E. *Creativity: The Human Brain in the Age of Innovation.* Oxford University Press; 2018:xiii, 274 pages.
21. Adorno TW. *Aesthetic Theory (R. Hullot-Kentor, Trans.).* University of Minnesota Press; 1997.
22. Adorno TW, Horkheimer M. *Dialectic of Enlightenment: Philosophical Fragments.* Translated by Edmund Jephcott. Stanford University Press 2002; 1944.
23. Abu Sitta S. The Implementation of the Right of Return. In: Carey R, ed. *The New Intifada: Resisting Israel's Apartheid.* Verso 2001:200-214.
24. Abunimah A. *One Country: A Bold Proposal to End the Israeli-Palestinian Impasse.* Macmillan; 2007.
25. Akram SM, Rampel T. Temporary Protection as an Instrument for Implementing the Right of Return for Palestinian Refugees. *Boston University International Law Journal.* 2004;22(1):1-162.
26. Bracka J. *Transitional Justice for Israel/Palestine: Truth-Telling and Empathy in Ongoing Conflict.* Springer International Publishing; 2021.
27. Bisharat GE. Maximizing Rights: The One State Solution to the Palestinian-Israeli Conflict. *Global Jurist.* 2008;8(2 (Frontiers) Article 1)
28. Faris HA, ed. *The Failure of the Two-State Solution: The Prospects of One State in the Israel-Palestine Conflict.* I.B. Tauris / Bloomsbury Publishing; 2013.
29. Farsakh L. The One-State Solution and the Israeli-Palestinian Conflict: Palestinian Challenges and Prospects. *Middle East Journal.* 2011;65(1):55-71.

30. Munayyer Y. There Will Be a One-State Solution — But What Kind of State Will It Be? *Foreign Affairs*. 2019;98(6):30-37.
31. Sohl A. Implementing the Right of Return. *Socialism and Democracy*. 2002;16(2):54-58.

Acknowledgements

To my love, our children and dog, for nourishing my heart, mind, and soul, and holding me steady.

To Sylvia Posadas: my editor, political analysis partner, transoceanic best mate, favorite poet, muse, and nitpicker, who has collaborated with me creatively to improve my drafts. Your encouragement, wit, empathy, insight, and countless late-night conversations have been instrumental in bringing my writings to life for over a decade, including this volume.

To George Hudes, whose patience, humor, friendship, and reverence for truth and morality set me off on this path of introspection and accountability.

And finally, to Caroline and Bob Blanchard, who believed in me and taught me how to think like a scientist.

I remain deeply grateful to all those who continue to struggle for truth, dignity, and justice.

~ YL

Index